Repairing the Missional Breach

Repairing the Missional Breach

Why the Church Isn't Making Disciples and How We Can Fix It

KEVIN BLACKWELL

Foreword by J. D. Payne

WIPF & STOCK · Eugene, Oregon

REPAIRING THE MISSIONAL BREACH
Why the Church Isn't Making Disciples and How We Can Fix It

Copyright © 2024 Kevin Blackwell. All rights reserved. Except for brief quotations in critical publications or reviews, no part of this book may be reproduced in any manner without prior written permission from the publisher. Write: Permissions, Wipf and Stock Publishers, 199 W. 8th Ave., Suite 3, Eugene, OR 97401.

Wipf & Stock
An Imprint of Wipf and Stock Publishers
199 W. 8th Ave., Suite 3
Eugene, OR 97401

www.wipfandstock.com

PAPERBACK ISBN: 978-1-6667-8724-5
HARDCOVER ISBN: 978-1-6667-8725-2
EBOOK ISBN: 978-1-6667-8726-9

04/01/24

Scripture quotations are taken from the New King James Version® and the New Living Translation©. New King James Version Copyright © 1982 by Thomas Nelson. Used by permission. All rights reserved. New Living Translation Version 1996, 2004, 2015 by Tyndale House Foundation. Used by permission of Tyndale House Publishers, Carol Stream, Illinois 60188. All rights reserved.

This book is dedicated to my wife Lorrie Blackwell. The copious amount of research and writing involved in this work could not have been accomplished without her love, support, understanding, encouragement, and prayers

Contents

Acknowledgments | ix

Foreword | xi

Introduction | xv

CHAPTER 1
    How Did It All Go Wrong? Defining Disciple Making
    and Church Movements | 1

CHAPTER 2
    The Need for Rediscovery: The Methods and Model
    of Jesus as Disciple Maker | 15

CHAPTER 3
    The Age of Church Growth and Pragmatism: A History
    and Critique of the Church Growth Movement | 42

CHAPTER 4
    An Emergent Generosity of Orthodoxy: A History
    and Critique of the Emergent Church Movement | 77

CHAPTER 5
    If Everything is Missional, Is Anything Truly Missional?
    A History and Critique of the Missional Church Movement | 110

CHAPTER 6
    Toward A Faithful Missional Future: Ministry Shifts
    Needed to Repair the Breach | 144

Bibliography | 177

Acknowledgments

THE WORK IN YOUR HAND is the result of hundreds of hours of research and writing that could not have been accomplished without the encouragement of several of my colleagues at Samford University. I am indebted to the outstanding work of Dr. J.D. Payne. As one of the leading missiologists in the world, his writings have had a profound impact on thousands. His work on ecclesial movements has had a substantial impact on this writing and his constant encouragement throughout the writing process has been critical. I am also indebted to Dr. Scott Guffin, whose feedback has been critical to the finished product. His research on the Church Growth Movement was extremely helpful and informative for this writing. Scott spent more than a few hours allowing me to read and re-read the manuscript to him, giving me helpful advice along the way. I am also indebted to Dr. Beck Taylor, President of Samford University, for his encouragement to see this project through. His friendship has been a great source of inspiration. Dr. Andy Westmoreland, President Emeritus of Samford University, has pushed me for more than a decade to strive to accomplish more than I ever thought possible. I will always cherish my friendship with my former boss, and I continue to learn so much from our conversations.

I cannot imagine what my life would be like had I not responded positively to a lunch invitation from Robert Mullins several years ago. He is the greatest disciple making pastor I have ever met, and his example, encouragement, and teaching has been critical to my own personal and spiritual formation as a disciple maker. I am also indebted to Daniel Edmonds. He has been talking about this subject longer than anyone I know. His ministry is an inspiration to hundreds of pastors like me.

The feedback I received during the formation of this book from Drs. Jason Duesing and Camden Pulliam has been indispensable to this work. The encouragement I have received from my friends at Midwestern Baptist

Acknowledgments

Theological Seminary has been one of the greatest gifts ever given to me by the Lord.

I am indebted to my parents, Terry and Jean Blackwell, for teaching me about Jesus and instilling in me a love for the local church. They are two of the most faithful believers I have ever known and serve the Lord with a daily commitment. Thank you to the faithful flock at Cottage Hill Baptist Church for the decades you have spent teaching me the Scriptures and showing me what it means to be on mission for Jesus.

Finally, without the encouragement of my family, this book would never have been possible. Thank you, Lorrie, Maggie, Andie, Averie, and Brodie, for allowing me to work late into the night and stay after work hours at the office to complete this book. I promise to give back the time that this book has taken from you.

Foreword

OUR LIVES ARE PART of a story. Chapters came before ours. Our chapter is being written. Lord willing, future chapters will develop from ours. In order to be wise stewards with the mysteries of Christ during our time, we need to understand where we have been, make necessary adjustments in the present, and plan for the future. Such is a way reflective of the apostolic imagination. And the work you are about to read will assist you with your part of the story.

As a college student in the early 1990s, I recall reading a seminary's periodical that spoke of "church growth." That sounded interesting and important, especially since I remembered a conversation with my pastor who shared about his ministry of growing churches. A few months later, I had graduated, was pastoring a church, and was on my way to seminary to study church growth. While there, I was exposed to a host of new terms related to this movement birthed in the mid-twentieth century. But my concern was on the present, not the past. *Just tell me what I need to do today to experience church growth. Don't give me the backstory—such is unimportant.* I was mistaken.

By the time I started doctoral studies, I was exposed to something new. The year 1998 had arrived, and Darrell Guder's *The Missional Church* was hot off the press. However, I found it strange. Why all this talk about reaching unbelievers in North America? *Nothing new here.* My denomination focused on evangelism. My church focused on evangelism. I had a focus on evangelism. Why are these writers saying we are not engaging the context when, for me and my tribe, such was not the case? I was mistaken. Why all the hoopla over the term *missional*? And who is this Lesslie Newbigin guy? Though I understood my tribe, I did not realize what had been occurring for the past ninety years throughout the broader body of Christ and influencing my ministry. Contexts had been shifting. I had a great deal to learn about the previous chapters to make wise ministerial decisions in the present.

Close to this time rumblings were felt. Folks were talking about the *emerging* and *emergent church*. Now, I was a seminary professor and had been serving with newly planted churches seeking to exegete and engage cultures. My students were asking questions. My colleagues were asking questions. I had questions. So, I threw myself into study and taught a course on what was occurring in the new emerging and emergent movements. How could we be more effective in today's ministry? Part of the answer required connecting our present chapter with previous chapters in recent church history.

Kevin Blackwell understands that the church in the North American context has been going through change and experiencing significant challenges. Though the movements of yesteryear provided assistance along the way, he notes in *Repairing the Missional Breach*, "movements by their very nature have beginnings and endings." Such is indeed true. Many of us saw the Church Growth Movement slowly fade in prominence. Something had ended when we (The American Society for Church Growth) changed our name to The Great Commission Research Network. Many of us experienced the very sharp rise and decline of the emerging/emergent church movements.

Many of us saw the birth of the missional church movement in North America. The river of that movement quickly became several streams moving in different directions. And they dried up within twenty years.

Few today discuss the Church Growth Movement, Missional Church Movement, and Emerging/Emergent Movement. They have become passé. However, while such is no longer fashionable, their influence remains. Sadly, younger generations do not know their history. Ministers today feel the effect of something but cannot articulate what that something is. Most do not know the chapters of the story before their time.

Movements create a lasting wake. Long after the boat has passed the waves continue to arrive on the shore. Those on land see the whitecaps, hear the crashing sound, and feel the water's effects, but whenever they look out to sea, nothing is there. The ship has sailed.

Here is the chapter in which we find ourselves at this point in the story. Churches and leaders know something has happened but are uncertain of the past. Herein lies a great strength of *Repairing the Missional Breach*. Blackwell has taken decades of modern church history, particularly focused

Foreword

on the United States, and summarized it for us. He helps us understand the chapters that came before our part of the story. Drawing attention to the origins and developments of three significant movements and the theological views of their leaders, Blackwell takes us on a journey of understanding.

But this book is not a dry history lesson.

History has a purpose and effect on the present. And it is here that Blackwell raises an important question: If these movements were focused on the Great Commission, then what was the impact on disciple making? His conclusion is that though intentions were good, the results were not encouraging.

If this book concluded here, then it would be a noble work and would make its contribution to the field. A great deal of missiological writings fail to bend toward the practical. However, Blackwell does not write as an ivory-tower academician. Drawing from years of pastoral ministry, he calls the church not to a new movement, but to a renewed commitment to the way of Jesus.

A "full hermeneutic of the Great Commission," he writes, encompasses both evangelism and discipleship into a holistic process beginning with conversion and moving toward a multiplying disciple maker mature in the faith. His work draws from biblical studies and shows the dangers of bifurcating the Great Commission into evangelism or discipleship. When this happens, Blackwell observes, "one will always receive lesser attention."

I commend *Repairing the Missional Breach* to you. This book will assist you in understanding three of the most important movements to affect US evangelicals in the past eighty years. You will gain a better understanding of the chapters written before now and how best to embrace what Blackwell calls "missional disciple making" for the present.

Our chapter continues. May we be wise stewards with the Great Commission as we serve God's will in our generation.

J. D. Payne, Ph.D., Professor of Christian Ministry, Samford University

Introduction

When people are disciples, they will find a way to make other disciples. In fact, they won't be able to stop themselves from doing it.[1]

—Bill Hull

THE BOOK YOU HOLD in your hand is the result of almost a decade of thinking about how the church can be more effective in making disciples. Though I have earned five post-secondary degrees from seminaries and a Christian university, I rarely if ever heard the term disciple making in any of my classes, nor did I learn what a disciple making church ought to look like. I was introduced to dozens of church growth strategies, and learned theological concepts, church history, and denominational polity, but somehow graduated each time without a thorough knowledge of what it meant to be a disciple making pastor. Though I have served churches for over thirty years and attended dozens of conferences, training, and workshops on ministry, it was not until the last few years that any training on disciple making has been made aware to me. Since being introduced to disciple making, I have been on a passionate journey to explore, understand, and develop a biblical understanding of what it means to make disciples, be an intentional disciple maker, develop a process for implementation in my church, and train the next generation of church leaders on the subject. I am convinced that churches that are intentional in making disciples offer the greatest hope for effective ministry in a postmodern cultural context. I am indebted to those people who have been on the front lines of this issue in decades past, their work has impacted me in ways that are hard to describe. I have gleaned from the wisdom of Robert Coleman, A. B. Bruce, Carl W.

---

1. Hull, *Disciple Making Church*, 56.

Introduction

Wilson, J. D. Payne, Bill Hull, Dann Spader, David Platt, Robby Gallaty, Craig Etheredge, and the immense impact of Dawson Trotman.

LEARNING FROM MY MISTAKES

For almost a decade I was the pastor of a church that enjoyed a wonderful season of growth, new members, and revitalization. When I began my tenure, the church was averaging around 90 in attendance, and most of the congregation was older. There was great concern among members regarding the future of the congregation. I led the church to make outreach and evangelism a priority, and though it didn't happen overnight, growth began to take place. Much of this growth was young families including many new believers. During my pastorate, we baptized 300 people, increased our attendance to just over 400, refurbished buildings, and built new spaces. It was the most vibrant, Spirit-filled congregation I have ever been a part of and to this day, I love the people in that congregation. I remember one particular Sunday when I gave the invitation and people lined the center aisle of the church to join, so much so that the line extended from the altar to the vestibule. When someone would decide to follow Christ, I would speak with them, line up their baptism, and then invite them to participate in a four-week new member's class. Yet, I was often frustrated at the lack of assimilation of these new members and exasperated by efforts to keep them committed. In my mind, it just didn't make sense that a new believer would stop coming to church, nor did it make sense that they wouldn't take advantage of one of our discipleship opportunities. As a pastor, I found myself being more of a sheep chaser than a disciple maker. I left that pastorate thankful for all that God did but frustrated at the lack of long-term results.

The lack of long-term results, however, rested squarely on my shoulders. Hardly a day goes by that I don't grieve the lack of disciple making intentionality in my pastoral leadership at that church. The Lord called me away from that congregation to a new work at Samford University, and in the coming years, I watched from a distance as the church began to lose members. While there were other significant factors in play, the long-term sustainability of the membership and continued growth were hindered by the fact that I didn't adequately equip the church to embody a full hermeneutic of the Great Commission. We made new converts, received new church members, and built new buildings, but failed in the most important

INTRODUCTION

component, creating a culture of disciple making. I hope that somehow, this book ensures that other church leaders will not make these same mistakes. I hope to also reveal in this writing that my failures are in many ways a microcosm of the failures of the American evangelical church over the past five decades. Also, I have a feeling that my leadership failures place me in good company with many reading this book. Some of you recognize that my experience is your current situation. After hundreds of conversations with church leaders, I am convinced that very few have ever implemented a process for disciple making in their church. Unfortunately, this reality is a product of the failures of the church to faithfully live out the disciple making commission of Jesus. It is my prayer that this book can assist you in understanding the biblical mandate, why so many have gotten it wrong, and what can be done to make it right.

MY DISCIPLE MAKING AWAKENING

About two years after I came to Samford, I received an email from a pastor inviting me to lunch. Little did I know that this lunch conversation would change the direction of my ministry and impact my life profoundly. At the time, my friend was serving as the pastor of a church that had been revitalized under his leadership. Though the church was on a county road in rural Alabama between a state prison and a water treatment plant, that congregation was making disciples like few other churches in our state. As we sat down for lunch we exchanged perfunctory greetings, and then unbeknownst to me, my new pastor friend began to disciple me on what it means to be a disciple making church leader. He asked me a question that challenged me like no other question before, he asked, "Who are you discipling?" I honestly didn't know how to respond. My first thought was to give him a full list of all the classes I was currently teaching as well as my preaching schedule for the month, but I knew that this was not what he was asking. I did not have a good answer for him. Over that next hour, I listened as intently as I have ever listened to anyone of what God had taught him about making disciples. That conversation between us is still ongoing to this very day. I left that lunch determined I would never give another blank stare to anyone who asked me that question. It propelled me into a theological deep dive into learning as much as possible so that I could answer three essential questions: What do the Gospels tell us about the model and methods of Jesus in making disciples? Do I have a full hermeneutical

Introduction

understanding of the Great Commission of Jesus Christ found in Matthew 28:19-20? What are the implications of the answers to these two questions for my life, ministry, and the church? This book reveals the results of my multi-year search to find the answers to these questions.

Only a few weeks after this conversation, I was preaching at a church where I was serving as interim pastor. The church was located in the town I grew up in, and many of the congregants had known me most of my life. After I preached that morning, I gave my usual invitation for people to place their trust in Jesus, and from the back of the sanctuary, a man began to make his way down the aisle. As he approached, I recognized him as a childhood friend that I had lost contact with for many years. I led him to Christ that morning and immediately felt the Lord saying to me, "What are you going to do now?" After the service I invited my childhood friend to enter into a disciple making relationship with me and with excitement, he agreed to weekly meetings. The following Sunday, I baptized him and began discipling him that afternoon. I took time to hear his story, seeking to determine where his starting point was regarding biblical knowledge. He shared with me his life story which included drug use, prison time, and a divorce. We started our disciple making journey together in the table of contents of the Bible and met for several weeks after that. As embarrassing as it is to admit, after years of ministry this was the first time I had ever intentionally, relationally, and personally discipled a new believer. I found it to be a life-giving experience for both of us. Since discipling that first disciple, I have been ferociously committed to personal disciple making.

For the past few years, I have been serving on staff at a local church as disciple making and teaching pastor. After failing to develop and implement a process of disciple making at my previous church, God has been gracious to allow me to lead a congregation to embrace a culture of disciple making. In my years of serving that church, there have been hundreds of people saved, discipled, and sent out as disciple makers. I am still growing in my understanding of what it means to be a disciple maker, but once I began to be obedient to the call it has brought me more joy than I have ever experienced in ministry. I want you to experience the same joy.

WHERE NO BOOK HAS GONE BEFORE

For the remainder of this book, I want to lead you on an investigation into the last fifty years of the American evangelical church, which has been

INTRODUCTION

impacted by three significant ecclesial movements. While some good has come from each movement, there has been a lack of long-term disciple making results, which has led to a significant decline in church attendance and church membership. This is important because to understand where we need to go, we need to understand how we got here. Without a doubt, making disciples is the priority of the New Testament church, however, over the past fifty years in American evangelicalism there has been a breach of Christ's Great Commission as found most succinctly in Matthew 28:19–20. Much of this failure can be attributed to wrong doctrine, lack of missional clarity, a truncated soteriology, and over-programmed methodology within three major ecclesial movements that took American evangelicalism by storm. These three movements are the Church Growth, Emergent Church, and Missional Church movements. To my knowledge, no book has told the history of these movements, examined the missional theology of its leaders, and analyzed the movement's disciple making results. A large part of this present work encompasses all of these components. I hope that this book will contribute to a greater understanding of where the American church has been over the past five decades, expose missional breaches, and offer insights into how it can be more faithful as a disciple making entity in the future. In these pages, you will find a brief historical narrative of these movements, descriptions, and critiques of the foundational theological concepts of the movements and their leaders, and formative conclusions to present a missionally faithful future for the American evangelical church. I have written this book for both the academy and church. I hope that the material contributes to the training of those who will serve the church and benefits those already serving in leadership roles. The content is a blend of academic and practical, which has been intentionally balanced.

In analyzing the disciple making results of the church, I have limited the years of focus from 1970 to the present day. Part of that is for brevity, but also for knowing that most of the people who will read this book have been, at least partially impacted by one, if not all of these three movements. The year 1970 has been chosen as the beginning of research on ecclesial movements within the American evangelical church because it corresponds with the publication of Donald McGavran's influential book, *Understanding Church Growth*, which many consider to be the beginning of the Church Growth Movement.[2] The implications of this work were seismic.

---

2. In his book, *Book of Church Growth*, Rainer views the publication of *Understanding Church Growth* in 1970 as the final significant development of the formation of

Introduction

The publication of McGavran's book was termed by C. Peter Wagner as the "Magna Carta of the Church Growth Movement."[3]

The timeframe chosen represents these three significant movements that brought cathartic shifts to the American ecclesial landscape and is narrow enough to provide a snapshot of how we have arrived at the place we currently find ourselves in American Evangelicalism. To evaluate the disciple making foci of these ecclesial movements the disciple making model and methods of Jesus Christ have been chosen as the primary example. In the final chapter, I bring formative conclusions from my research of the New Testament model of disciple making as found in the ministry of Jesus. These conclusions will suggest a faithful Biblical approach to the Great Commission as a missional priority for the future American evangelical church. Thus, the book calls for a rediscovery, return, and implementation of the disciple making model and methods of Jesus Christ to reach postmodern American generations.

In an effort to turn the tide of declining church attendance and religious activity in the United States, the movements under examination all began with pure intentions. The leaders longed to see a renewal of evangelism, baptisms, and church attendance among the people for whom they felt called to minister. While some good has come from each of the three movements, there has been a breach in fidelity to certain aspects of the commission to make disciples. Since 1970 there has been a shift in American Evangelicalism from the commission to make disciples to a consumeristic pragmatism and at times a misguided orthodoxy. One of the most significant conclusions to be found from this shift was that religious activity does not necessarily equate to the making and maturing of multiplying disciples.[4] Certain aspects of the ecclesial movements in question

---

the Church Growth Movement. Rainer, *The Book of Church Growth*, 38. There is some disagreement on the year in which the movement began. For example, Payne argues the origins of the movement is 1955 with the publication of McGavran's *Bridges of God*. Payne, *Kingdom Expressions*, 11.

3. Wagner, *Your Church Can Grow*, 14.

4. Central to this conclusion is the results of Willow Creek Community Church's findings from a multiple-year qualitative study of its ministry. Seeking to find which programs were most effective in helping people grow spiritually, the results were termed by Bill Hybels as "mind-blowing" and "shocking." The conclusion can be summed up in this way, "Increasing levels of participation in these sets of activities does NOT predict whether someone's becoming more of a disciple of Christ. It does NOT predict whether they love God more or they love people more." This study will be examined more closely in the chapter analyzing the Church Growth Movement. See "Willow Creek Repents?"

Introduction

have led the church to increased activity, but not toward lasting disciple making results. Bill Hull agrees,

> I think the problem at its root is that we have accepted a non-discipleship Christianity that leads to plenty of motion, activity, and conferences but no lasting transformation. By transformation, I mean consistent long-range change into the likeness of Jesus.[5]

Dallas Willard also asserts, "For at least several decades the churches of the Western world have not made discipleship a condition of being a Christian . . . So far as the visible Christian institutions of our day are concerned, discipleship is optional."[6] Not only have certain aspects of the ecclesial movements morphed into iterations that offer inadequate disciple making processes, but, as mentioned, even the theologies of evangelism and soteriology have been, at times, less than orthodox.

The first chapter will offer an overview of how ecclesial movements have been defined and a brief history of the use of the term disciple making and how this Great Commission mandate has been misunderstood and misused. I am indebted to the research of my colleague J.D. Payne and the wonderful writings of Gary McIntosh on ecclesial movements in America. Also tightly wrapped into this discussion is how the American evangelical church has understood and practiced evangelism and discipleship in recent decades. This practice has often included a bifurcation of evangelism and discipleship, which I argue is unbiblical and dangerous.

Chapter two will serve as the evaluative model and method for analyzing disciple making within the three ecclesial movements mentioned as well as provide a missional road map for a faithful future of making disciples. The chapter will present a thorough exegesis of the disciple making model and methods of Jesus as seen in the four gospels. Primary to this examination is the question, "How did Jesus make and develop disciples?" A. B. Bruce's book *The Training of the Twelve*, first published in 1871, has become a primary resource for modern theologians and ecclesiologists seeking to answer similar questions. Bruce's purpose for writing was to give a detailed account of the methods of Jesus and how he managed the training of the disciples. His chronological approach brings out the intentionality of the methods Jesus used to produce disciples who would later begin a worldwide expansion of making disciples. He states, "From the evangelic records

---

5. Hull, *Jesus Christ Disciplemaker*, 10.
6. Willard, *Great Omission*, 4.

Introduction

it appears that Jesus began at a very early period of His ministry to gather around Him a company of disciples, with a view to the preparation of an agency for carrying on the work of the divine kingdom."[7] Bruce's contribution to this discussion is key as he offers a thorough exegetical introspection into the process of training disciples.

Heavily influenced by Bruce, Robert Coleman wrote *The Master Plan of Evangelism* in 1963. In his book, Coleman offers eight distinct stages of the disciple's development as disciple makers under the tutelage of Jesus Christ. His stages include selection, association, consecration, impartation, demonstration, delegation, supervision, and reproduction. His practical insights and ecclesial focus on the disciple making methods of Jesus are foundational to the second chapter. Bill Hull bridges the first-century model of Jesus to the twenty-first-century church in his book, *Jesus Christ Disciplemaker*, first published in 1984 with a second edition released in 2004. Hull gives exegesis on the Great Commission and applies it to the modern-day church. He argues that Jesus took the disciples through four distinct stages of the disciple making process, all of which are still applicable to the modern-day church. These three books serve as the primary resources for chapter two. Much of the exegesis of the chapter depends on the excellent work accomplished by Robert L. Thomas and Stanley N. Gundry's *Harmony of the Gospels*. Heavily influenced by A. T. Robertson and John A. Broadus' chronological gospel harmonies of the nineteenth century. Thomas and Gundry's side-by-side comparative verses reveal the gospel writer's exposition of the events of Jesus' life and ministry. A chronological harmonization is an essential tool in determining the process and methods of Jesus in preparing His disciples for gospel expansion.

Chapters three, four, and five offer a brief history, analysis, and critique of three ecclesial movements in the United States over the past fifty years: Church Growth Movement (chapter three), Emergent Church Movement (chapter four), and Missional Church Movement (chapter five). There have been many critiques written about the Church Growth and Emergent Church Movements, while the critiques and analyses of the Missional Church Movement are evolving. The central figure for the Church Growth Movement was Donald McGavran and much of the writing and research in chapter three will surround McGavran's ministry, theology of evangelism, and its orthopraxical implications.

---

7. Bruce, *Training of the Twelve*, 13.

Introduction

Chapter four examines and critiques the Emergent Church Movement with most of the attention given to the key contributor to the theology of the movement, Brian McLaren. There is found in the chapter what I believe to be a helpful exposition of the theology of McLaren. Also included are key theological themes and ideologies of the Emergent Movement as its leaders sought to engage with postmodern thinkers to reach them for Christ and increase church participation. Many within the movement saw themselves as missionaries sent to reach the postmodern generations.

Chapter five examines and critiques the Missional Church Movement which launched in 1998 with the publication of Darrell Guder's *Missional Church: A Vision For The Sending Of The Church In North America*. The term *missional* is so often used in present-day American evangelicalism that it is difficult to determine exactly what it means and how it should be parsed. There is inherent within the title of *missional* a certain elasticity. Van Gelder and Zscheile's *The Missional Church in Perspective*, published in 2011, helps to shape and define the term *missional*. Most writings under the subject of *missional* refer to how a church sees and implements the *missio Dei* (mission of God) in its local context. Lesslie Newbigin's church-centered understanding of missions was formative to the leading thinkers of the Missional Church Movement, so much so that he could rightly be called the father of the movement. In the chapter, I have benefited from the research of my Samford colleague, J.D. Payne. His chapter on "The Missional Church" in *Kingdom Expressions* is an excellent tool offering a brief, but exceptionally rich outline. Roxburgh and Boren's *Introducing the Missional Church* was also critical in offering a proper evaluation of the movement.

Formative recommendations are offered in chapter six related to an effective future for the American evangelical church. The challenge presented by postmodernism's view of the church and the postmodern view of epistemology is also an important part of the chapter. Following this investigation, I offer an exegesis of postmodern culture and formative ministry shifts that I believe must occur to reach the present and future generations.

While the American church struggles for breath in the deep waters of postmodern and post-Christian culture, there has never been a harvest as prepared for the laborers as now. A new vision of church ministry and missions must be embraced; a vision that not only invites people to "come and attend" church but more importantly through a holistic approach to the

Introduction

Great Commission, equips and produces disciple making disciples. What is needed is a drastic change in mindset in which the American evangelical church sees itself not as the disciples preaching to the Jews in Jerusalem, but more like Paul preaching to the Hellenistic philosophers on Mars Hill. A faithful missional focus will involve relational investment and winsome dialogue with unreached people and intentional disciple making with the goal of not only growing church membership but making replicating disciples through the methods and model of Jesus. Robert Coleman states, "This is the problem of our methodology today. Well-intended ceremonies, programs, organizations, commissions, and crusades of human ingenuity are trying valiantly to do a job that can only be done by people in the power of the Holy Spirit." He continues, "Unless the personal mission of the Master is vitally incorporated into the policy and fabric of all these plans, the church cannot function as she should."[8]

This present work calls for a new disciple making movement that is biblically faithful, Christ-centered, ecclesial-focused, and culturally relevant to the present postmodern audience. The call of this book is for a fresh, new fidelity to a Christ-centered model of disciple making, along with a full hermeneutic of the Great Commission which will lead to a more faithful biblical model. The call is not for a new movement but for a rediscovery. If the American evangelical church is going to be effective in making disciples, there must be a comprehensive understanding and application of the biblical model of Jesus Christ as disciple maker. There must also be an effort to reflect on past attempts to effectively engage culture, grow churches, and make disciples while finding and correcting gaps in orthodoxy and orthopraxy related to the ecclesial movements of the past. What is needed is not another ten-to-fifteen-year movement, but rather a return to an ancient example by which all future trends and movements can be criticized.

It is incumbent upon the present and future church to effectively exegete its current evolving culture, while also remembering that Jesus Christ is and was the architect and builder of the church. Jesus has given the church a promise that He would build "His church" (Matthew 16:18), and through the power of the Holy Spirit and in fidelity to the Holy Scriptures, this will continue to be the promise for the present and future church. While culture evolves, the disciple making model of Jesus as displayed in the Gospels is unchangeable. In conclusion, this present work is a clarion

---

8. Coleman, *Master Plan*, 97.

Introduction

call to the American evangelical church to return to its apostolic mission to make and mature disciples as Jesus commissioned His church. This book will argue not for a new discovery but for a rediscovery of the model and methods of Jesus Christ in making disciples who make disciples.

Chapter 1

How Did It All Go Wrong?

Defining Disciple Making and Church Movements

The relevance of all that we do waits on its verdict, and in turn, the destiny of the multitudes hangs in the balance.[1]

—Robert Coleman

AUGUST 29, 2005, IS a day that forever changed the city of New Orleans, LA. Hurricane Katrina, a powerful category three storm, made landfall near the border of Louisiana and Mississippi. The storm surge of 15 to 19 feet overwhelmed the levee system of New Orleans. In just a few hours 80 percent of the city was flooded with some parts inundated with 20 feet of water. In the early 20th century city planners along with the Army Corp of Engineers developed and constructed a system of drainage canals and levees to protect New Orleans from just such a disaster. Around 50 percent of the city sits below sea level and to make matters worse it is surrounded by the Mississippi River to the south, Lake Pontchartrain to the north, and marshlands to the east and west. Though there had been storm events, nothing had ever tested the 350 miles of levee system quite like Katrina did. By the time the storm had passed, there were more than 50 breaches in the levee system which resulted in over 1,000 fatalities resulting in one of the greatest disasters in US history. It was determined that the failures of the levees resulted from instability and erosion at the base of the structures. The integrity of

---

1. Coleman, *Master Plan of Evangelism*, 121.

the walls once tested, did not hold up to the deluge of storm surge due to imperfections that had existed below the surface. These imperfections eventually resulted in catastrophic breaches. The lessons learned from Hurricane Katrina resulted in a massive effort to rebuild and strengthen the levees to prevent this tragedy from happening again.

Breaches begin as small cracks that might seem insignificant, but when tested can lead to tragic inundation. Over the past several decades the missional focus of the American evangelical church has suffered from a gradual erosion of its fidelity to make disciples. The decline of Christianity in America, and the Western world in general, is a result of this erosion. What we are now experiencing is a breach of mission and most of it has happened as a slow erosion. There are hermeneutical cracks that have developed over time in how the church views the Great Commission of Christ. These have gone unnoticed until the surge of secularism and postmodern thought inundated Western culture, testing the integrity of the church's missional strategy. This book is a call to strengthen the missional integrity of the church so that these breaches can be fixed, and the church can be more faithful in its disciple making mission.

THE MISSIONAL BREACH

Somewhere in America today a pastor is sitting in his office completely exasperated. Though he has been serving the church for a few years now, it just hasn't gone as he planned when he took the position. He has been faithful in preparing God-honoring biblical sermons and delivering them with passion and excitement Sunday after Sunday. He has been diligent in visiting his people, loving, and shepherding them, examining the demographics of his community, and evaluating ministries, staff, and administrative structures. He has constructed a vision plan for the church and has worked tirelessly to get everyone on board so that sustained growth will take place in the coming years. Yet, despite all this ministry, planning, evaluation, and effort, the church continues to be ineffective in fulfilling its mission. A couple of years ago the pastor decided to focus on evangelism and spent much time training his people and organizing various evangelistic outreach events. This went well and people were converted, but most of those new believers ultimately did not assimilate into the congregation and have fallen away. As a result, the pastor determined that the church had a discipleship problem, and this became the new focus. The church began new discipleship programs to balance out the evangelistic outreach, but the new programs took time, resources, and attention away from evangelism. It was much harder to find the right balance between evangelism and discipleship than the pastor could have ever imagined. He hoped that his well-prepared sermons, skillful leadership, strategic vision, gifted staff, new church structures, evangelism training, and robust discipleship classes would have jump-started the church into a new season of ministry effectiveness. This, however, has not come to fruition. He now has a church busy with activities and exhausted volunteers without much fruit to show for the efforts. He sits in his office praying for a new movement in his church while wondering, what am I missing? What if, however, the answer to the pastor's dilemma wasn't nearly as complicated as he imagined it to be?

A pastor sitting in his office frustrated at the church's ineffectiveness in evangelism and discipleship must be a strange concept for the Savior, designer, and builder of the church. I don't believe that Jesus ever intended for any church leader to go through this particular struggle. If you asked Jesus, "How should the church most effectively do evangelism and discipleship?" He would likely say, "Are you asking me how the church can effectively make disciples?" The question would be foreign to first-century Christians because they viewed their mission as disciple making. The church isn't commissioned to do evangelism or discipleship, it is only commissioned to make disciples, which encompasses both. I believe that church leaders spend the majority of their time developing plans that focus on one of three primary areas: increasing their audience, increasing baptisms, or creating discipleship programs. Many of these plans are so complex that they drain the church's energy, and as a result, several churches are struggling today with ministry fatigue. This dilemma epitomizes how ministry in the twenty-first century has gone wrong. If a church is truly making disciples, then it is accomplishing all three of these without as much effort. This approach will take a long-term commitment that yields better results incrementally and not instantly, but the long-term investment will be worth it. Simply put, the church cannot fulfill the Great Commission with new evangelism and discipleship strategies that become fads or movements and then fade every few years. In our efforts to fulfill the Great Commission, the church has made converts without making disciples, and that is the great missional breach of the modern-day church. This is what has gone wrong, terribly wrong. Church leaders have sought to mass-produce disciples from the pulpit and design ornate visionary strategies that have yielded only momentary, fleeting results. When church leaders divide the Great Commission into evangelism and discipleship, one will always receive lesser attention, and this dividing missional "crack" has resulted in the breach. It is best to view the Great Commission as one comprehensive process resulting in a fully trained and sent disciple. It might seem a provocative thought, but I argue that the hermeneutically unwarranted bifurcation of Matthew 28:19-20 has led the modern-day church to a place of ineffectiveness. It is my hope and prayer that this writing will challenge this type of thinking and precipitate change in the way the local church views Great Commission success so that we can shore up the levees.

The present American evangelical church finds itself in a peculiar place where growth, sustainability, and viability are becoming increasingly difficult. Craig Ott summarizes the situation in this way, "If current leaders do not develop new leaders who will spiritually shepherd and further guide the movement, it will become susceptible to conflict, false teaching, syncretism, and other problems."[2] The "movement" Ott calls for is a disciple making movement and this movement is as old as Christendom. It is the movement established by Jesus himself. I often hear church leaders speak of the need for a new movement in the American evangelical church. I have grown weary of these types of discussions because, for the past century, the church has been in an endless cycle of "the next great thing." These new movements often begin with a group of church leaders asking how best to shore up the missional cracks to reach a current and future generation, in other words, most movements are shaped by looking forward. What if, however, the answer is not in looking forward, but rather in casting our reflections to the past to learn and replicate how Jesus began the church? The Gospels and the book of Acts give us insight into the movement that Jesus began through the choosing, equipping, empowering, and sending of a group of followers to make disciples of all nations. This is the movement. It is not "the next great thing," but rather it is the only thing that matters. The disciple making movement of Jesus, as displayed through his ministry, and commissioned to his disciples, didn't come with an expiration date. While methods certainly need to be adapted to best communicate the gospel to cultures, the missional disciple making movement of Jesus remains the *primum prioritas* for the church. All ecclesial movements must be judged on this missional priority. Church leaders must recommit themselves to this movement and develop other leaders committed to the same cause.

2. Ott, *Church on Mission*, 115.

The reality, however, is that most church leaders are not committed as disciple makers personally, nor do they have a strategy to develop multiplying disciples in their church. As with the pastor mentioned previously, these church leaders are busy with the duties of ministry, thinking about a new vision for the church, or in search of the next thing that will bring new life into their church. The ecclesial movements of the past fifty years lacked a total commitment and comprehensive hermeneutical understanding of what it meant to equip a generation of believers to make disciples. Today, we are suffering from these missional breaches and the lack of multiplying disciples has caught up to the modern-day church. Something needs to change. It is time to shore up the levees. Just as the engineers learned lessons from the floods of Katrina, we as church leaders and missionaries to our generation must also learn lessons to assist us in being more faithful in our mission to make disciples.

DEFINING ECCLESIAL MOVEMENTS

If we are to examine the past several decades of ecclesial movements in America then perhaps a responsible question at this point is, what are ecclesial movements and how should they be defined? The initial task of defining the term *movement* is not easy due to the difficulty of differentiating between an ecclesial *trend* and an ecclesial *movement*. J. D. Payne's work on American ecclesial movements speaks to the challenge of defining movements. He states, "A trend tends to be a general direction in which something is moving, developing, or progressing, often for at least a decade before it can be labeled a trend." He continues, "A movement tends to be more developed than a trend. It often has a clear focus, specific leadership, and complex structures, all related to accomplishing a particular objective."[3] Payne finds that the three movements in question (Church Growth, Emergent, and Missional) share commonalities that led to the origins of movements. First, they shared a desire to increase church attendance. Second, they shared a common goal of better contextualizing the gospel to their audience. Third, these specific ecclesial movements were generally not tied to any specific denomination but rather shared methodologies and involved theological diversity. Fourth, Payne sees each movement as having shared the common goal of seeing more people come to faith in Jesus.[4]

3. Payne, *Kingdom Expressions*, xii.
4. Payne, *Kingdom Expressions*, x, xi.

Gary McIntosh argues that ecclesial movements are generally never static, thus the descriptor *movement*. According to McIntosh ecclesial movements are precipitated as a new idea, set of ideas, or a philosophy to turn the tide of decline in church attendance. These movements generally have formative thinkers, events, or writings that help to shape the methodology and practice of the practitioners of the movement.[5] McIntosh gives further explanation as to the commonalities of ecclesial movements in America over the past fifty years. First, movements come and go as godly people seek to help the church be as vital as possible. Second, since the 1950s ecclesial movements tend to have a vital lifespan of about fifteen years before giving way to another set of ideas or new thinkers. Third, each ecclesial movement seeks to balance perceived excesses or omissions found in earlier movements. There will always be in the capitalistic market of America a group of people who offer new corrections or new strategies for the American evangelical church. An example of this is the church health paradigm written by Rick Warren, a noted disciple of Donald McGavran, who felt that the Church Growth Movement had neglected the inner health of the church.[6] Fourth, each new generation of believers needs to recast old ideas in a new language for its own time. Finally, McIntosh suggests that every decade church leaders ought to assess their fidelity to the *missio Dei* of the local church and how effective they are in carrying out their missional purpose.[7]

After much research, I have determined that an ecclesial *movement* can be defined as a church-centered ideology comprising a cross-section of evangelical[8] Christians transcending denominations and polity with the common goal of increasing church attendance and seeing people come to Christ. The ecclesial movements in focus envisioned not only an ideal missional strategy for their time but also the boundless opportunities available for the expansion of the Christian mission in the future. Each of the

---

5. McIntosh points to the mid-1960s as the start of ecclesial movements in America as the historic churches and denominations began to decline in attendance. The response to this decline led church and denominational leaders to ask unprecedented questions, do research, and take action to turn the decline. Thus, he begins his writing with the Church Renewal Movement of the 1960s and early 1970s. McIntosh, "Church Movements of the Last Fifty Years in North America," 40.

6. McIntosh, *Church Movements*, 48.

7. McIntosh, *Church Movements*, 47–48.

8. Though church movements are much broader, I have chosen to keep the focus of this book on modern church movements within American evangelicalism.

ecclesial movements under investigation in this book sought, or is still seeking, to influence future generations of church leaders and thinkers toward lasting change in ministry and evangelization. It is reasonable to assume that no leaders in the respective ecclesial movements of the past fifty years in America sought to start a trend, but rather a seismic shift in ecclesial approaches in light of the social milieu of their time. In other words, these movements represent their attempts to shore up the missional levees.

DEFINING DISCIPLE MAKING

The term *disciple making* is extracted directly from the words of Jesus in Matt 28:19, and it has become a popular term in the past twenty years related to both missions and the local church. For this book *disciple making* is defined by Jesus through His use of the term *make disciples*, or in the Greek, *matheteusate*. The word is in the imperative mood and implies a call to action meaning there is something that must be done. When combined with verse twenty the church is being commissioned to make disciples and teach them to be fully mature followers of Jesus. Using Jesus' words in this passage to define *disciple making* produces a homogenizing of evangelism and discipleship into a holistic process with the result being a disciple/follower who is mature in doctrine and equipped to make more disciples. Though the word *evangelism* is not used by Jesus in this verse, certainly there is an assumption that the new disciple has been converted. Craig Etheredge states, "In the New Testament, the term "disciple" becomes synonymous with a "believer" in Jesus Christ. When you look at the Gospels the term disciple is the primary term used to describe a follower of Jesus. The term was used 261 times in the Gospels and the Book of Acts."[9] I define *disciple making* as encompassing both evangelism and discipleship into one holistic process to lead a person from a conversion to a spiritually mature multiplying disciple maker. In other words, evangelism, and discipleship as conjoined twins that if separated will result in tragedy.

The term *disciple making* is relatively new in American evangelicalism and has mostly been used by missiologists. David Garrison's publication, *Church Planting Movements*, defines church planting beyond the scope of simply creating new churches. He terms the end vision of the movement as a group of people who have been reached, discipled, and begin replicating and multiplying. He states, "A Church Planting Movement occurs when

---

9. Etheredge, *Bold Moves*, 52.

the vision of churches planting churches spreads from the missionary and professional church planter into the churches themselves so that by their very nature, they are winning the lost and reproducing themselves."[10] This definition caught on within missional church planting circles giving way to a disciple making movement within international missiological communities. An example of this is found in David Watson's book, *Contagious Disciple Making*, in which the term was used to describe multiplying movements in India and Africa. Using his experience working overseas, Watson and his organization *Cityteam*, began to perform similar work of discipling new believers for replication in the United States. Watson and his colleagues had worked with the church planting movement as defined by David Garrison and were heavily influenced by Garrison's definition of church planting. The term *disciple making movement* was birthed due to Watson and his team placing a new complementary title on Garrison's definition of church planting, thus the two terms were merged.[11] Though the title *disciple making movement* was birthed it was largely missiological and only slightly ecclesiological.

One of the first uses of the term *disciple making* in an American ecclesial context is found in LeRoy Eims's book, *The Lost Art of Disciple Making* published in 1978. Eims sought to examine the growth process in the life of a Christian from their new birth to becoming a worker for Christ. In so doing, he offers recommendations to churches to nurture disciples to develop disciple makers. Eims wrote his book during the heart of the Church Growth Movement in the United States, which trended toward quick-fix programmatic solutions for seeing increases in church activity and attendance. *The Lost Art of Disciple Making* was a rare monograph in the late 1970s American ecclesial literature in that it suggested a slow and steady process of disciple making rather than the quick-fix concepts found in most books at that time. He writes, "The concepts and principles we will be suggesting, and examining do not emerge from a philosophy of speedy growth and instant maturity. True growth takes time and tears

---

10. Garrison, *Church Planting Movements*, 9.

11. An example of the terms *church planting movement* and *disciple making movement* as a coherent missiological principle is found in Watson's statement in his book. He states, "If you really want to start a disciple making movement anywhere in the world and witness God's work as he starts a church planting movement, invest in teaching, training, and mentoring leaders to obey all the commands of Christ." Watson and Watson, *Contagious Disciple Making*, 7.

and love and patience."[12] As the Church Growth Movement was beginning to wane, Bill Hull wrote his seminal work, *The Disciple Making Pastor* in 1988. Hull's use of the term *disciple making* had a Christological focus as he sought to influence pastors to imitate the disciple making heart of Jesus. In many ways, Hull's publication is a critique of the more than two-decade influence of the Church Growth Movement at the time of his first edition. The later iterations of the Church Growth Movement were by that time creating a competitive consumeristic mindset in churches, which would continue well beyond the end of the 1980s. Hull states, "I maintain that the evangelical church is weak, self-indulgent, and superficial, that it has been thoroughly discipled by its culture."[13] He states the purpose of the book and thus offers the term disciple making, "The book's objective is to give pastors the philosophical base and the model by which they can implement disciple making in their churches." He continues, "I have built the model around the training methods of Jesus."[14]

Both Eims and Hull were heavily influenced by the research and writing of Robert Coleman, who wrote the forward in *The Lost Art of Disciple Making* and *The Disciple Making Pastor*. Interestingly, Coleman never uses the term *disciple making* in his monumental work, *The Master Plan of Evangelism*. Though he doesn't use the term *disciple making* the concept is central to the heart and message of his work. It combines a thorough examination of the model and methods of Jesus as a disciple maker with an ecclesiological application in each chapter under the title, "The Principle Observed." Instead of using the term *disciple making* he instead uses the term *evangelism*, which is a trait shared by Donald McGavran, though they differ in their translation and the orthopraxy of the term. McGavran and Coleman's use of the word *evangelism*, instead of *disciple making*, presents the possibility of a misunderstanding and confusion of both terms.

NOT EVANGELISM AND DISCIPLESHIP, BUT DISCIPLE MAKING

As previously mentioned, the neglect of disciple making within the American evangelical church is attributed to the unbiblical divide between evangelism and discipleship. This bifurcation is one of the greatest

---

12. Eims, *Lost Art of Disciple Making*, 12.
13. Hull, *Disciple Making Pastor*, 23.
14. Hull, *Disciple Making Pastor*, 31.

detriments to effective disciple making. The division is due in large part to the unintended results of Donald McGavran's bifurcated understanding of the Great Commission, the programmatical influence of the Church Growth Movement, and Rick Warren's five purposes of the local church as found in his widely distributed book *Purpose Driven Church*.[15] In his book, Warren encourages churches to major on five biblical purposes, two of which include evangelism to reach the lost, and discipleship to grow the saved.[16] This division was replicated by thousands of churches and more than a few evangelical denominations in the late 1990s and early 2000s. This bifurcation unintentionally created a dichotomous approach to the Great Commission in certain sectors of American evangelicalism. Carl Wilson states, "The church in general has gone through periods when leaders set evangelism against discipleship. The conditions of the church in general call people back to see that the true presentation of the good news of the kingdom of Christ involves both."[17] Wilson also sees this unneeded bifurcation as a trick of Satan. He asks the question, "Where in the Scriptures do Jesus or the apostles separate the two ideas or debate one against the other?"[18] I believe it is also important to extrapolate the difference between the term *discipleship* and the term *disciple making*. Dann Spader offers insightful commentary on the way these two terms have been used over the past decades. He states:

> Our command is not discipleship but disciple-making. *Discipleship* normally refers to what you do with Christians. The term *discipleship* makes most people think of deeper Bible studies or weightier content for Christians. This is important, but it isn't our mandate.

---

15. Rick Warren attributes much of his success in church growth to Donald McGavran's principles. He states, "The day I read McGavran, I felt God directing me to invest the rest of my life discovering the principles—biblical, cultural, and leadership principles— that produce healthy, growing churches." It is safe to say that Warren is a McGavran disciple and a product of the Church Growth Movement. Warren, *The Purpose Driven Church*, 30.

16. Much like McGavran, Rick Warren saw Jesus' words, "Go and make disciples" as a commission of evangelism. He termed purpose number 3 as "go and make disciples", yet his focus is strictly evangelism within that purpose. Purpose number four is "baptize them," and purpose number five is "teaching them to obey." Warren's five purpose approach compartmentalized the Great Commission thus bifurcating the comprehensivenature of the Great Commission as found in Matthew 28:18-20. Rick Warren, *The Purpose Driven Church*, 104–106.

17. Wilson, *With Christ in the School of Disciple Building*, 310.

18. Wilson, *With Christ in the School of Disciple Building*, 310.

How Did It All Go Wrong?

> Our mandate is *disciple-making*, which is the whole process from unbeliever to fully trained, reproducing disciple-maker.[19]

The separation of evangelism and disciple making can be traced back to the 1850s when philosophical commentary began to be widely distributed in the American church. Mendell Taylor states that the term *evangelism* was a recent development in the mid-1800s in the American ecclesial culture and was first penned by a man named Charles Adams.[20] According to Carl Wilson, the divide between evangelism and disciple making was exacerbated when a man named Horace Bushnell wrote a book entitled *Christian Nurture* calling the church back to disciple making. Unfortunately, Bushnell's liberal view of atonement undercut his intentions and motives. Bushnell, however, did begin a conversation about maturing Christians which emphasized growth in the Christian life and many influential writings followed. Many of these writings were penned by theological liberals, and the topic began to be shunned by those with conservative theological convictions. The tragedy is that disciple making became associated with modern liberal philosophical thinking and many avoided being associated with it. Wilson states, "Hence the area of disciple-building, or Christian education, was abandoned to unbiblical thinkers. This led in practice to treating evangelism and disciple-building as two separate processes."[21] One of the leaders of the Church Growth Movement, C. Peter Wagner referred to disciple making as "a torpedo to evangelism" even implying that it hindered the fulfillment of Christ's commission to his church.[22]

The church must return to a comprehensive understanding of the Great Commission to make disciples and avoid the temptation to dichotomize the process. Evangelism and discipleship are together disciple making as interdependent commands, rather than independent doctrines and practices. Common sense informs us that when we dichotomize something from a whole to parts, the risk is that one of the parts will be less emphasized or even worse, neglected completely. I believe this has been the story of the church for at least the past five decades. For years I have experienced churches that were either great at evangelism or discipleship, but rarely have I experienced a church that placed a priority on both. The church may

---

19. Spader, *4 Chair Discipling*, 42.
20. Taylor, *Exploring Evangelism*, 19.
21. Wilson, *With Christ in the School of Disciple Building*, 311.
22. Wagner, "Lausanne Twelve Months Later," *Christianity Today*, 8.

speak of both, and even hold evangelism and discipleship as a high priority in mission statements or list them as core values, but in my experience, a church rarely embodies a full embrace or understanding of both. Some of this can be attributed to a truncated soteriology in evangelicalism where regeneration and justification are often the focus to the detriment of the essential nature of the ongoing work of the Spirit through sanctification. There is no full biblical understanding of the doctrine of salvation without a commitment to a thorough theology of discipleship. This is why there must be a rediscovery of a full hermeneutic of disciple making as displayed in the New Testament.

The three ecclesial movements in focus in this book were all successful in getting people back in church, providing outreach tools and practical help, and placing a strong emphasis on missions, however, none of them emphasized disciple making as a priority, nor did they prioritize a full hermeneutic of the Great Commission. This has led many churches to an emphasis on outreach, missions, and evangelism, but often without a well-defined strategy or process of growing disciples and training followers of Christ to be disciple makers. Dallas Willard certainly believes this to be true when he states, "This most recent version of evangelicalism lacks a theology of discipleship. Specifically, it lacks a clear teaching on how what happens at conversion continues on without breaking into an even fuller life in the Kingdom of God."[23]

The bottom line is this: in our passion to see people saved we have neglected a passion to see them embrace God's full plan of sanctification. Most every sermon I have heard on Matt 28:19-20 places emphasis on evangelism, yet ironically the word evangelism is not found anywhere in the Matthean Commission. The Greek word most often associated with evangelism, *euaggelion*, is not used by Jesus in this passage. Certainly, the act of telling the good news is implied within the command to "go and make disciples," however, most homiletical outlines give primacy to evangelism over verse twenty's call to "teach them to observe." Herein lies the heart of the issue, when we preach a dichotomous approach to the commission of Jesus, rather than embrace the full hermeneutic of "make disciples," *matheteusate*, we minimalize one of the most important commands found in the New Testament. Jesus doesn't command the church to "get people saved," "make converts," "make new Christians," or "find new church members." The commission of Jesus to His church is much more comprehensive

---

23. Willard, *Discipleship*, 236.

and will take much more time and relational investment. Has the church fulfilled the Great Commission of Christ when people are converted? Has the Great Commission been fulfilled in the baptismal waters? What is the real mark of completion?

The church is called to make followers, disciples, and learners of Christ who are discipled into a deeper theological understanding which propels them to replicate this cathartic spiritual experience in the lives of those around them. We do not send out converts to a life of missions, we send out justified, regenerated, growing followers of Christ whose hearts have been fixed on a life of pursuing the one who has given them His righteousness. This is a process, and it is hard, time-consuming, messy, and exhilarating. A full hermeneutical understanding of the heart of Christ for the lost must include this type of focus. If the church only sees itself as rescuing people from hell, it has minimized the mission of God. To accomplish this the church must return to the Scriptures and ask hard questions related to its mission. We must not allow our missiology to be constructed by church growth experts, theologians, gurus, pragmatic strategies, sociological frameworks, or popular authors. There has never been a more important time to take a fresh look at the methods and model of Jesus and rediscover his heart for the perpetuity of missional disciple making. When we choose man-centered methodologies for fulfilling the Great Commission, we are essentially expressing the belief that our ways of reaching the world are better and improved from the example of Jesus as found in the Gospels.

CONCLUSION

What is needed today is a comprehensive approach to the Great Commission as well as a rediscovery of the ministry of Jesus with his disciples. An embrace of a full hermeneutic of the Great Commission will ensure that the missional levees are strong as the church casts its eyes toward making disciples for future generations. The initial scenes in the Gospels are of the coming of Christ through the incarnation and advent. God sent his Son into this world to redeem it and bring reconciliation as the Second Adam (Rom 5:15-18). The final scenes are of the death and resurrection of Christ as the atoning sacrifice and the firstborn who would rise from the dead (Col 1:18). These sections of the gospel writings receive most of the doctrinal attention of the church (and they are very important), however, there is another section of Scripture, larger in content, that is often seen simply as the ministry actions of Jesus but hold no real significance to the daily lives of believers. Within this large section of the Gospels, however, is contained the blueprint for the modern church to replicate as it seeks to fulfill the mission of Christ to make disciples. In the ministry of Jesus, we see not only evangelism (the telling of the good news) and discipleship (the sanctification of his followers), but models and methods for making mature, world-changing, gospel-heralding disciples whose hearts have been cast toward an eternal mission. In essence, we see the making of disciples who make disciples. In the next chapter, we will take a deep dive into how Jesus made disciples.

Chapter 2

The Need for Rediscovery

The Methods and Model of Jesus as Disciple Maker

"Follow Me," said Jesus to the fishermen of Bethsaida, "and I will make you fishers of men." These words show that the great Founder of the faith desired not only to have disciples, but to have about Him men whom He might train to make disciples of others: to cast the net of divine truth into the sea of the world, and to land on the shores of the divine kingdom a great multitude of believing souls.[1]

—A.B. Bruce

There is found in the Gospels a distinct method and a discernable model of disciple making utilized by Jesus Christ. In support of this argument, the chapter will feature an examination of the current scholarship on this subject, as well as an exegetical study of the ministry of Jesus in the Gospels. An initial question worthy of consideration is whether there is a discernable disciple making pattern found in Jesus' ministry as revealed in the Gospels There is some disagreement related to whether the disciples replicated a plan handed down to them by Christ in establishing the early church.[2] In this chapter, however, I utilize scholars who not only recognize

---

1. Bruce, *Training of the Twelve*, 14
2. For example, Michael Green refers to the missionary efforts of the apostles in Acts as haphazard. He states, "It would be a gross mistake to suppose that the apostles sat down and worked out a plan of campaign. The spread of Christianity was largely accomplished by informal missionaries and must have been to a large extent haphazard and spontaneous." Green, *Evangelism*, 356.

a discernable disciple making pattern in the ministry of Jesus but have written extensively about it. If there is no discernable method or pattern to replicate, then it must be assumed that the intent of Jesus' ministry was primarily to provide atonement, teach lessons, preach sermons, and perform miracles without training his disciples of God's eternal plan to take the *missio Dei* beyond the Jewish people. If indeed training the twelve was part of his plan, then a discernable model and method would certainly be recognizable and replicable, and his church would be foolish not to rediscover and recenter the very core of its mission around it.

Coleman states, "In fact, at first glance, it might even appear that Jesus had no plan. Another approach might discover some particular technique but miss the underlying pattern of it all. This is one of the marvels of his strategy. It is so unassuming and silent that it is unnoticed by the hurried churchman."[3] The ministry of Jesus, however, was not only redemptive, but it certainly was replicable. The Son was sent not only to redeem and atone but to train and equip his followers to begin a worldwide movement of disciple making. The disciples were being sent and commissioned to begin a global movement of disciple making which eventually would reach beyond the Jews.

The "mystery," as revealed in Ephesians 3:1–6 and Colossians 1:24–27, of the *missio Dei* was to include the Gentiles as kingdom people. Craig Ott asserts, "This is a reflection of the very character of God. The election of Abraham, Israel, and the church should not be understood in an exclusive sense, because that election is for the sake of blessing the nations (Gen 12:3; 17:16; 18:18; 22:18)."[4] To accomplish this global vision the Gospels reveal that God sent a substitutionary missional agent, namely Jesus Christ. The four Gospels narrate the story of how he reached, called, and equipped a small band of disciple makers who would take the good news to the nations. Carl W. Wilson states, "It is obvious from the Scriptures that Jesus was not only interested in what men believed about him but how the leaders and disciples, submitted to his lordship, would proclaim him as King and then build his church."[5]

The commonality among all attempts to articulate a discernable pattern of disciple making in the ministry of Jesus is the use of chronological harmonizing of the Gospels, which homogenizes the four Gospels

---

3. Coleman, *Master Plan*, 18.
4. Ott, *Church on Mission*, 80.
5. Wilson, *With Christ*, 10.

into a historical narrative. Robert Thomas and Stanley Gundry write of the benefits of studying the ministry of Christ in chronological harmony, "It may be affirmed that the harmonies of the Gospels are not only legitimate but necessary to the fullest comprehension of the person and work of Jesus Christ."[6] Robert Coleman articulates a reliance on such chronological studies for his research and sees within this harmonizing a ministry pattern in the work of Christ. He writes, "Everything he did and said was part of the whole pattern. It had significance because it contributed to the ultimate purpose of his life in redeeming the world for God. This was the motivating vision governing his behavior." He continues, "That is why it is so important to observe the way Jesus maneuvered to achieve his objective. The Master disclosed God's strategy for world conquest. It is tremendously revealing to study it."[7]

CHALLENGES TO THE EARLY DISCIPLE MAKING MOVEMENT

There is an assumption that the challenge of Jesus and the disciples to begin a disciple making movement in their day was much easier than the cultural complexities of which the church in America finds itself today.[8] As difficult as it is to imagine a disciple making movement in, as some call it, a post-Christian, postmodern America, it is equally difficult to imagine a similar movement in a pre-Christian, pre-modern world. The setting in which Jesus began his ministry was not too different from American culture today. First-century Palestine was multi-cultural including a combination of Aramaic, Greek and Roman influences. The people looked Jewish but spoke Aramaic and Greek, and many had embraced a belief system that was not as much God-honoring, as it was nationalistic and political. At every turn, Jesus was challenged by the religious leaders of his day and mocked by the irreligious pagan Romans. In the book of Acts, the gospel spread throughout the Roman Empire which was filled with hedonistic philosophies, emperor worship, and rampant debased immorality. Gospel multiplication took place during the apostolic age even though Christian persecution was in style, Roman culture considered the death of Jesus on a cross to be offensive, and the Jews saw the crucifixion of Jesus as God's

---

6. Gundry and Thomas, *NIV Harmony of the Gospels*, 252.
7. Coleman, *Master Plan*, 24.
8. Green, *Evangelism*, 50.

curse. A good indication of this is found in Paul's words to the Corinthians, "So when we preach that Christ was crucified, the Jews are offended, and the Gentiles say it's all nonsense" (1 Cor 1:23).

The challenges faced by the first-century evangelists to continue the disciple making movement of Jesus were immense. The message of Jesus was particularly offensive to the Jews because almost every major Christian theological assertion was an affront to the tenets of the Jewish religion. The message of Christ was difficult for Jews to believe during the lifetime of Christ, but even more difficult after his death.[9] The thought of worshiping a crucified Messiah was blasphemous to the Jews and to become a follower of Christ would be to the exclusion of family, friends, and society. Extending the disciple making movement to the pagans of the Roman Empire also presented many challenges. The state religion of the Roman Empire was emperor worship, and the emperor was seen as the *pontifex maximus*. There was an expectation that Roman citizens would participate in the state worship of the pagan Roman gods, which would be recompense for the protection the gods gave to the empire. The worship of the citizenry was a matter of state security, though personal belief was a private matter. It wasn't that the Roman authorities cared what the Christian citizens believed, but their lack of participation in the state cult was paramount to treason. Green writes, "The Roman attitude to private religious convictions, superstitions, was once again entirely tolerant, so long as public decency and order were not outraged by the cult in question."[10]

Nero's accusations of arson against the early believers criminalized their belief system and caused them to be castigated to the utmost extremes. These accusations took place in AD 64 only thirty-one years after the Great Commission and the expanding propagation of the Christian message. Essentially to join the Christian cult was seen as punitive and criminal resulting in court-ordered martyrdom.[11] As Jesus hands to the small band of disciples the disciple making mandate on the hill of commission, he is sending them and their eventual disciples into a dangerous world in which many believed the Christian message was anathema. It was a world filled with Jews who were offended by the cursed crucifixion, and pagans who viewed the Christology of the disciples as unpatriotic, nonsense, and criminal. Despite all of this hostility, the disciple making movement of

---

9. Green, *Evangelism*, 52.
10. Green, *Evangelism*, 59.
11. Green, *Evangelism*, 60.

Jesus flourished through his subsequent followers, empowered by the Holy Spirit.

At a time when church leaders are struggling to lead effective ministries against the stream of postmodern culture, it would be appropriate to remember that the Christian message has always been counterculture. The temptation for church leaders in postmodern America is to resign to a false belief that the present culture is impossible to reach, but if Jesus and the apostles could launch a movement of disciple making in a pre-modern, ancient culture entrenched in pluralistic worldviews then logically the same could happen today. It will not happen, however, without an intentional methodological shift in ministry practice; a shift that not only focuses on the message of Jesus in the Gospels but also takes the church back to the disciple making methods and model of Jesus. Without this rediscovery and return to the original principles of worldwide outreach, the church will continue to flounder in lethargy and ineffectiveness.

THE DISCIPLE MAKING METHODS OF JESUS

What are the replicable methods of Jesus in reaching and training disciples? The first disciple making method of Jesus was the power of relationships. It is not an oversimplification to state that the entirety of Jesus' method for disciple making centered on the power of relationships with people, specifically the men whom God gave him to disciple. His method of making disciples through relationships was adaptable. He would intentionally enter someone's life and demonstrate a remarkable ability to understand how best to communicate with them.[12] In his book *Learning Evangelism From Jesus*, Jerram Barrs surmises that Jesus' ability to relate with people was the key component of success in His evangelistic ministry. He writes, "It is very evident from these studies that Jesus used a great variety of means to communicate the truth to people and to break through the barriers that rebellious human beings erect between their hearts and the Lord."[13] He writes of the relational adaptability of Jesus, "We cannot read through the encounters that Jesus has with individuals and groups and then draw the conclusion that there is a 'one size fits all' approach."[14]

---

12. Hull, *Jesus Christ Disciplemaker*, 53.
13. Barrs, *Learning Evangelism*, 249.
14. Barrs, *Learning Evangelism*, 249.

This method of Jesus is not only a New Testament phenomenon, but rather it is consistently displayed as God's primary missional method throughout the entirety of the Bible. It is evident even in the Garden of Eden that God is a highly relational mission-centered God. His purpose has always been to redeem his people from the clutches of death and separation and reach them to restore his relationship with them. His covenant with Abraham in Genesis 12 was dependent upon a relationship through which the whole world would be blessed. Through the seed of Abraham, a new way of righteousness would be found as imputed to men in the person and work of Jesus Christ. In God's covenant relationship with David the Messianic lineage[15] would be established and secured. The model of the propagation of the *missio Dei* has historically been accomplished through God relating with the people he created through covenants and callings. The relationship that Jesus enjoyed with the men he called to be his disciples is certainly proof of this missional method. Wilson agrees, "The second step in Jesus' ministry was to gather a group of penitent men and to disclose to them that he was Messiah and Lord. First, he taught them who he was. Then he led them to experience his power—to trust that knowledge about him."[16] This was not only true of his interactions with his twelve, but with all those Jesus encountered in his ministry.

Jesus modeled a rare ability to meet people where they were, without any expectation of their worthiness. Barrs writes, "As we read the four Gospels, we learn that Jesus is the best example of how we are to relate to those we meet, whatever their views, whatever their way of life."[17] In Jesus the church finds the best way to live before unbelievers, to love them, serve them, and through relational discernment speak truth to them in a transformational way. The lessons that the apostles learned from their training would lead them to connect relationally with those whom they had no prior relationship with and with those outside of the Hebraic Covenant.[18]

The prayer of Jesus in John 17 contains a petition with a tone of victorious success in finishing the task given to him by the Father. The task was the training of the disciples to be disciple makers. "I have glorified you on

---

15. 1 Chronicles 17:11–14.

16. Wilson, *With Christ*, 34. Wilson lists as the first method of disciple making, repentance.

17. Barrs, *Learning Evangelism*, 17.

18. Peter's interactions with Cornelius and his family in Acts 10 is a great example of how the apostles adapted their training to connect relationally without people outside of their culture.

the earth. I have finished the work which you have given me to do" (John 17:4). The redemption of humankind could not have been the "work" to which Jesus is referring because that had not yet been accomplished. The "work" was to train the small band of disciples to share the gospel and make disciples. A. B. Bruce agrees:

> In the intercessory prayer, e.g., He speaks of the training He had given these men as if it had been the principal part of His own earthly ministry. And such, in one sense, it really was. The careful, painstaking education of the disciples secured the Teacher's influence on the world should be permanent: that His kingdom should be founded on the rock of deep and indestructible convictions in the minds of the few, not on the shifting sands of superficial evanescent impressions on the minds of the many.[19]

Dann Spader suggests that Jesus' ministry methods can be summed up through four relational principles: First, Jesus was deeply committed to relational ministry. "After these things, Jesus and His disciples came into the land of Judaea, and there he remained with them and baptized" (John 3:22). He wanted them to know him intimately and he took time to invest in them. Second, Jesus invested in a few to reach many with the message of salvation. Within eighteen months of beginning his ministry, Jesus identified five individuals (James, John, Simon, Andrew, and Matthew) and challenged them to go deeper with him. He taught these men to be "fishers of men." Third, Jesus often slipped away to pray. More than forty-five times in the Gospels, Jesus found a quiet place to pray and spend time with his Father. His relationship with the world and his disciples was greatly enhanced through his relationship with his Father through prayer. Jesus models for the church that reaching a culture will involve an impregnating power that can only come from copious amounts of prayer. Fourth, Jesus loved sinners profoundly. He was a "friend of sinners"[20] who often intentionally sought those in his culture who were farthest away from God. He associated with those that others condemned, including his own disciples. Rather than condemn sinners, he often sought after them with a redemptive purpose. He said, "For God did not send His Son into the world to condemn the world, but that the world through Him might be saved" (John 3:17). Jesus balanced his efforts between winning the lost, building believers, and equipping workers. He understood that his mandate from the

---

19. Bruce, *Training of the Twelve*, 14.
20. Matthew 11:19.

Father was to make disciples who were equipped to make more disciples, and this was primarily accomplished through relationships. Spader states, "His goal was multiplication, and with laser focus, he trained his few disciples to multiply their lives in others. And in the Great Commission, which is a great summary of his life, he told his disciples to go and repeat the process with others."[21]

A second method used by Jesus in disciple making was his consistent investment and concentration on the few, rather than the multitude. According to Coleman, God's mission has always been centered on the "Principle of concentration."[22] He argues:

> The Old Testament records how God selected a comparatively small nation of Israel through which to affect his redemptive purpose for mankind. Even within the nation, the leadership was concentrated usually within family lines, especially the Davidic branch of Judah.[23]

This principle of concentration[24] was one of Jesus' leading methods in starting a disciple making movement. Because Jesus staked all his ministry on these few men, thousands of followers could walk away from him in John 6:66, yet because the men remained with him the movement of global disciple making was never threatened. The small group of disciples were individually being transformed and equipped so they could in turn transform and mold others into conformity with Christ. The smaller the group, the more relational the bond, and the more manageable the training. The Gospels reveal Jesus spending time with his few disciples forty-six times, and only seventeen times with the multitudes.[25] His priority was on the men whom God had given to him for training and releasing.

Paul also replicated the method and encouraged Timothy to make it a ministry priority, "And the things that you have heard from me among many witnesses, commit these to faithful men who will be able to teach others also" (2 Tim 2:2). Disciples are never mass-produced; they are always intently trained through a relationship. The method of Jesus for

---

21. Spader, *4 Chair Discipling*, 14–15.
22. Coleman, *Master Plan*, 111.
23. Coleman, *Master Plan*, 111.
24. The principle of concentration can be summed up this way, "The more concentrated the size of the group being taught, the greater the opportunity for effective instruction." Coleman, *The Master Plan*, 25.
25. Spader, *4 Chair Discipling*, 81.

The Need for Rediscovery

making disciples was highly dependent upon these intimate relationships which is why he spent so much time investing in a few. Bill Hull asserts, "Jesus determined that the strategy necessary to rescue this planet from the clutches of the enemy involves people. This fact might seem so obvious that it need not be mentioned. Yet in the latter part of this century, there is perhaps no more blatant error among Christians than the dismissal of this simple idea."[26] E. M Bounds agrees with this assertion:

> We are constantly on a stretch if not a strain, to devise new methods, new plans, and new organizations to advance the church and secure enlargement and efficiency for the Gospel. This trend of the day has a tendency to lose sight of the man or sink the man in the plan or organization. God's plan is to make much of the man, far more of him than of anything else. Men are God's method. The church is looking for better methods: God is looking for better men.[27]

Coleman states, "It all started with Jesus calling a few men to follow him. This revealed immediately the direction his evangelistic strategy would take. His concern was not with programs to reach the multitudes, but with men whom the multitudes would follow. Men were to be his method of winning the world to God."[28]

The public ministry of Jesus did not begin with him seeking a large audience, but rather seeking men to train. John 1:35–51 reveals the initial interactions with the first followers of Jesus. These followers were won through a variety of means: the first two were won by the testimony of John (v. 36): Simon Peter by the testimony of his brother Andrew who likely was one of the initial two followers along with the gospel writer, John (vv. 40–42): Philip followed Jesus after given an invitation (v. 43). Nathaniel by the testimony of Philip (vv. 46–47). Each of these men was persuaded of the Messiahship of Jesus both through John's testimony and through a conversation with Jesus in his home (v. 39).[29] As Jesus called these initial men into a disciple making relationship his desire was not to teach them

---

26. Hull, *Jesus Christ Disciplemaker*, 35.
27. Bounds, *Power Through Prayer*, 5.
28. Coleman, *Master Plan*, 27.
29. Gundry and Thomas, *NIV Harmony of the Gospels*, 48. In the footnotes on this page Gundry and Thomas note that these initial disciples did not become permanent followers at this point because at least two of them returned to their occupation as fishermen for a brief time.

a set of rules or to train them in religious rituals, as Jews these young men would have been well acquainted with all those things. Jesus was inviting them into a personal relationship with him.

As the company of disciples around Jesus grew, in the middle of his second year of ministry it became necessary for him to narrow his group to a smaller number. At this point, he "called his disciples, and he chose from them twelve, whom also he named apostles" (Luke 6:13–17). Even within the small group of twelve Peter, James, and John seemed to enjoy a greater privilege of experiences and teaching than the others.[30] Certainly, Jesus cared about the multitudes and crowds evidenced by his feeding and compassion for them in Matthew 14, but he chose to devote himself to a few men rather than the masses.[31] In so doing the masses could be reached through the few whose lives were indelibly touched and transformed by the vast amount of time they spent training under the tutelage of the world's greatest disciple maker.

A. B. Bruce views the selection of a few men by Jesus as a necessity and a major part of his method for winning the world. He writes, "It is probable that the selection of a limited number to be his close and constant companions had become a necessity to Christ, in consequence of his very success in gaining disciples."[32] The larger crowds would at times become an incumbrance on the ministry of Jesus (John 6) and an impediment to his movements. Bruce continues, "But it was his wish that certain selected men should be with him at all times and in all places."[33] These men would be more than mere traveling companions, they were to be students of His, fellow laborers in the work of the kingdom. This small band of young Jewish men were chosen to be trained agents for the propagation of the faith after Jesus ascended to his Father. His laser-like focus on them for a three-year ministry intensive was critical to the success of the disciple making movement. Bruce states:

> From the time of their being chosen, indeed, the twelve entered on a regular apprenticeship for the great office of apostleship, in the course which they were to learn, in the privacy of an intimate daily

---

30. Counted among such privileges were a visit to the sick room of Jairus's daughter in Mark 5:37, the Mount of Transfiguration in Mark 9:2; Matt 17:1; Luke 9:28; and close proximity in the Garden of Gethsemane as Jesus prayed.

31. Coleman, *Master Plan*, 29.

32. Bruce, *Training of the Twelve*, 23.

33. Bruce, *Training of the Twelve* 23.

The Need for Rediscovery

fellowship with their Master, what they should be, do, believe, and teach, as His witnesses and ambassadors to the world. Henceforth the training of these men was to be a constant and prominent part of Christ's personal work. He was to make it His business to tell them in darkness what they should afterwards speak in the daylight, and, and to whisper in their ear what in after years they should preach upon the housetops.[34]

A third method that Jesus used in disciple making was his frequent use of Scripture in training his disciples. Even a casual reading of the Gospels reveals that Jesus held a high view of Scripture and taught others to do the same. Eighty times in the Gospels Jesus quotes from more than seventy chapters from twenty-four different Old Testament books.[35] The frequent use of Scripture in his time with the disciples is extraordinary with at least sixty-six references to the Old Testament in the four Gospels and the more than ninety allusions to it in his speaking with others.[36] His rebuke of the Sadducees reveals his high view of the authority of Scripture, "You are in error because you do not know the Scripture" (Matt 22:29). He made sure that none of his followers would suffer the same error. It is evident in Jesus' many interactions with his disciples, the crowds, and individuals that he spoke often about the different aspects of the truths of Scripture. This approach varied depending upon the person he was speaking with and their spiritual condition including their knowledge of Scripture. Barrs writes of Jesus' use of the truths of Scripture:

> To some he taught the gracious nature of God's kingdom; to some he taught the law; to some he spoke about the idolatry of money; to others he revealed his own forgiving love; to others he spoke of himself as the Messiah who would reveal all truth; to yet others he gave the challenge of the necessity of urgent repentance.[37]

Jesus did not question the historical validity of the Old Testament Scriptures; he simply taught them and applied them to the lives of those he discipled. He knew better than anyone that each Scripture was inspired by the Holy Spirit (Mark 12:36; Matt 22:43) and he viewed them as the Word of God (John 10:35; Mark 7:13; Matt 15:6). Jesus clearly saw all Scripture as pointing to him, "You search the Scriptures because you think that in them

34. Bruce, *Training of the Twelve* 23.
35. Spader, *Walking as Jesus Walked*, 107.
36. Coleman, *Master Plan*, 65.
37. Barrs, *Learning Evangelism*, 249.

you have eternal life; and it is they that bear witness about me" (John 5:39). He also states the same belief in Matthew 5:17–18, "Do not think that I have come to abolish the Law or the Prophets; I have not come to abolish them but to fulfill them. For truly, I say to you, until heaven and earth pass away, not an iota, not a dot, will pass from the Law until all is accomplished." Coleman writes, "Jesus utilized this ready source of sure knowledge in his work. This was the food which nourished his soul and fortified his heart against temptation. But above all, it was his textbook for teaching in public and private the eternal truth of God."[38]

His consistent use of Scripture in the training of his disciples was proof of his desire for them to know and use the Scriptures in their own life and in their own disciple making. Because Jesus often taught his disciples from Scripture, they were being equipped with at least some level of hermeneutical application. Jesus displayed an uncanny ability of memorization and comprehension of the Old Testament which the disciples would later replicate in their preaching in the book of Acts.[39] The result of Jesus impressing upon his disciples a love and commitment to Scripture is seen in their apostolic ministries as the Bible became for them the objective basis of their faith in Christ and foundational to their preaching ministries. Hull agrees, "Jesus emphasized early in his ministry the power of the Scriptures and the necessity of knowing them. Jewish men believed in the supernatural nature of Scripture, but few had experienced more than an academic interaction. Christ desired something more than a mere exercise of the mind."[40]

The fourth method used by Jesus in disciple making was kingdom-centered teaching and preaching. The message of Jesus was highly focused upon the already and not yet kingdom. The kingdom of God has been inaugurated, but it has yet to be consummated; it has come, but it is still coming. John the Baptist proclaimed, "Repent, for the kingdom of heaven is near" (Matt 3:2) and Jesus continued his cousin's central theme in his preaching. Green asserts, "The Messianic good news begins with the Messianic forerunner, John the Baptist. He exhorted and preached good news to the people. The good news begins with his repentance preaching and announcement of the coming kingdom. His story is, in fact, the beginning of the gospel."[41] The message of John was also the message of Jesus, "The

38. Coleman, *Master Plan*, 117.
39. Green, *Evangelism*, 100.
40. Hull, *Jesus Christ: Disciplemaker*, 89.

The Need for Rediscovery

kingdom of God is near. Repent and believe the good news" (Mark 1:15). Jesus, however, did more than announce the advent of the kingdom, he taught His followers the nature of the kingdom, the character of its citizens and how it should be expanded. A. B. Bruce sees these aspects clearly in both the Sermon on the Mount and in the parables of Jesus. He states, "In the great discourse delivered on the mountaintop, the qualifications for citizenship in the kingdom of heaven were set forth, first positively, and then comparatively."[42]

The Beatitudes contain the citizen qualities which ought to define the very nature of the disciples and would serve as an ethic, per say, of the "salt and light" character which his followers were commanded to richly display. The Sermon on the Mount offered a different type of righteousness apart from that which was known by the religious leaders of the day. "For I tell you, unless your righteousness exceeds that of the scribes and Pharisees, you will never enter the kingdom of heaven" (Matt 5:20). The disciples would receive and exhibit an imputed righteousness which would eventually become the center of the apostolic *kerygma* in the Book of Acts. Certain parables also display the heart of what Jesus wanted His disciples to know about the kingdom. A. B. Bruce says:

> But there is a special group of eight which appear to have been spoken about the same period, and to have been designed to serve one object, to exhibit in simple pictures the outstanding features of the kingdom of heaven in its nature and progress, and in its relations to diverse classes of men.[43]

Bruce writes of two parables which, in his opinion, were of particular importance in forming the disciple's understanding of the already/not yet kingdom: the parable of the sower, and the parable of the wheat and tares. The parable of the sower would prepare the disciples for the various responses and receptions that they could expect to receive from the kingdom message they would proclaim as disciple makers. The parable of the wheat and tares reveals the coming separation of the lost and saved at the final judgment, which would serve as a reminder to the disciples that they were not the final judges, only the proclaimers of the good news. The parable would also serve as a warning of the coming judgement which brought an urgency to the disciple making ministry of the early church.

41. Green, *Evangelism*, 79.
42. Bruce, *Training of the Twelve*, 29.
43. Bruce, *Training of the Twelve*, 30–31.

Wilson views the kingdom ministry and message of Jesus as one of the preeminent subjects of his time with the disciples. He writes that Jesus taught his disciples three main kingdom principles while with them. First, the principle of continued kingdom extension to new people, which Jesus had modeled for them throughout Judea, Jerusalem, Samaria, and Galilee. Second, the principle of reaching and helping the unwanted and sinners, to forgive and accept them so they could enter the kingdom, which Jesus dramatically illustrated. Third, the adaptation of new kingdom methods, in line with the New Covenant, which was initiated by Jesus and passed down to his followers. The focus of Jesus was not on the law or old legal practices, but on people who were not previously seen as worthy of reaching.[44]

Hull defines the central message of Jesus as the *Kingdom Gospel*. He summarizes it this way, "It is the proclamation of the rule and reign of Christ over all of life."[45] The *Kingdom Gospel* of Jesus inaugurates God's effective will having already arrived and in the process of expanding. His kingdom is becoming a reality in the lives of people who have accepted him and includes a call to self-denial in which the kingdom becomes a priority. In this call for self-denial, there is a growing awareness that believers are to give their lives away to others so that the kingdom expands. Inherent in the *Kingdom Gospel* is a call to discipleship. Hull views the acceptance of the *Kingdom Gospel* as a call to be a committed disciple of Christ, learning from him and submitting to his leadership and teaching.[46]

A full summation of his methods of disciple making is clearly seen in his words to the disciples,

> "Abide in Me, and I in you. As the branch cannot bear fruit of itself unless it abides in the vine, neither can you, unless you abide in me. I am the vine; you are the branches. He who abides in me, and I in him, bears much fruit; for without me you can do nothing" (John 15:4–5).

The challenge of Jesus found in these verses encapsulates His method of winning the world. No method would be effective unless the disciples first learned the value of abiding with Christ. Their level of effectiveness would have a direct correlation with their intimacy with Christ. Jesus desired that the disciples understand that abiding involves a growing sense that "apart from me you can do nothing" (v.5). The secret of the disciples'

---

44. Wilson, *With Christ*, 44.
45. Hull, *Conversion and Discipleship*, 38.
46. Hull, *Conversion and Discipleship*, 39.

effective gospel work was the realization that they were weak. Jesus desired for them to see abiding in him not as an option, but a necessity. The disciples would find success not in a strategy, but in their relationship with him, and through that relationship all of the disciple making methods would be personified. In other words, Jesus did not give them a strategy, he was the strategy. Christ calls believers first to abide with him before calling them to go and do outreach for him. The promise to "bear much fruit" is contingent upon the depth of the disciple's abiding relationship with Jesus. Their effective work was not dependent upon their charisma or natural abilities, it would be directly related to their abiding relationship with Jesus.

THE DISCIPLE MAKING MODEL OF JESUS

A study of the Gospel narratives reveals an intentional process that Jesus used to make disciples who would later make many more disciples. Spader states, "Jesus understood that just as plants follow a natural, organic process of development, so too can human disciples. Jesus did not take any shortcuts with the process of disciple making. Instead, he developed his disciples naturally and intentionally."[47] An examination of the Gospels shows that disciple making is an organic movement stemming from the example of Jesus as he prepared a few young men to replicate a process of which they had been the beneficiaries. David Platt writes:

> This is how the gospel penetrated the world during the first century: through self-denying, Spirit-empowered disciples of Jesus who were making disciples of Jesus. Followers of Jesus were fishing for men. Disciples were making disciples. Christians were not known for association with Christ and his church; instead, they were known for complete abandonment to Christ and his cause.[48]

Various Views of the Disciple Making Model of Jesus

While there is agreement among several scholars that a discernable model of disciple making used by Jesus is discoverable, there is some disagreement as to the chronology and cathartic events. Dann Spader reveals a four-tiered process that he extrapolates from four encounters between Jesus and His

---

47. Spader, *4 Chair Discipling*, 41.
48. Platt, *Follow Me*, 179.

disciples. Spader's "4 chaired discipling" approach involves three invitations from Jesus and one command: The invitation to "come and see" as found in John 1:38-39. The invitation to "follow me" from John 1:43 and in Mark 2:13–14. The invitation in Matthew 4:19 and Mark 1:16–17 to "come and follow me and I will make you to be fishers of men." The command to "go and bear much fruit" from John 15:16. Spader's focus is not necessarily on the chronology, for example, the transition from "come and see" to "come and follow" is almost instantaneous. Bill Hull also finds four phases in the development of trained disciple makers in the ministry of Jesus, though his phases differ slightly from Spader. Hull views the following four phases as integral for disciple training: The *Come and see* phase inaugurated by Jesus' invitation in John 1:35, which lasted four months and encompasses the first four chapters of John's gospel. The *Come and follow me* phase begins in Mark 1:16–20 and Matthew 4:18–22. In this phase, Hull describes the disciple's work as watching rather than working. He sees this phase as being ten months in length. The *Come and be with me* phase was initiated by the calling of the twelve in Mark chapter three and lasted twenty months. He states, "During the come and be with me phase, Jesus' trainees made the critical transition from established disciples to equipped laborers."[49] The *Remain in me* phase launched them from the Mount of Olives in John 15 to the Great Commission in Matthew 28.

    Robert Coleman offers eight guiding principles which he calls "The Master's Plan."[50] He describes, "The steps are not to be understood as invariably coming in this sequence as if the last were not initiated until the others had been mastered. The outline is intended only to give structure to his method and to bring out the progressive logic of the plan."[51] Coleman argues that these eight disciple making principles of Jesus are to be replicated and serve as an example for the church. Coleman's eight principles include: Selection—The selection of the twelve in which Jesus enlisted men who could bear witness and carry on his work. Association—Jesus made a practice of being with them, letting his disciples follow him. Consecration—As disciples (learners) these men were expected to be loyal followers and Jesus would consistently challenge them in their commitment. Impartation—Jesus gave to them the Holy Spirit (John 20:22) thus empowering them to know the love of God for a lost world. The disciples were expected

---

49. Hull, *Jesus Christ: Disciplemaker*, 145.
50. Coleman, *Master Plan*, 18.
51. Coleman, *Master Plan*, 19.

to allow the Holy Spirit to control their lives.[52] Demonstration—Jesus saw to it that the disciples learned his way of having a relationship with God and men. Delegation—There was always an expectation laid out by Jesus that eventually the disciples would have to take over his work and go out into the world with his message. Supervision—Coleman states, "His questions, illustrations, warnings, and admonitions were calculated to bring out those things that they needed to know in order to fulfill his work."[53] Reproduction—His work with the disciples was expected to expand in an ever-enlarging circumference until the world knew the Master.

A. B. Bruce's *The Training of the Twelve* is highly detailed and intensive in exegetical insights offering a chronological approach to the way Jesus selected and prepared these men as disciple makers. Bruce's approach is different than the previously mentioned authors, though the latter scholars have all been influenced by Bruce. The book doesn't compartmentalize the training into phases or moments but rather offers readers a view into the way Jesus taught them, the content of his teaching, and chapters dedicated to knowing the disciples more intimately. Bruce highlights various lessons Jesus taught the disciples including religious liberty, the doctrine of the cross, humility, last things, and prayer. While Bruce doesn't offer a neatly packaged outline, he does reveal a clear selection, association, and sending model from Jesus in training these men.

Carl W. Wilson views the disciple making model of Jesus as containing seven ministry developments. First, ministry begins with repentance. He states, "Repentance was always the initial objective in the ministry of Jesus and his apostles."[54] Second, opening the eyes of the disciples to trust Christ as Lord. This was accomplished by Jesus teaching them who he was and then he led them to experience his power. Third, the disciples yielded themselves to follow Christ in ministry. Much of this was accomplished, according to Wilson, for about six months when Jesus ministered and performed miracles in Judea and Jerusalem. It was during this stage of ministry development that Jesus called some of these believing disciples to follow him in regular association. Fourth, growing the disciples in their knowledge of the kingdom government. This period of training men for ministry generated great expectations about the kingdom that would come and was already at hand. Wilson states, "The twelve who stood

---

52. Coleman, *Master Plan*, 57.
53. Coleman, *Master Plan*, 81.
54. Wilson, *With Christ*, 30.

with him were not entrusted to lead and build the kingdom."⁵⁵ There is among scholars varying views of the intricacies of this process, but there is general agreement based on a chronological study of the Gospel narratives. Fifth, the shift from valuing earthly rewards to heavenly and eternal rewards. This stage of ministry development, according to Wilson, was key in strengthening the core commitment of the disciples. He asserts, "The climax to this fifth step was the teaching about what would inaugurate the transition of Jesus' earthly ministry to his reign in the heavenly realms: the Crucifixion, Resurrection, and the Ascension to the right hand of God."⁵⁶ Sixth, the preparation of Jesus to equip the disciples to operate as a body of believers toward each other, toward the Old Covenant worship group, and the world in general. Wilson views this stage of development as being six months from Feast of Tabernacles to the week before the final Feast of the Passover.⁵⁷ In this stage Jesus formed the disciples into a body that could cooperatively make disciples in a hostile world, offering preparation for the storms ahead. Seventh, Jesus' victory through death and resurrection by the Holy Spirit. The maturity of the disciples grew expeditiously during this final phase of less than two months. Wilson summarizes, "This step is critical for the fulfillment of Jesus' personal redemptive work, and it is important in bringing together all the former steps of ministry development for building His disciples and the church."⁵⁸

A SYNTHESIS OF THE DISCIPLE MAKING MODEL OF JESUS

The challenge of distilling the grand mission of Jesus into a tightly packed process is daunting and certainly, there is still much research to be accomplished. Coleman states, "The boundless dimensions of the Lord of Glory simply cannot be confined within any human interpretation of his perfection, and the longer one looks at him, the more one sees this to be the case."⁵⁹ In spite of the difficulties of such an endeavor there is a general process to follow, but the process doesn't begin until one decides to first

---

55. Wilson, *With Christ Building*, 49.

56. Wilson, *With Christ*, 53.

57. This ministry development phase is found in Matt 17:24—18:35; Mark 9:33–50; Luke 9:46–62; Matt 8:19–22. Wilson, *With Christ*, 62.

58. Wilson, *With Christ*, 71.

59. Coleman, *Master Plan*, 22.

The Need for Rediscovery

answer the call without worry of where the process might lead. Bonhoeffer asserts:

> And if we answer the call to discipleship, where will it lead us? What decisions and partings will it demand? To answer this question, we shall have to go to him, for only he knows the answer. Only Jesus Christ, who bids us follow him, knows the journey's end. But we do know that it will be a road of boundless mercy. Discipleship means joy.[60]

The process of becoming multiplying disciples began with a simple invitation which an unnamed disciple, presumably John, Andrew, Peter, Philip, and Nathaniel accepted because they believed that in Jesus was the road to boundless mercy and joy.[61]

The first phase of the disciple making model of Jesus is the *come and see* invitation. John gives us this initial encounter between Jesus and His first disciples:

> The following day John was again standing with two of his disciples. As Jesus walked by, John looked at him and declared, "Look! There is the Lamb of God!" When John's two disciples heard this, they followed Jesus. Jesus looked around and saw them following. "What do you want?" He asked them. They replied, "Rabbi (which means teacher), "where are you staying?" "Come and see," he said. It was about four o'clock in the afternoon when they went with him to the place where he was staying, and they remained with him the rest of the day (John 1:35–39 NLT).

The request of Andrew and the anonymous disciple to know where Jesus was staying was simply a desire to sit down with him to probe into the meaning of John the Baptist's declaration that Jesus was the Lamb of God. The question "Rabbi, where are you staying?" implies a request for an undisturbed conversation.[62] Hobbs states that it is likely that the other disciple

---

60. Bonhoeffer, *Cost of Discipleship*, 38.

61. In speculation that the unnamed disciple was the Gospel writer, Bruce states, "What if John were himself one of the five who on the present occasion became acquainted with Jesus? That would make a wide difference between him and the other evangelists, who could know of the incidents here related, if they knew of them at all, only at second hand. It would not be surprising that to his latest hour John remembered with emotion the first time he saw the Incarnate Word and deemed the minutest memorials of that time unspeakably precious." Bruce, *Training of the Twelve*, 8.

62. Harris, *Exegetical Guide to the Greek New Testament: John*, 48.

was John, the author of the gospel.[63] Gerald Borchert says, "Disciples, learners, or followers in the first century were quite literally people who followed a teacher and learned from both the words and actions of their mentor. The fact that they asked Jesus where he was staying or abiding (*meneis*) confirmed their intention of becoming his disciples."[64] F. F. Bruce comments, "So they went with him to his lodging and spent the rest of the day with him. The 'tenth hour' was about 4 p.m., when men began to leave their work for the day. What he said to them is not recorded, but it was enough to convince them."[65]

The actions of the disciples following their time with Jesus prove that they were believers and that the Messianic title that John the Baptist gave to Christ was indeed accurate.[66] "One of the two who heard John speak, and followed him, was Andrew, Simon Peter's brother. He first found his own brother Simon, and said to him, 'We have found the Messiah,' which is translated, the Christ" (John 1:40-41). Hull writes:

> They asked in bewildered unison, "Where are you staying?" In their awkward way, they were asking if they could tag along with him. Jesus answered with a simple invitation: "come and see." In effect he was saying, "Come with me, and you can see how I live." This invitation doesn't initially seem very significant but with these words Jesus launched the first phase of his ministry. John 1:39 indicates that they stayed the remainder of the day with Jesus. We can only guess the content of their discussions, but we can observe that as on many other occasions, they came away with their hearts aflame.[67]

During this first phase, the disciples were with Jesus for only four months following this initial conversation, then they likely went home while the seed planted in their hearts became deep convictions regarding

---

63. Hobbs, *Gospel of John*, 18.
64. Borchert, *John 1-11*, 141.
65. Bruce, *Gospel of John*, 56.
66. There is some disagreement among scholars as to the moment the disciples believed that Jesus was the Messiah. For example, Carl W. Wilson believes that the disciples didn't trust Jesus as the Messiah until they experienced his power at the wedding at Cana in Galilee. He bases this belief on John 2:11, "This, the first of his signs, Jesus did at Cana in Galilee, and manifested his glory. And his disciples believed in him." Wilson, *With Christ in the School of Disciple Building*, 35.
67. Hull, *Jesus Christ Disciplemaker*, 32–33.

The Need for Rediscovery

their belief in Jesus.[68] Before these men were disciple makers, they had to be disciples, and this only happens when belief in Jesus as the Messiah begins. Bonhoeffer states, "The first step places the disciple in the situation in which faith is possible."[69] Jesus did not tell them only to believe, but likely showed them why they should believe in him as the Messiah. F. F. Bruce states, "The invitation for which, perhaps, they had scarcely dared to hope was forthcoming at once, as it still is to those who wish to get to know him better: 'come and you will see.'"[70] At the beginning of his gospel ministry, Jesus launched His plan to make disciples of all nations with the simplest of invitations to a few inquisitive minds, "come and see." The first phase of their development resulted in their belief, but not necessarily their followship. Thomas and Gundry write, "Yet they (the disciples) did not become his permanent followers at this point, because at least two of them returned to their occupation as fishermen."[71]

The second phase of the disciple making process of Jesus is the *come and follow me* or *associate with me* phase. Developing disciples takes time and frequent association. The new phase of the initial disciple's relationship with Jesus began with invitations such as found in John 1:43, where John writes, "The following day Jesus wanted to go to Galilee, and He found Philip and said to him, 'follow me.'" The invitation to Philip was simple and direct, "Come and follow me," The verb, follow me, is in the present imperative active form and means to "keep on following me."[72] Once a person professed their belief, then Jesus invited them to follow Him or observe him in greater depth. *Follow Me* or *come and associate with me* occurs here for the first time in the gospel and it is accompanied by a tone of authority in his command. F. F. Bruce imagines this scene as, "A hand on the shoulder and the words to match the action: 'You come along with me.'"[73] Coleman summarizes this phase as he states, "Having called his men, Jesus made a practice of being with them. This was the essence of his training program—just letting his disciples follow him."[74]

---

68. Hull, *Jesus Christ Disciplemaker*, 62.
69. Bonhoeffer, *Cost of Discipleship*, 62.
70. F. F. Bruce, *Gospel of John*, 56.
71. Gundry and Thomas, *The NIV Harmony of the Gospels*, 48.
72. Hughes, *John*, 50.
73. Bruce, *Gospel of John*, 59.
74. Coleman, *Master Plan*, 37.

Platt says, "When Jesus came on the scene in human history and began calling followers to himself, he did not say, 'follow certain rules. Observe specific regulations. Perform ritual duties. Pursue a particular path.' Instead, he said, 'follow me.'"[75] Jesus' invitation to follow him was at first, an invitation to observe him and be with him. The founding of the whole Christian movement was initiated through the simple acts of Jesus investing in his life embedding his teachings in his followers and developing them into authentic disciples. Alan Hirsch asserts, "Jesus had, through living with them and showing them God's way, somehow succeeded in embedding his life and gospel in them."[76] He didn't initially ask anything of these men other than to come and spend time walking in His footsteps. Robby Gallaty states, "First, Jesus ministered, and the disciples watched him."[77] Jesus spent time with his disciples primarily to reveal to them the authority given to him by the Father so that before his ascension he could effectively pass on this authority to them. Jesus embodied spiritual authority without abusing it. His influence on the disciples had everything to do with his authority given by the Father.[78]

The call of Jesus to follow him is a deeper and more involved call than the initial "come and see" invitation and moves these initial disciples from being curious to being committed to Jesus. John 3:22 states, "Then Jesus and his disciples left Jerusalem and went into the Judean countryside. Jesus spent some time with them there, baptizing people." He spent time with them in the initial months of his ministry because Jesus understood the importance of deepening his relationship with these men. Gundry and Thomas view the time frame of John chapters one through five as a one-year ministry beginning with Jesus' baptism and ending with a Passover, not mentioned in the biblical record, that came a few months after Jesus's statement of John 4:35.[79] Regardless of the exact amount of time, it is impossible to imagine that these men could have multiplied believers if not first they had the opportunity to learn intently from Jesus through their frequent association in this phase.

In this first year of ministry, Jesus took them to many locations and exposed them to various ministry settings: He took them to a wedding party

---

75. Platt, *Follow Me*, 54.
76. Hirsch, *Forgotten Ways*, 102-103.
77. Gallaty, *Rediscovering Discipleship*, 36.
78. Hirsch, *Forgotten Ways*, 118.
79. Gundry and Thomas, *NIV Harmony of the Gospels*, 318.

The Need for Rediscovery

(John 2:2), to Capernaum (John 2:12), to Jerusalem for the Passover (John 2:13), to meetings with religious leaders (John 3), to the Judean countryside (John 3:22), and into Samaria (John 4:4). In these initial encounters Jesus taught them what a disciple maker does, and he also discipled them in the Scriptures. While there are various opinions as to the timeframe of these initial encounters between Jesus and his disciples, one thing is clear, Jesus used this time to invest in his disciples. Coleman writes, "By responding to this initial call believers in effect enrolled themselves in the Master's school where their understanding could be enlarged, and their faith established."[80] Bonhoeffer agrees:

> When the Bible speaks of following Jesus, it is proclaiming a discipleship that will liberate mankind from all man-made dogmas, from every burden and oppression, from every anxiety and torture which afflicts the conscience. If they follow Jesus, men escape from the hard yoke of their own laws and submit to the kindly yoke of Jesus Christ.[81]

By inviting these men to follow him, Jesus called them to a life of legitimate apprenticeship into his way of living. He deemed their participation in his community to be necessary and useful to his purposes and he established their position as peripheral participants in the community.[82] More than that, Jesus' invitation was for his disciples to learn the authority and truth embodied in Christ, which would ultimately be given to them at Pentecost. A. B. Bruce conflates the "come and see" and the initial "follow me" into one phase, which he refers to the first phase. In this phase, He believes they were simply believers in Jesus, and occasional companions at convenient, particularly festive events. He states, "Of this earliest stage of intercourse of the disciples with their Master we have some memorials in the four first chapters of John's gospel, which tell how some of them first became acquainted with Jesus."[83]

The third phase of the disciple making process of Jesus is the *Come and I will make you fishers of men* phase. Two parallel passages of scripture record the call of Jesus to the disciples, which moved them from simply

---

80. Coleman, *Master Plan*, 43.
81. Bonhoeffer, *Cost of Discipleship*, 37.
82. Csinos, "'Come, Follow Me': Apprenticeship in Jesus' Approach to Education," 53.
83. Bruce, *Training of the Twelve*, 13. He includes in this phase the marriage in Cana, the Passover in Jerusalem, a visit to the scene of the John the Baptists ministry, and the return journey through Samaria from the south to Galilee.

following him, to now working with him. Matthew 4:18–22 and Mark 1:14–20 reveal a deeper challenge in which these men would become active in ministry as the invitation given by Jesus indicates a process of ministry formation. While the invitation looks similar to the second phase, "follow me," it now comes with added responsibilities and expectations. Blomberg reminds readers that the parallel accounts in Matthew and Mark are not the first time Jesus encountered these men as some surmise, "Simon and Andrew have already encountered Jesus when Andrew was a disciple of John (John 1:35–41), so Jesus' call is not as abrupt as might otherwise be imagined."[84] Mark 1:14 is a new phase in the ministry of Christ. A chronological study of the ministry of Jesus reveals that there is more than one year between verses 13 and 14 of Mark chapter one.[85] Mark chooses to focus on the final eighteen months of the ministry of Jesus mostly spent around the Sea of Galilee. Only the gospel of John focuses on the Judean ministry of Jesus in the first year of his ministry. The arrest of John marks the beginning of the Galilean ministry of Christ. Mark only mentions the arrest of John in chapter one but gives no details of the context in which his arrest took place. He will give further details of the reason for John's arrest and subsequent beheading in Mark 6:14–29. The first part of Mark 1:14 is of extreme importance because it sets the stage for the entirety of Mark's narrative.[86] The phrase "after John was delivered" denotes a transition of leadership, the passing of the baton from John to Jesus.

For the first year of Jesus' ministry, we find him mostly in Judea and Samaria with only a brief visit to Galilee (John 4:43–54) in which he heals a nobleman's son. There is little question that Mark 1:14 is a transition point for Jesus as he, in a sense, moves his ministry location to Capernaum and makes his miracles, sermons, and interaction much more public and exponentially expand his outreach. Another view of Mark's statement in 1:14 is given by Stein:

> Mark 1:14 is best understood more as a theological statement than as a chronological one. Mark was aware that John's ministry continued for a time, but he wanted by this statement to tell his readers that with John the Baptist the old covenant came to a close. He was the last of the Old Testament prophets. Jesus, on the other

---

84. Blomberg, *Matthew*, New American Commentary.
85. Ziman, *Life of Jesus*, 226.
86. Brooks, *Mark*, 47.

hand, inaugurated the new covenant. John and Jesus belong to two different eras: the time of prophecy and the time of fulfillment.[87]

As Mark 1:14 reveals a transition in the ministry of Jesus, Mark 1:16–18 reveals a transition in the ministry of the disciples. In Mark 1:17, Jesus once again invites them to "follow me" but this time adds "and I will make you become fishers of men." Jesus had been with these men for many months, but this invitation is a call to a higher level of commitment and a more intentional focus on making disciples. He would shortly send them out two by two into the towns and villages of Galilee (Luke 10), but first he invites them into a deeper level of commitment which would necessitate a greater sacrifice. The response of Peter, Andrew, James, and John is magnanimous. It is said of Peter and Andrew that they "immediately left their nets and followed Him" (Mark 1:18). James and John's response was just as radical as they "left their father Zebedee in the boat with the hired servants and went after him" (Mark 1:20). Hull refers to this part of the process as the "come and be with me" phase based on Matthew 9:37-38. It is evident that Jesus is moving these men to a deeper level of "being fishers of men."

The fourth phase of the disciple making model of Jesus is the *go and bear fruit phase* and it is the deepest level of the process of disciple making. On the last night of his pre-resurrection ministry, Jesus enjoys the Passover meal with his disciples and then, in a dramatic illustration of servitude, he washes their feet. As they made their way from the upper room to the Garden of Gethsemane, Jesus stopped in a vineyard for his final great lesson for these men. John records the event in John 15:1-8. In his last "I AM" statement Jesus says in verse one, "I am the vine, and my Father is the vinedresser." He would later add, "Abide in me, and I in you. As the branch cannot bear fruit of itself unless it abides in the vine, neither can you, unless you abide in me. I am the vine; you are the branches. He who abides in me, and I in him, bears much fruit; for without me you can do nothing" (vv. 4-5). The moment in the vineyard was the crescendo of his disciple making training as Jesus shared his highest expectation for them. His expectation was multiplication and reproduction. Coleman writes:

> It was clear that the life-sustaining power of the vine was not to be bestowed endlessly on lifeless branches. Any branch that lived on the vine had to produce to survive for that was its intended nature. Jesus then made the application to his disciples. As surely as they were participants in his life, even so they would bear his fruit

---

87. Stein, *Jesus the Messiah*, 112.

(John 15:5; 8), and furthermore, their fruit would remain (John 15:16). A barren Christian is a contradiction. A tree is known by its fruit.[88]

The challenge is clear, the expectation is that the disciples would bear much fruit, which would be the result of their abiding or remaining intimate with Christ. There is debate about precisely what the "fruit" is in this verse. Carson points out, that this fruit embraces "all of the believer's life and the product of his witness."[89] F. F. Bruce believes it to be the fruit of the Spirit,[90] but in the context of the commissioning content of chapters fourteen through sixteen, it seems more likely that Carson's view is the correct interpretation. Using Carson's interpretation, the command is to remain connected to the vine and the result would be a branch filled with the fruit of being a disciple.

Fruit bearing is dependent upon the depth of which a disciple remains or abides with Christ. Just as the gardener expected the branch to bear fruit, so Jesus also would expect this inner circle of men to replicate themselves by spreading the gospel and making disciples throughout the region. Jesus' lesson to the disciples is that fruit-bearing glorifies the Father and ultimately this is the truest sign of being a disciple maker (John 15:8). This phase includes the cross event, resurrection, restoration of the disciples' faith, the Great Commission, and ascension. Shortly after the ascension, the Holy Spirit would rest upon the disciples and the global endeavor of gospel proclamation and disciple making would begin.

What is clear in the Gospel narratives is that Jesus spent copious amounts of time investing in these few men and was highly dependent upon them to take his message to a lost world. He called to himself a few untrained and uneducated Jewish boys, and through his relational investment, ministry example, scriptural teachings, missional commission, and subsequent empowering they were prepared to multiply a movement.[91] Bill Hull summarizes the final phase and its impact on the world, "The three years spent with Jesus would expand as these eleven men would become hundreds, thousands, and millions. And so, the mature fruit of discipleship

---

88. Coleman, *Master Plan*, 100.
89. Carson, *Gospel According to John*, 517.
90. Bruce, *Gospel of John*, 309.
91. Platt, *Radical*, 89.

has been progressively pruned and harvested throughout the ages, all to the glory of the one who started the whole process."[92]

CONCLUSION

The goal of this chapter has been to give an overview of the various methods Jesus used in his disciple making model and to give a purview of the scholarly views of the model. Using the exegesis of five scholars, and hermeneutical observations a discernable, replicable Christ-centered model has been offered. In the book of Acts, the disciples used the methods and model of Jesus to expand the church to the uttermost parts of the world. The real work for the modern-day American evangelical church is to take the Christ-centered methods, model them, and adapt them with an ecclesial flair. Hull argues, "Failure to contextualize disciple making into our society and time has led to today's weak church. Discipling should remain at the heart of the church, but it needs a multidimensional focus, one with broader applications."[93] What Hull is arguing for is a church-centered model which takes the methods and model of the Christ-centered plan and adapts according to the giftedness and diversity of the members of the church body. The placing of Christ's methods and model within an ecclesial structure is not an easy endeavor and will take a skilled and biblically astute leader. The reality of Scripture is that our missional God enacted a worldwide strategy for global impact centered on the redemptive work of Christ and his subsequent training of the twelve. The entire focus of this chapter can be summarized by the following statement by Robert Coleman:

> His (Jesus) whole evangelistic strategy—indeed, the fulfillment of his very purpose in coming into the world, dying on the cross, and rising from the grave—depended on the faithfulness of his chosen disciples to this task. This was the way his church was to win, through the dedicated lives of those who knew the Savior so well that his Spirit and method constrained them to tell others. As simple as it may seem, this was the way the Gospel would conquer. He had no other plan.[94]

---

92. Hull, *Jesus Christ, Disciplemaker*, 227.
93. Hull, *Disciple Making Church*, 35.
94. Coleman, *Mater Plan*, 91.

Chapter 3

The Age of Church Growth and Pragmatism

A History and Critique of the Church Growth Movement

> The great century of Christian missions may well be followed by a greater century of the Christian churches.[1]
>
> —Donald A. McGavran

THE FOLLOWING CHAPTER WILL offer insights into the Church Growth Movement, including its formation, key contributors, and foundational methodological principles. Included in this chapter will be an analysis and philosophical critique of the movement as well as Donald McGavran's theology of evangelism and its influence. Donald A. McGavran is widely considered to be the founder of the Church Growth Movement and the main influencer of the missiology, theology, and methodology of the principles associated with it.[2] While the Church Growth Movement has its share of critics, many of which will be examined in this chapter, its impact on the

---

1. McGavran, *Bridges of God*, 158.
2. Wagner writes in the preface to the third (1990) edition of *Understanding Church Growth*, "When, one or two generations from now, historians of religion look back to the twentieth century, McGavran will most likely be remembered chiefly as the father of the Church Growth Movement. Donald A. McGavran, *Understanding Church Growth*, viii.

The Age of Church Growth and Pragmatism

American ecclesial scene has been massive, particularly the missiological philosophies of McGavran.

In his book, *The Book of Church Growth*, Thom Rainer offers a concise, yet informative definition of the Church Growth Movement, "The Church Growth Movement includes all the resources of people, institutions, and publications dedicated to expounding the concepts and practicing the principles of church growth, beginning with the foundational work of Donald McGavran in 1955."[3] As Rainer alludes, the origins of the Church Growth Movement began with the publication of McGavran's *The Bridges of God: A Study in the Strategy of Missions*. The Church Growth Movement in America began to take shape in the 1970s through the influence of the Fuller School of World Mission and Institute of Church Growth as McGavran's missiological principles were applied to the American church to re-engage in Great Commission work. McGavran's merging of biblical, theological, and social studies resulted in the development of church growth principles that, when applied to the mission field, would serve to plant growing churches and fulfill the Great Commission.[4]

The publication of *The Bridges of God* was the origin of the Church Growth Movement, but the release of *Understanding Church Growth* in 1970 was a significant development in bringing McGavran's missiological principles to an American church audience. Both of these books articulate McGavran's missiological principles, but *Understanding Church Growth* reveals how these principles could be deployed in American churches. The book lays out and promotes the theology, sociology, and methodology of church growth which would define a generation's view of how to catapult congregations to growth and vitality. The *American Society for Church Growth* was founded in 1985 by two of McGavran's disciples, C. Peter Wagner, and George Hunter III. The goal of the ASCG was to implement and promote the foundational principles of McGavran and was a large influencer on American church culture for many years. The society's formal definition of church growth was widely accepted as the standard moniker of the Church Growth Movement and McGavran's inclusion in the statement added to his continued impact on the movement:

> Church growth is that discipline which investigates the nature, expansion, planting, multiplication, function, and health of Christian churches as they related to the effective implantation of God's

3. Rainer, *Book of Church Growth*, 23.
4. Payne, *Kingdom Expressions*, 14.

commission to "make disciples of all peoples" (Matt 28:18–20). Students of church growth strive to integrate the eternal theological principles of God's word concerning the expansion of the church with the best insights of contemporary social and behavioral sciences, employing as the initial frame of reference the foundational work done by Donald McGavran.[5]

McGavran's heavy academic influence caused the Church Growth Movement to become more than a church movement, but also a legitimate academic field of study. It developed into a credible academic focus as institutions of Christian higher education responded to the desire of church leaders to study McGavran's principles and apply them in an ecclesial context. During the movement colleges and universities added church growth courses to their curriculum and offered lectureships and professorships in the discipline.[6]

McGavran's influence on church growth yielded to C. Peter Wagner after the publication of *Understanding Church Growth* in 1970, yet he continued to make significant contributions. Much of the work of the Church Growth Movement from 1970 to the early 1990s was carried on by McGavran's faculty at Fuller. Other publications of influence include *How to Grow a Church*, written with Win Arn, and C. Peter Wagner's *Your Church Can Grow: Seven Vital Signs of a Healthy Church*, each of which was of paramount importance to the expansion of the Church Growth Movement in America. McGavran's writings, his influence on C. Peter Wagner, Win Arn, George Hunter III, Elmer Towns, and many others, along with the development of the School of World Missions at Fuller, proved to be formative in the Church Growth Movement. Later iterations of the movement are the Church Health, Seeker Sensitive and Attractional Movements with leaders of these adaptations impacted by McGavran's missiological and evangelistic principles. Leaders of these movements include Rick Warren, Bill Hybels, Stephen A. Macchia, and Lyle Schaller.[7] McGavran was the most influential missiologist of the late twentieth century, and together with C. Peter Wagner the Church Growth Movement took shape as they, along with others, produced a large number of congregational resources.[8]

---

5. C. Peter Wagner, *Strategies for Church Growth*, 114. Today the *American Society for Church Growth* is known as the *Great Commission Research Network*.

6. Payne, *Kingdom Expressions*, 13.

7. McIntosh, "Church Movements," 40.

8. Payne, *Kingdom Expressions*, 18.

The Age of Church Growth and Pragmatism

MCGAVRAN AS MISSIONARY AND ACADEMICIAN

The Church Growth Movement is more than Donald McGavran, but it is not less. The church growth principles of McGavran became a rallying point for many church leaders in the later twentieth century. The movement transcended denominational and doctrinal fences and brought together those who understood that a new evangelistic emphasis was needed in America. Speaking of the ecumenical nature of the movement Rainer writes, "The movement claims supporters from virtually all denominations and bodies of believers, especially in North America."[9] As McGavran's missiological principles began to be applied to the American evangelical church, *church growth* became the buzz phrase that occupied a generation of ecclesiologists.[10] Jeff Walters states, "No individual system of thought or theology rises in a vacuum. Donald McGavran's theology and that of the Church Growth Movement was heavily influenced by his missionary upbringing, his denominational heritage, his education, and his missiological studies."[11]

Influence of McGavran's Upbringing and Mission Work

Donald Anderson McGavran was born in Damoh, India, on December 15, 1897, to missionary parents.[12] His parents, John and Helen, served in India for many years and their service to the people in that region made an indelible mark on the lives of their children, especially Donald. He was saved and baptized at the church his father served during a missionary furlough, the First Christian Church of Tulsa, Oklahoma. At a YMCA camp in Wisconsin during his college years, he surrendered his life to Christian work. Though resistant at first to a life of ministry, eventually he prayed, "Very well, Lord. It is clear to me: either I give up all claims to being a Christian, or I go all the way. Since that is the situation, I choose to go all the way."[13] That decision was made formally when Donald and his wife Mary attended the Eighth International Convention of the Student Volunteer Movement for Foreign

---

9. Rainer, *Book of Church Growth*, 66.

10. Lawless, "Donald McGavran, C. Peter Wagner, and Church Growth Evangelism," in *A History of Evangelism in North America*, 291.

11. Walters, "Donald McGavran's Theological Foundations for 'Effective Evangelism,'" 51.

12. McIntosh, *Donald A McGavran*, 49.

13. McIntosh, *Donald A McGavran*, 65.

Missions in Des Moines, Iowa in 1919. At that convention, Donald and Mary made commitments to give their lives to missionary service. Reflecting on that decision McGavran wrote:

> There it became clear to me that God was calling me to be a missionary, that he was commanding me to carry out the Great Commission. Doing just that has ever since been the ruling purpose of my life. True, I have from time to time swerved from that purpose but never for long. That decision lies at the root of the church-growth movement.[14]

In 1923 Donald and Mary joined eighty-seven other missionaries traveling to India through the United Christian Missionary Society (Disciples of Christ). The ten fields managed by the society in India were seeing little church growth, however, the focus of Donald and Mary's work would initially be on education, medicine, and evangelism. Though church growth was not initially his primary focus, it soon became his passion. After one year of language study, McGavran was given the duty of overseeing mission schools in addition to teaching Bible and English classes in the high schools. He was later named Director of Education for the mission schools in what had now become fourteen mission stations.[15] After the death of their daughter, McGavran returned to the United States to be with family in 1930. That summer he began PhD studies in Religious Education from Union Theological Seminary in New York being taught by professors from Columbia University. Upon his graduation in 1932, Donald and his family traveled back to India for their second term of duty. The research of McGavran during his PhD studies focused on the education and beliefs of Hinduism. His research would be valuable to his ongoing mission and religious education work in India.

Returning to India, McGavran was elected as executive secretary-treasurer of the India mission of the United Christian Missionary Society (UCMS). Serving as the treasurer for a large mission society was difficult, but it was especially difficult during The Great Depression. Funding from home had been cut by half, and sometimes only twenty-five percent of the funding made it to the mission.[16] With fewer dollars, McGavran had to be careful as to how the money was spent increasing the importance of an effective return on the investments. Being in charge of the distribution

---

14. McGavran, "My Pilgrimage in Mission," 53.
15. Works, Jr., "Donald A. McGavran: The Development of a Legacy," 6.
16. McIntosh, *Donald A. McGavran*, 88.

he began to be concerned as to how the money was spent and the lack of results of converts and new churches including how little the churches were growing. His curiosity as to why more people were not being evangelized and why churches were not growing eventually led him to begin asking the questions that would become foundational to his book *The Bridges of God* and ultimately the tenets of the Church Growth Movement. This is evident in McGavran's stated purpose of writing *The Bridges of God*, "This book is written in the hope that it will shed light on that process and help direct the attention of those who love the Lord to the highways of the Spirit along which his redemptive church can advance."[17]

McGavran's Missiological and Theological Influencers

The years of 1933-1955 were formative to McGavran's missiological soteriology and would become the major impetus for the Church Growth Movement. It was during this time that Donald McGavran began seriously thinking about church growth. This new focus led him to research how churches grew with his work being heavily influenced by J. Waskom Pickett. The results of the research were published under the title, *Christian Missions in Mid-India*.[18] His insights were also heavily influenced by William Carey, John R. Mott, Roland Allen, Kenneth Scott Latourette,[19] and the writings of his own father.[20] Pickett was especially influential to McGavran's missiological concepts. Pickett served for forty-six years as pastor, editor, publisher, secretary of Christian councils, and bishop in the Methodist Church. At the National Christian Council session, members debated the importance of "mass movements" as a measure of missiological success. This crisis precipitated missionary leader John R. Mott to commission research on these "mass movements" to ascertain their effectiveness.[21]

---

17. McGavran, *Bridges of God*, 4.

18. Suarez, "Donald McGavran's Understanding of Conversion," 182–183.

19. Latourette wrote in the introduction to *The Bridges of God*, "It is one of the most important books on missionary methods that have appeared in many years," xiv.

20. McGavran's father John G. McGavran served on the mission field for thirty-eight years. He was known to missionaries of all denominations in the Hindi-speaking world of mid-India as the editor of the *Sahayak Patrika*. McIntosh, *Donald A McGavran*, 82.

21. Pickett's study was the result of criticism from Christian leaders of the mass conversions taking place in India. These Christian leaders assumed that large groups of Indian people coming to Christ would result in a lack of proper Christian training which, in their view, is best offered one convert at a time. Contrary to these assumptions,

Pickett was asked by the National Christian Council of India, Burma, and Ceylon to make an extensive study of Christian mass movements in India. His study sought to find out how effective mass movements were at winning and maturing new Christian believers. The results of Pickett's study were published in *Christian Mass Movements in India* in 1933.

After reading Pickett's research McGavran stated, "There came a book sent by God, and its name was *Christian Mass Movements in India*."[22] These influences, especially Pickett's research, began to change the way McGavran viewed missions.[23] Evidence of Pickett's influence on the later Church Growth Movement is found in the content of the book that they would eventually co-author. In the book, *Church Growth and Group Conversion*, McGavran wrote the dedication, and his words reveal his thinking that became so foundational to the Church Growth Movement. He wrote, "Dedicated to those men and women who labor for the growth of the Churches, discarding theories of church growth which do not work and learning and practicing productive patterns which actually disciple the peoples and increase the Household of God."[24]

Rainer emphasizes Pickett's influence on McGavran and subsequently on the Church Growth Movement in three areas. First, a normative principle[25] for worship and ministry led to pragmatic approaches, which Rainer summarizes as, "If it is not unbiblical, and if it contributes to the growth of the church, then do it."[26] Second is Pickett's introduction to McGavran of how people come to Christ through "mass movements." Rainer points out that McGavran chose to use the term "people movements" rather than "mass movements" because mass movements implied "unthinking

---

Pickett found that those won to Christ through mass movements were growing in their faith and making substantial life changes as a result. McIntosh explains the result of Pickett's research, "Hindu and Muslim observers admitted that Christianity had lifted the untouchables (members of low-caste Hindu groups). The major conclusion resulting from Pickett's intense study was that mass movements, or group movements, as some preferred to call them, were valid and legitimate in God's plan for India's redemption." McIntosh, *Donald A. McGavran*, 90–91.

22. McIntosh, *Donald A. McGavran*, 90.

23. J. Waskom Pickett's influence on McGavran was significant. McGavran has stated, "I lit my candle at Pickett's fire." McGavran and Hunter, III, *Church Growth*, 14.

24. Pickett, Warnshuis, Singh, and McGavran, *Church Growth and Group Conversion*. The first edition was published in 1936.

25. The normative principle states that anything that is not forbidden in Scripture is acceptable in worship and ministry.

26. Rainer, *Book of Church Growth*, 30.

The Age of Church Growth and Pragmatism

acceptance of Christ by great masses."[27] Third is Pickett's emphasis on the importance of the receptivity of people to accept Christ. Rainer writes, "Perhaps the clearest church growth principle that has emerged from Pickett to McGavran to modern church growth is the principle of receptivity."[28] Pickett emphasized that resources of people, money, and energy, in a world of limited resources, should be directed toward people who are most likely to hear and obey the gospel.[29]

The influence of John R. Mott on McGavran and the pragmatic emphasis of the Church Growth Movement is also substantial. Mott was active in the Student Volunteer Movement, the Intercollegiate Young Men's Christian Association, the general YMCA, and the International Missionary Council. He was a unique voice of pragmatic missional approach particularly related to the evangelization of people through the development of indigenous growing churches.[30] Although Mott was generally supportive of the Mission Station[31] approach, he insisted that the ultimate goal of mission work was not to give agricultural, medical, and economic assistance, but rather, "The primary emphasis should continue to be placed on evangelism and religious education."[32] Mott's pragmatic approach is also seen in his foreword to McGavran and Pickett's book *Church Growth and Group Conversion*:

> The distinctive and important contribution of this most instructive, stimulating, and reassuring book has been that of setting forth with clarity and frankness why on the one hand the work of so many church and mission stations has been so comparatively sterile, and why in other cases their labors have been attended with wonderful fruitfulness. It raises the serious question of whether the time has not come in field after field, not only in India but also

---

27. Rainer, *Book of Church Growth*, 30.
28. Rainer, *Book of Church Growth*, 30.
29. Rainer, *Book of Church Growth*, 30.
30. Fisher, *John R. Mott*, 6, 10.
31. McGavran criticized the well-established missiological strategy of a *mission station* approach in *The Bridges of God*. Rather than *mission station* he used the term *gathered colony*. He defines the mission station approach, "Under the present strategy, Christian leaders tend to think of missions as a conglomerate mass of mixed chicken-raising, evangelism, medicine, loving service, educational illumination, and better farming, out of which some time and somehow, a Christian civilization will arise! The treatment for all such splendid and self-sacrificing mission work is the same: pray for it and support it." McGavran, *The Bridges of God*, 103.
32. Fisher, *Mott*, 155.

in other lands, when there should be a major shift in emphasis and a marked reallocation of resources of men and money.[33]

As a result of these influences, McGavran's missiological views began to change. As he worked within the conservative mission station approach in India, he was frustrated by the lack of results. He gradually reverted to his formative years as a child when he first learned that the Great Commission of Christ was to win the world and save lost humanity. Regarding his changing views, he wrote:

> As my convictions about mission and church growth were being molded in the 1930s and 40s, they ran headlong into the thrust that mission is doing many good things in addition to evangelism. I could not accept this way of thinking about missions. These good deeds must, of course, be done, and Christians will do them. I myself was doing many of them. But they must never replace the essential task of mission, discipling the peoples of the earth.[34]

He and Mary would travel for five years, 1954-1959, on the mission field studying how churches were growing and this time provided significant research for the study of church growth throughout the world. McIntosh writes, "The studies had added considerably to Donald's understanding, and he published a second book, *How Churches Grow: The New Frontiers of Mission*."[35] In *The Bridges of God*, McGavran showed how people movements impacted the growth of the church. In this new book, however, he demonstrated that churches grow in many different ways, depending on their circumstances. The book was the first full expression of his church growth missiology.[36]

McGavran as an Academician

McGavran served American Christian higher education institutions, which became laboratories for his church growth philosophies drawing significant interest from church and denominational leaders from across the globe.

---

33. John R. Mott, foreword to *Church Growth and Group Conversion*, v. After the original publication of this book in 1936 there were subsequent editions in 1938, 1956, 1962, and 1973. Mott's foreword first appeared in the 1938 edition.
34. McGavran, "My Pilgrimage in Mission," 54.
35. McIntosh, *Donald A. McGavran*, 145.
36. McIntosh, *Donald A. McGavran*, 145.

The Age of Church Growth and Pragmatism

His fusion of academics with ecclesiological and evangelistic principles is quite significant as he was able to bridge the gap that had developed between academic institutions and congregations.[37] *Effective Evangelism* was one of the final writings of McGavran and in it, he explains the gap that had developed between Christian higher education and churches. He writes, "Though we might be tempted to separate theological education from evangelism, we are reminded of our eternal God's command to disciple all the peoples of the earth and His promise that in Abraham all the peoples of the world would be blessed."[38] During McGavran's life, he served as a faculty member in nine institutions of higher learning, and during that time he perceived that most schools didn't count evangelism or church growth as an important part of their curriculum. He writes in *Effective Evangelism*, "Under the impact of the worldwide church growth movement this regrettable state of affairs is changing."[39] McGavran is often remembered for his missiology and his impact on churches, but perhaps overlooked is his significant contribution to the pedagogy of Christian higher education.

McGavran, through his research, grew continually frustrated about the lack of evangelistic church growth on the mission field. He believed that the reason for this was the lack of proper evangelistic and church growth training the missionaries were receiving in theological institutions. He writes, "As I pondered these things, it became clear to me that I ought to resign from the missionary society and start an institute of church growth. This would enroll career missionaries from many denominations."[40] His decision to begin an institute of church growth began the institutionalization of the Church Growth Movement and changed the trajectory of McGavran's life and ministry. In 1959, he approached the presidents of three seminaries with the idea of starting an institute and was turned down by all three. Unperturbed he shared his dream with the president of the Northwest Christian College in Eugene Oregon, where he was teaching during the spring semester of 1959. Northwest president, Dr. Ross Griffeth replied

---

37. McGavran shares his frustration with the disconnect between the academy and the Great Commission in the first chapter of Effective Evangelism. He writes, "Do theological seminaries have anything to do with effective evangelism? Or are seminaries and Bible colleges concerned only with correct views of the Bible and with inculcating true doctrines." McGavran, *Effective Evangelism*, 1.

38. McGavran, *Effective Evangelism*, 1.

39. McGavran, *Effective Evangelism*, 2.

40. McGavran, *Effective Evangelism*, 69.

to McGavran's request, "We would be happy to have you as a member of our faculty. You could begin the Institute of Church Growth here."[41] In 1960, after completing his missionary assignment, McGavran moved to Eugene to begin working on creating the Institute at Northwest Christian College. The Institute opened on January 2, 1961, with one student. Over the next four years, fifty-seven missionaries studied at the Institute while on Furlough, and one of those students, Alan Tippett, would eventually become the second member of the church growth faculty.[42]

Though the Institute at Northwest was foundational to the institutionalization of the movement, it had its share of struggles particularly financially, and in establishing an accredited graduate degree program. The first two building blocks for the Church Growth Movement would be the founding of the Institute of Church Growth at Northwest, and the second was just as significant, the beginning of the *Church Growth Bulletin* in 1964. The first issue of the *Church Growth Bulletin* was published in September of that year, and it proved to be a key communication piece during the infancy of the Church Growth Movement.[43] These developments along with a church growth four-day seminar for missionaries on furlough sponsored by the Evangelical Foreign Missions Association, further propagated church growth thinking.[44] McGavran noted the various contributions made to the Church Growth Movement at Northwest Christian College:

> Thus, at the Institute of Church Growth between January of 1961 and June of 1965 many notable contributions to church growth thinking were made. Year by year leaders of the universal church had impressed upon them that the actual winning of men and women to Christ and the multiplication of congregations, far from being the concern only of missionary societies and professional evangelists, were the concern of the entire church. Seminary professors, mission executives, and all leaders of all denominations needed to know what was actually happening in regard to the discipling of the unsaved in their own nations and in all other nations. It was not enough to shepherd existing churches and proclaim the gospel widely. The goal was much more than that. The goal was to multiply sound, believing, Spirit-filled congregations

---

41. McGavran, *Effective Evangelism*, 69.
42. McIntosh, *Donald A. McGavran*, 152.
43. McIntosh, *Donald A. McGavran*, 164.
44. McGavran, *Effective Evangelism*, 71–72.

in every segment of society in North America and other five continents as well.[45]

By 1965 it was becoming increasingly clear that the Institute of Church Growth at Northwest would close due to financial issues. During this same time, the president of Fuller Theological Seminary in Pasadena, California David Hubbard, invited McGavran to Fuller to discuss a dream the school had of establishing a school of evangelism. The result of that meeting which took place in February of 1965, was to explore the possibility of getting the Institute of Church Growth to move to Fuller as the nucleus of the school of mission. As a step of preparation for establishing the new school, President Hubbard asked Donald McGavran to write a brief statement as to the kind of graduate school of world missions and evangelism he envisioned at Fuller Theological Seminary. His statement emitted excitement and was formative to the decision to start the school. He wrote:

> Training missionaries and nationals in harvesting evangelism with a minor emphasis on seed sowing evangelism, training men to know how churches grow, discovering by rigorous research what methods God has blessed to church multiplication, furnishing missionaries those knowledges and skills, language skills, understanding of younger churches, nationalism, the science of man, the need for both Christian unity and doctrinal truth, etc. These things which help them be effective witnesses in today's world.[46]

McGavran was soon hired as founding Dean of the School of World Missions at Fuller Theological Seminary where he secured Tippett as its first faculty member. During his time as Dean of the school McGavran continued to research church growth, developed case studies, and taught his missiological principles to others. The first year of classes began with fifteen students but eventually grew to become one of the most influential schools of missiology in the world. By the fall of 1971 the school had a faculty of six, a student body of more than eighty missionaries and nationals, from forty-one countries.[47] In *Effective Evangelism*, McGavran offers a view into the ground-breaking curriculum and training given at Fuller:

> The School of World Mission used the sciences of man, such as sociology and anthropology, to increase understanding of the

---

45. McGavran, *Effective Evangelism*, 77–78.
46. McIntosh, *Donald A McGavran*, 174.
47. McIntosh, *Donald A McGavran*, 212.

complex and little-known process of church growth out of non-Christian populations. In training missionaries these sciences have often been used to reduce the Westerners' ethnocentrism—his smug sense of superiority. The School of World Mission did not use sciences that way. It used them to obtain more and better church growth, that men may be reconciled to God.[48]

The group of faculty members hired between 1965–1971 includes Edwin Orr, Ralph Winter, Charles Kraft, Arthur Glasser, and C. Peter Wagner. They became known as the "Pasadena gang" and they were clearly the most associated people with the work of church growth. Win Arn, was later added to the group and eventually founded the Institute of American Church Growth in 1972, and John Wimber eventually became founding director of the Department of Church Growth at Fuller Evangelistic Association.[49]

Along with the work of the Fuller school, the ongoing influence of the annual church growth seminar must also be considered. The seminar, held at Biola College in Los Angeles, was a continuation of the seminar begun by the Evangelical Foreign Missions Association, originally held in Winona Lake, Indiana. It was from these lectures delivered by McGavran at the seminar that his book *Understanding Church Growth*, was published.[50] McGavran's work at Fuller, along with C. Peter Wagner and others, would come to have a dramatic impact on the American ecclesial landscape. Though Thom Rainer and Lifeway Resources contributed substantially to the perpetuation of the Church Growth Movement,[51] the Pasadena gang remains the seminal voice of the movement.

THE CHURCH GROWTH MOVEMENT AND THE AMERICAN CHURCH

According to Lyle Schaller, the most momentous development of religion in America during the 1970s was the emergence of the Church Growth Movement.[52] Before the 1970s the focus of church growth was on mission

48. McGavran, *Effective Evangelism*, 81–82.
49. Rainer, *Book of Church Growth*, 41.
50. McGavran, *Effective Evangelism*, 72.
51. Rainer was honored on November 11, 2010, as the recipient of the Donald A. McGavran Award for outstanding leadership in church growth. The award was presented to Rainer by the *Great Commission Research Network*.
52. Schaller, foreword to *Church Growth*, 7.

The Age of Church Growth and Pragmatism

fields apart from North America, however, McGavran's writings along with the growing influence of the Fuller School of Missions and the Institute of Church Growth were key to bringing missiological concepts to an American ecclesial audience. A key event occurred in 1972 as a pastor from Pasadena, Chuck Miller, remarked to C. Peter Wagner, "I would like to learn church growth thinking so that I can be all that God wants me to be." Wagner replied, "You can't do that because you haven't been in the Third World for three years and Dr. McGavran does not want to do the American scene." Upon hearing the request of Pastor Miller, McGavran agreed without hesitation saying, "I don't see why we can't do this." [53] The result of Pastor Miller's question was a class taught by Wagner and McGavran on church growth for American church leaders. The class brought together a group of eighteen area pastors, including Chuck Miller, at the Lake Avenue Congregational Church. McGavran and Wagner taught through the book, *Understanding Church Growth* which they covered chapter-by-chapter and the pastors discussed application to their own church situation. Excitement about what the pastors learned ignited a passion in some of the men who attended, including Win Arn.[54]

Another significant contribution to the establishment of the Church Growth Movement in America was the publication of *How to Grow a Church* written by Donald McGavran and Win Arn. The book was dramatically different than McGavran's previous books which usually presented a highly technical writing style geared toward overseas mission efforts. The book was written for an American church audience in an easy-to-understand dialogue between McGavran and Arn.[55] Before the book's publication very few pastors in America were familiar with McGavran's principles and had not read his books, but the publications of *Understanding Church Growth* and *How to Grow a Church*, changed everything. McGavran's principles were beginning to be widely considered in an American ecclesial context. Donald McGavran retired from his position as Dean of the School of Missions and Institute of Church Growth in 1973, though he would remain on faculty. His retirement led to opportunities for both Wagner and Arn to display the Institute of Church Growth concepts more prominently to an American audience.

---

53. Chuck Miller telephone interview by David L. Cook as recorded in David Lowell Cook's "The Americanization of the Church Growth Movement," 19.

54. Cook, *Americanization*, 20.

55. Rainer, *Book of Church Growth*, 44.

C. Peter Wagner and the Church Growth Movement

It was C. Peter Wagner, more than anyone else, that kept church growth at the forefront of American evangelicalism. Though Wagner's initial response to McGavran's *The Bridges of God* was negative,[56] he eventually began to deeply appreciate the teachings of McGavran when he entered Fuller Theological Seminary in 1967. Rainer writes of Wagner's influence on the proliferation of McGavran's church growth principles, "Whereas Fuller Seminary gave the movement its institutional staying power, Wagner provided the personal leadership to keep church growth at the forefront of evangelical Christianity."[57] Wagner's publication of *Church Growth and the Whole Gospel* in 1981 propelled him as the leader of the movement. His service in many prominent positions was also critical to keeping church growth principles mainstream in American evangelicalism. He was a charter member of the Lausanne Committee for World Evangelization when it was formed in 1974. He served on the Executive Committee for six years. Due to his positions of influence within the Lausanne committee, church growth played a major role in the path toward the rising influence of modern evangelicalism.

McGavran's missionary spirit was the pioneering influence on the Church Growth Movement, but it was Wagner's persistent writing and salesmanship that kept the flame of church growth alive for more than two decades. His most important tool in keeping the movement alive was his writings. In the decade of the 1970s, he wrote several books explaining the practical application of the church growth theories which had their moorings in McGavran's missiology. Unlike McGavran, however, Wagner focused almost exclusively on the American ecclesial scene and targeted evangelical pastors and church members. His book *Your Church Can Grow* sold over 100,000 copies, as well as *Your Spiritual Gifts Can Help Your Church Grow*.[58] Wagner described his book, *Your Church Can Grow* as "one of the first systematic attempts to apply the scientific principles of

---

56. Wagner said of his reading of *The Bridges of God*, "So I finished the book and put it on the shelf for cockroach food. I went on to some other books and forgot about it." Rainer, *The Book of Church Growth*, 53.

57. Rainer, *Book of Church Growth*, 51. Rainer also refers to Wagner as the "chief spokesperson for the Church Growth Movement," 51.

58. Rainer, *Book of Church Growth*, 57.

The Age of Church Growth and Pragmatism

church growth as developed by Donald McGavran specifically to the North American scene."[59]

Other significant factors in bringing church growth into the American scene include the addition of a church growth component to the Doctor of Ministry program at Fuller's School of World Missions. This was heavily influenced by Wagner's desire to effectively train American evangelical pastors on the evangelistic principles of the movement. In 1974 when Fuller was overhauling the DMin curriculum Wagner pushed for the inclusion of an in-ministry model approach which included two units on American church growth. The two courses included: "Principles and Procedures of Church Growth" and "Church Growth Research." Additional courses were added to the program in 1978 which focused on the anthropology, theology, and history of church growth. These classes trained ministers in practical methodologies and theoretical principles that could be immediately applied to the American ecclesial setting. Wagner was the principal instructor in the Fuller Doctor of Ministry program teaching more than 2,000 students by 1988.[60] Also significant was Wagner's steering of the Charles Fuller Evangelistic Association toward becoming a leading church growth organization.

In the late 1970s, Peter Wagner began to turn his attention to the spiritual side of the Church Growth Movement as a response to the criticisms of those who claimed church growth was all pragmatic to the exclusion of the spiritual. For example, mission professor Herbert Kane criticized the movement saying, "The proponents of church growth, with few exceptions, have emphasized the human factors and all but overlooked the divine factor."[61] The influence of Pentecostalism within the Church Growth Movement began to increase due to Wagner's study of growing Latin churches in America, many of which practiced the charismatic gifts. Over the years of studying the effectiveness of these charismatic churches, he increasingly was influenced by Pentecostal spirituality. By the late 1970s, Wagner was lecturing on divine healing as a means of church growth, which propelled the impact of the Church Growth Movement into charismatic churches and denominations in the United States and beyond. One of the most controversial factors was Wagner's class offered at Fuller entitled, "Signs, Wonders and Church Growth." He taught the class with John Wimber, and

---

59. C. Peter Wagner, *Your Church Can Grow*, 10.
60. Cook, "Americanization of the Church Growth Movement," 21–22.
61. Kane, *Christian World Mission*, 212.

it was not unusual for students to stay after class and request prayer for divine healing. The course drew criticism from people all over the nation, especially from Fuller supporters. They felt that "Fuller Seminary was going charismatic."[62]

Wagner's newfound openness to charismatic gifts marked a new development of the Church Growth Movement, focusing more on the supernatural and departing from the movement's social science research approach. The bulk of his writing from this point forward would have a Pentecostal flare. Cook writes, "Most revealing in Wagner's Pentecostalization of the Church Growth Movement was his editing of the third edition of *Understanding Church Growth* to which he added a chapter on 'Divine Healing and Church Growth.'"[63]

Paradigm Shifts and Iterations of the Movement

Since the inception of the Church Growth Movement in America, it has taken on various iterations and synonymous terms. Other terms used for church growth in American ecclesial culture include evangelism, effective evangelism, missiology, conversion growth, quality growth, organic growth, and church planting and multiplication.[64] In an effort to employ social and demographic research tools to discover the responsive segments of society, the later iterations of the movement became increasingly pragmatic in approach. McIntosh recognizes at least four paradigm shifts that have taken place from its inception to the present day, at least as it is recognized among church leaders and the public in general.

In its inception, it was largely a *research-based paradigm* that sought facts related to church growth and decline. McGavran sought to answer the meta-question, "Why do some churches grow while others don't?" He identified four sub-questions that collectively would answer the meta-question, and these would be the basis for the entire Church Growth Movement. First, what are the causes of church growth? Second, what are the barriers to church growth? Third, what are the factors that can make the Christian faith a movement among some populations? Finally, what principles of church growth are reproducible?[65]

62. Cook, "Americanization," 27.
63. Cook, "Americanization," 27.
64. McIntosh, "Church Movements of the Last Fifty Years in North America," 40.
65. Hunter III, "Legacy of Donald A. McGavran," 158.

The Age of Church Growth and Pragmatism

In the 1980s as a response to the request of pastors to assist them in implementing the church growth principles as a strategic plan, it turned into a *business paradigm*. Strategic planning included setting numerical and ministry goals, improving facilities, and hiring the right kind of people to fulfill the strategic plans. Kennon L. Callahan was the leading proponent of this business approach to church growth. His book, *Twelve Keys to an Effective Church* published in 1983 was a prime example of the shift in literature toward a business approach to church growth. Callahan sought to assist churches in long-term planning to improve finances, worship services, leadership, accessibility, parking, seating, objectives, and small group discipleship. The next paradigm shift took place in the late 1980s with the writings of George Barna. He proposed a *marketing paradigm* for church growth in his book, *Marketing The Church* which was released in 1988. Barna suggested that the answer to the decline of church attendance in the United States was the use of a marketing orientation, something that most churches had never considered. He took the earlier business paradigm further by employing marketing approaches as a means to attract and win people to Christ and increase church attendance. Though his intentions were good, his approach ultimately was negatively received and was turned away by many church leaders. This caused a reaction that eventually led to the *church health paradigm* of the mid-1990s. The church health writings were only adaptations of earlier principles from McGavran and Win Arn's *How to Grow a Church*.

Three key books were published including *The Purpose Driven Church* by Rick Warren in 1995, *Natural Church Development* by Christian Schwarz in 1996, and *Becoming A Healthy Church* by Stephen A. Macchia in 1999. Of particular importance during this time was Warren's *purpose-driven* approach to healthy church growth. Warren admits that he was heavily impacted by McGavran's church growth principles while serving as a student missionary in Japan. While on the mission field, Warren discovered an article about Donald McGavran and the impact was significant. Warren writes, "The day I read the McGavran article, I felt God directing me to invest the rest of my life discovering the principles—biblical, cultural, and leadership principles—that produce healthy, growing churches. It was the beginning of a lifelong study."[66] His research of McGavran and the Church Growth Movement was so extensive that he wrote, "I've read nearly every

---

66. Warren, *Purpose Driven Church*, 30.

book in print on church growth."[67] Warren's demographic description of "Saddleback Sam"[68] as a target population is proof of the impact that McGavran's sociological approach had on his ministry.

The same could be said of several mega-churches in the 1990s as they employed variations of McGavran's Homogenous Unit Principle (HUP)[69] as a scientific method of better understanding those persons they were trying to reach.[70] Elmer Towns stated, "These churches know where people are in their thinking and life-style, and they know how to reach them."[71] Bill Hybels, founding pastor of Willow Creek Community Church, was also heavily impacted by McGavran's principles. Whereas Saddleback focused on "Sam" Willow Creek had their own general profile as a target audience, "Unchurched Harry."[72] Hybels was certainly impacted by McGavran's HUP as indicated by Town's summation of his views:

> Many pastors and churches are ineffective simply because they are trying to reach people with whom they have no natural affinity. He believes God uses individual pastor's unique gifts and passions to enable them to reach a specific group of people—the inner-city, urban fast-trackers, the working class, rural Midwesterners, university students, suburbanites, and so on.[73]

Has this approach led to effective disciple making? The result of the work to attract crowds to the church through programs and worship customized to meet the needs and match the preferences of a specific target has been historically effective at drawing crowds but did not create long-term results through equipped multiplying disciple makers.

A prime example of an attractional program-centered church's failure to make disciples was displayed in 2007 when the leaders of Willow Creek Community Church—one of America's largest and most influential

---

67. Warren, *Purpose Driven Church*, 17.

68. Warren, *Purpose Driven Church*, 155.

69. McGavran explains the HUP principle this way, "Men like to become Christians without crossing racial, linguistic, or class barriers." McGavran, *Understanding Church Growth*, 223.

70. Towns, *Inside Look*, 14.

71. Towns, *Inside Look*, 12.

72. Lee Strobel wrote a book entitled, *Inside the Mind of Unchurched Harry and Mark: How to Reach Friends and Family Who Avoid God and the Church* in 1993. It became the guidebook that Hybels used as a target demographic.

73. Towns, *Inside Look*, 47.

churches—presented the findings of a multi-year qualitative analysis of its ministry. Their philosophy of ministry up to that point was summed up in this way, "The church creates programs and activities. People participate in these activities. The outcome is spiritual maturity." The study consisted of evaluating the programs and activities of the church and their impact on the spiritual maturity and growth of the members. The results of their findings led the leadership to a very somber conclusion, "Increasing levels of participation in these sets of activities does NOT predict whether someone's becoming more of a disciple of Christ." As a result of their analysis, pastor Bill Hybels stated, "Some of the stuff that we have put millions of dollars into thinking it would really help our people grow and develop spiritually, when the data actually came back, it wasn't helping people that much." Hybels called this finding a wake-up call for his church. Though this example is specific to one church, the realities of the findings showed that increased activity and programming did not necessarily produce disciple making disciples. This is not to say that the activities and programs were not evangelistically infused, but were the results ultimately effective in equipping Christians to grow as disciples and make more disciples? It is entirely possible that the declining numbers of church attendance in the 2020s is directly related to the lack of effectiveness of the Church Growth Movement to create lasting disciple making impact.

CRITICISMS OF THE CHURCH GROWTH MOVEMENT IN AMERICA

From the very beginning of the Americanization of the Church Growth Movement, there were critics. Some of this is due to the unclear identity of what exactly the Church Growth Movement was. Church growth material during the decade of the 1970s was being produced at such an incredible rate by a cross-section of authors that it was difficult to determine who was the voice of the movement. The Church Growth Movement was not always responsive to criticisms due to McGavran's polemic approach as straightforward and uncompromising. Many of his writings were bold in assertion and unapologetic in tone, turning a deaf ear to the voices of the critics. The advances made in the Church Growth Movement in the 1970s also brought a gathered momentum of critical response, to which eventually the leaders of the movement would have to respond. Much of the criticism was due to what some saw as "evangelism without the Gospel."[74] One such critic, Tom Nees, said of the theology of evangelism of the Church Growth Movement, "It reduces initial Christian commitment to an inoffensive appeal avoiding the suggestion that to become a Christian one must turn from a social order that perpetuates injustice."[75] John H. Piet criticized McGavran's definition of evangelism as being too narrow of a description.[76] Wagner received the most criticism after the publication of *Understanding Church Growth*. His writing was criticized for not having a strategy for evangelism as part of his church growth strategies. As one commentator stated, "Wagner's methodology is a mixture of theological absolutism (i.e., the necessity for a born-again experience) and sociological utilitarianism."[77] Wagner's growing interest in the charismatic gifts also brought criticism as he and the Church Growth Movement in general were viewed as propaganda for Pentecostalism.

Some critics viewed the principles of the movement as too pragmatic, only focused on numerical increase. Part of this frustration was the belief that rapid conversions were producing immature Christians ultimately causing some to call for the stoppage of evangelism so that new converts could be matured. McGavran disagreed, "Much Christianization and many, many imperfect Christians!!" He continued, "What does Church Growth say to this? My answer is simple. Keep on baptizing as many as possible and teaching them all things whatsoever the Lord commanded as vigorously as possible."[78] Donald Drayton, a professor of theology at North Park Theological Seminary, wrote a scathing review of the Church Growth Movement in the *Christian Century*. He maintained, "The high commitment of Church Growth teaching to the social sciences, especially anthropology, has led to the incorporation of a large portion of the relativism and pragmatism of the modern worldview."

An unfair criticism was that McGavran and the Church Growth Movement were largely atheological. Much of this criticism is due to McGavran's impreciseness in his writings regarding his theological and

---

74. Rainer, *Book of Church Growth*, 45.

75. Rainer, *Book of Church Growth*, 45.

76. Rainer, *Book of Church Growth*, 45. Rainer points out that McGavran affirmed William Temple's definition of evangelism, "Evangelism is the winning of men to acknowledge Christ as their Savior and King, so that they give themselves to His service in the fellowship of His church."

77. Rainer, *Book of Church Growth*, 45.

78. McIntosh, *Donald A. McGavran*, 253.

soteriological beliefs. Walters states, "While he may never have delineated a precise theology of evangelism, one can find in McGavran's writings an orthodox, if sometimes incomplete, system regarding the working of God in the salvation of men."[79] McGavran recognized this criticism and addressed it in *Understanding Church Growth*. He argues:

> Church growth is basically a theological stance. God requires it. It looks to the Bible for direction as to what God wants done. It holds that belief in Jesus Christ, understood according to the Scriptures, is necessary for salvation. Church growth rises in unshakable theological conviction ... From the beginning the Church Growth Movement has been rooted in biblical, evangelical, conversionist theology.[80]

McGavran asserts that the leaders of the movement often withheld their personal theological convictions because of the movement's interdenominational milieu. It wasn't that the movement was atheological, only that the leaders knew that substantial theological differences existed within the various streams of the movement. Ultimately the focus of the movement was not on baptismal views, ecclesiological differences, the practice of spiritual gifts, or whether women should be ordained. The theological rallying point was, "Men and women without a personal relationship with Jesus Christ are doomed to a Christless eternity. The decisions they make for or against Jesus Christ in this life will make the difference."[81]

Receiving the most criticism was McGavran's Homogeneous Unit Principle (HUP). In his book, *The Bridges of God*, McGavran offers a careful examination of the social and cultural cohesion of which bridges could be built from which the gospel could be offered without considerable cultural obstacles. He argued that there could be significant factors affecting a group's receptivity or resistance to the gospel. He called for new converts to immerse and remain immersed in their cultures rather than their culture being inculcated into a Westernized Christian mindset using mission stations.[82] There must be, he argued, culturally relevant ways to present the gospel. By taking down the cultural barriers, large homogeneous units of

---

79. Walters, "Donald McGavran's Theological Foundations for 'Effective Evangelism,'" 50.

80. McGavran, *Understanding Church Growth*, 8.

81. McGavran, *Understanding Church Growth*, 9.

82. Van Engen, "Bridges of God: The Mission Legacy of Donald Anderson McGavran," 29.

people will be won to Christ as cultural *bridges* are built for them to travel across to become Christians, accept the gospel, and be won to Christ. Much of the criticism has come from those who see the HUP to be potentially racist and segregating in its praxis within American ecclesial entities.

In response to such criticism, McGavran wrote a letter explaining the principle in terms of missiological rather than ecclesiological:

> The HU principle arose facing the three billion who have yet to believe. Tremendous numbers of people are not becoming Christian because of unnecessary barriers (of language, culture, wealth, education, sophistication, imperialistic stance) erected by the advocates. The HU principle was first enunciated by a missionary carrying out what our Roman Catholic brethren call "the apostolate." The Early Church acted in accordance with the HU principle . . . Do, I beg of you, think of it primarily as a missionary and an evangelistic principle. There is danger, of course, that congregations (whether established in the HU principle or not) become exclusive, arrogant, and racist. That danger must be resolutely combated.[83]

McGavran's insistence that the HUP was a missiological principle denotes the fact that it was not created for an ecclesial context but was later adapted when his missiological principles became mainstream as church growth principles. For example, it is noted in *Church Growth: Strategies that Work*, "In the seventies, the principle began to be observed in American churches."[84] In a 1978 article in *Christianity Today* Peter Wager and Ray Stedman argue the merits of HUP. Stedman states, "A church can grow like that, but it does not fulfill the mind of the Lord for the church." Wagner acknowledges the ecclesial risk of the principle, "the homogeneous unit principle is a starting point. If it's an ending point, it is sub-Christian."[85]

Analysis of McGavran's Theology of Evangelism

McGavran's source of theology was his strong belief in the authority of Scripture. In an article on the central tenets of a theology of evangelism, he lists first, "The absolute inspiration and authority of the Bible."[86] Whatever

---

83. McIntosh, "Life of Donald McGavran: Coming of Age," 186–187.
84. McGavran and Hunter III, *Church Growth*, 31.
85. Wagner and Stedman, "Should the Church Be a Melting Pot?" 10.
86. McGavran, "Contemporary Evangelical Theology of Mission," 101.

one's opinion of McGavran's theology, it cannot be argued that he had a low view of Scripture, nor can it be proven that the Church Growth Movement was atheological. According to McGavran, the supreme reason for engaging in missions and evangelism can be summed up by one statement, "It is God's will that his church grow, that his lost children be found."[87] McGavran's idea of church growth was purely evangelistic, and he would use the term *church growth* synonymously with *effective evangelism* later in his life, this is especially seen in his book by that title.[88] He coined the term *church growth* to distinguish it from those that were offering social services or good deeds without an effective evangelism strategy, which he frequently observed on the mission field. McGavran's missiology, as he articulated in *The Bridges of God* and *Understanding Church Growth*, was based on a clear biblical theology in relation to the lostness of humanity and the redemption available through Christ. His definition of missions offers the theoretical foundations of the Church Growth Movement and gives insight into his theology of evangelism,

> Since God as revealed in the Bible has assigned the highest priority to bringing men and women into living relationship to Jesus Christ, we may define missions narrowly as an enterprise devoted to proclaiming the Good News of Jesus Christ and to persuading men (and women) to become His disciples and dependable members of His church.[89]

Any discussion of McGavran's theology of evangelism must include his view of the lost condition of humanity and God's *missio Dei*.[90] God desires that none perish and that all would come to repentance (2 Pet. 3:9).[91] His view of conversion is based upon a foundational belief of the authoritative Word of God as the only adequate source for a right theological perspective

---

87. Hunter, III, "Legacy of Donald A. McGavran," 159.

88. Suarez, "Donald McGavran's Understanding of Conversion," 187.

89. Donald A. McGavran, *Understanding Church Growth*, 35.

90. Both Donald McGavran and Lesslie Newbigin shared a common perspective related to the foundational missiological principle of the *missio Dei*. Both men emphasized the importance of the *missio Dei* as the main objective of the church. McGavran states, "In this world, mission must be what God desires. It is not a human activity but missio Dei, the mission of God, who himself remains in charge of it." McGavran, *Understanding Church Growth*, 20.

91. Van Engen, "Bridges of God: The Mission Legacy of Donald Anderson McGavran," 30.

on the human condition and God's remedy.⁹² In conversion, mankind is to leave behind unbiblical ideas such as polytheism or worldly philosophies before coming to God.⁹³ As seen already in this chapter McGavran's idea of conversion is rooted not only in theology but also in sociology and anthropology, through an ecclesiological context.⁹⁴ This is a key component in understanding his soteriology.

The Great Commission of Jesus Christ (Matt 28:19-20) is foundational to McGavran's theological expressions, and his interpretation of it is crucial to understanding his theology of evangelism and conversion. His use of the term *church growth* was simply a way to describe the essential work of the Great Commission. His view of the missionary enterprise of the church went beyond social services or good deeds, making the conversion of the people in mass movements the primary concern. McGavran stated, "These good deeds must, of course, be done, and Christians will do them. I myself was doing many of them. But they must never replace the essential task of missions, discipling the peoples on Earth."⁹⁵ McGavran used the term *discipling* to describe the process of "helping people turn from non-Christian faith to Christ."⁹⁶ In other words, one can equate his *discipling* with what most call *evangelism*. As stated previously, his definition of missions as "proclaiming Christ and persuading men to become His disciples and responsible members of His church,"⁹⁷ offers a two-fold articulation of evangelism and the fulfillment of the Great Commission. The key to understanding McGavran's theology of evangelism is found in this bifurcated definition encompassing both conversion and church membership. He believed that evangelism was incomplete if new believers did not become active participants in church membership.⁹⁸

---

92. Early in his theological development McGavran was influenced by liberal theologians within his own denomination and through Yale Divinity. His theological shift from liberalism to a conservative view of Scripture was in response to seeing firsthand the destructive nature of a low view of the historical critical approach. McGavran on the impact that liberalism had on his life after his Yale experience, "The Bible that I read for the next fifteen years had the various strands (J, E, D, P, etc.) underlined in different colors." McGavran, *Effective Evangelism*, 55.

93. McGavran, *Bridges of God*, 14.

94. Suarez, "Donald McGavran's Understanding of Conversion," 187.

95. McIntosh, *Donald A. McGavran*, 15.

96. McGavran, *Bridges of God*, 15.

97. McGavran, *Understanding Church Growth*, 35.

98. Walters, "Donald McGavran's Theological Foundations for 'Effective Evangelism,'"

The Age of Church Growth and Pragmatism

In examining McGavran's theology of evangelism it is important to remember that he writes as a missionary first whose intent is to reach a "people," rather than a "person." The dual nature of his theology of evangelism is fleshed out in his book *The Bridges of God* in which he describes his view of Matthew 28:19-20. He believed that the convert must experience a new birth. McGavran states, "The Christianization of peoples is not assisted by slighting or forgetting real personal conversion. There is no substitute for justification by faith in Jesus Christ or for the gift of the Holy Spirit."[99] He explains conversion or *discipling* takes place when people feel "united around Jesus Christ as Lord and Savior, believe themselves to be members of His Church, and realize that 'our folk are Christians, our book is the Bible, and our house of worship is the church.'"[100] The second stage of evangelism found in the Great Commission was "teaching them all things" or as McGavran called it, *perfecting*.[101] In the *perfecting* stage, the members of the Christian community experience an ethical change. He states, "This is a bringing about of an ethical change in the discipled group, an increasing achievement of a thoroughly Christian way of life."[102] This two-fold approach to the Great Commission would have a lasting impact on his writings on church growth throughout his life, the Church Growth Movement, and eventually on American evangelicalism in general.

Finally, in reflecting on Donald McGavran's theology of evangelism, his development of the HUP was paramount in his belief of how to best evangelize people. This was a critical concept that galvanized his theology, sociology, and anthropology into one coherent process of mass evangelization. He defined these units as any group of people with some commonality in the way they communicated and related to each other. McGavran tied this into the Great Commission as he believed making disciples, *panta ta ethne* (Matt 28:19), was a mandate to reach the families, clans, tribes, castes, and ethnic groups—that is the peoples of humanity. Much of the affinity group outreach in the modern church today has its etymology in McGavran's homogeneous view of people movements.[103]

53.

99. McGavran, *Bridges of God*, 11.
100. McGavran, *Bridges of God*, 14.
101. McGavran, *Bridges of God*, 14.
102. McGavran, *Bridges of God*, 15.
103. McGavran, *Bridges of God*, 15.

Donald McGavran's contributions to the missional re-focusing of the North American evangelical church is substantial, and the benefits that sprang from his research and teaching have far outweighed the criticisms over the decades. An important question, however, must be asked related to the residual ecclesial impact of his views. Have McGavran's principles had negative implications on the disciple making foci of the local church in North American ecclesial practice? To answer that question I offer two primary critiques of McGavran's missiological/church growth principles. First, his view of Matthew 28:19–20 as a two-fold, bifurcated commission, and second, his homogeneous unit principle.

McGavran's interpretation of the Great Commission plays a significant role in what he viewed as *effective evangelism*. Darrell Guder argues that McGavran's distinction between *discipling* and *perfecting* demonstrates a reductionist understanding of the gospel.[104] Disciple making is not a two-pronged approach, but rather a comprehensive approach that sees the Great Commission as one process. The Great Commission of Jesus is the missiological/evangelistic thrust of his church and the church's approach to it calls for a full hermeneutic of the Great Commission. A holistic process-driven approach sees the Great Commission not as a call to convert and then teach, but rather as a way of connecting the *going* to the *baptizing* and *teaching*. Both *discipling* and *perfecting* are simultaneously included. McGavran's choice of terms to explain his bifurcated understanding of Matthew 28:19-20 is also problematic. He used the term *discipling* in a way no one else ever has, thus his use of this term has been widely misunderstood. His use of these terms created an unneeded and unbiblical split in the process of people growing as disciples of Jesus.[105]

In McGavran's defense, he would later give clarity to his views on Matthew 28:19-20 in his book, *How Churches Grow* (1959). There he clarified that the two stages of *discipling* and *perfecting* were virtually indistinguishable. As men turn to Christ, they are expected to grow in faith even as they are leading others to Christ and in turn, making more disciples. Though he would try and explain his thoughts as a coherent whole, his *discipling* and *perfecting* approach would eventually lead to churches and ministries offering evangelistic programming and discipleship opportunities as

---

104. Suarez, "Donald McGavran's Understanding of Conversion," 188.

105. Van Engen, "Centrist View: Church Growth is based on an evangelistically focused and a missiologically applied theology," in *Evaluating the Church Growth Movement*, 142.

separate entities. The results of this type of compartmentalized approach to the Great Commission would naturally evolve into churches creating and heavily investing in evangelistic attractional approaches to reach people while falling short in "teaching them to observe all things." Exegetically, it is difficult, if not impossible, to separate the two commands.[106] In the preface to the 1990 edition of *Understanding Church Growth*, C. Peter Wagner writes of the procedural issues in distinguishing McGavran's *discipling* and *perfecting* as "two discreet stages" of Christianization.[107] In an effort to clarify, Wagner's description of the Great Commission as "two discreet stages" only further complicated the unwarranted bifurcation. McGavran's distinction between *discipling* and *perfecting* did not have adequate theological or hermeneutical support, thus he opened himself to theological criticism and ultimately restricted the disciple making modalities of the Church Growth Movement.[108]

Although McGavran's writings support his view that salvation is by faith alone through grace alone, his fusing of ecclesiology with soteriology has invited criticism from theologians. Church membership was seen by McGavran as the final process of disciple making and he insisted that it was a necessary part of the conversion. McGavran contends that church membership is "the normal fulfillment of conversion."[109] He expounds, "The primary mission of the church is to tell everyone everywhere of God's provision for salvation and to enroll in the ark of salvation—the church of Jesus Christ—as many as believe."[110] The typological reference of the ark of salvation as the church is an unfortunate exegetical conclusion. McGavran treads unbiblical ground in blurring the lines between ecclesiology and soteriology. Should new believers become active members of local churches? Absolutely. Should church membership be equated with a visible sign of soteriological completion? Absolutely not.

---

106. Guder, "Evangelism and the Debate Over Church Growth," 149.

107. McGavran, *Understanding Church Growth*, , x.

108. Suarez, "Donald McGavran's Understanding of Conversion," 197. Suarez's criticism of McGavran's discipling and perfecting view is fair, however, it is my belief that McGavran's true intentions were not to create two stages. There was a bit of nebulousness in how he used these terms which has led to criticism. Therefore, the criticism might be more with how McGavran was perceived rather than his actual view of the Great Commission.

109. McGavran, "Contemporary Evangelical Theology of Missions" in *Contemporary Theology of Missions*, edited by Gladder and McGavran, 103.

110. McGavran, "Contemporary", 105.

As stated, McGavran's missiological HUP sought opportunities to reduce the barriers of a person coming to Christ in such a way that the person would not have to leave family, language, and culture. As a part of the pragmatic approach of church growth which quantified how a church was growing (i.e., through biological reproduction, conversion, or transfer growth), it was just as important to know what social groups were being reached as part of that growth. Jon Bialecki explains the HUP approach at the ecclesial level:

> By charting how various churches were growing and what kind of growth they were experiencing, it would now be possible to allocate resources, both human and financial, in places where there would be the most reward for the investment. For McGavran, the parable of the sower did not mean that the proverbial seeds are to be scattered indiscriminately, but rather that some soils were better than others.[111]

There are two primary criticisms related to this principle. First, there is a segmentation of theology and praxis seen in methodology that is influenced more by anthropology and sociology than theology. Gailyn Van Rheenen states that since methodologies and strategies are never theologically neutral, they "should be shaped by the gospel itself."[112] Second, a homogeneous church offers too narrow of an ethnic focus and does not reflect the true biblical church as more of a mosaic of various ethnicities representing an accurate picture of the kingdom. The picture given by Luke in Acts of the church in Antioch (Acts 13) certainly presents a mosaic of cultures united as one body of believers. Ephesians 2:14-18 presents a church where Christ has "broken down the middle wall of separation" (Eph. 2:14). John saw the final eschatological reality of great multitudes in heaven from every tongue and tribe singing at the marriage supper of the Lamb (Rev. 19:1-10). The growing diversity of the population in North America will require a diverse mosaic, rather than a homogeneous approach to disciple making and evangelism. In conclusion, while McGavran presents a faithful orthodoxy some features of his orthopraxical modalities are problematic for the American Evangelical church as it seeks to fulfill its mission to make disciples through the process of the Great Commission in an ever-growing diverse population.

---

111. Bialecki, "Third Wave and the Third World: C. Peter Wagner, John Wimber, and the Pedagogy of Global Renewal in the Late Twentieth Century," 189.

112. Van Rheenen, "Reformist View," 177.

The Age of Church Growth and Pragmatism

ANALYSIS OF DISCIPLE MAKING IN THE CHURCH GROWTH MOVEMENT

The Church Growth Movement generally had the right orthodoxy related to a high view of Scripture, the sufficiency of Christ as the only way to salvation, substitutionary atonement, the depravity of man, and the church as the redeemed body of believers.[113] This chapter has sought to show that it was the orthopraxy of the movement that lacked a comprehensive agenda in making a long-term impact in producing disciples who make disciples. Later iterations of the movements relied heavily on pragmatic approaches which focused on reaching the multitudes with a "do whatever gets them to church" mentality. Herbert Kane's criticism, "The proponents of church growth, with few exceptions, have emphasized the human factors and all but overlooked the divine factor," [114] is not altogether inaccurate. Wagner stated:

> We believe in pragmatically sound methods. We devise methods and policies in light of what God has blessed, and what he has obviously not blessed. Industry calls this, "modifying operation in light of feedback." We teach men to be ruthless in regard to method. If it does not work to the glory of God, throw it away and get something that does.[115]

How exactly would the leaders of the Church Growth Movement define what is working or not working? Generally, effective churches were seen in light of quantifiable results, and ineffective churches were the ones not growing. McGavran espoused an approach to church growth that essentially removed all the impediments and barriers that kept people from attending. Churches are encouraged to find their homogeneous target, find out what their culture enjoys most about church, and shape programming to match their whims. This approach naturally, over time, leads to churches marketing themselves to a customer base through attractive seeker-sensitive approaches which perpetuates a consumeristic mindset. McGavran states, "The correct policy of evangelism is to disciple each homogeneous unit out

---

113. A slight caveat to this would be Wagner's later iterations into a hyper-Pentecostalism which eventually infiltrated the movement and ultimately, in the opinion of this researcher, caused its ecclesial decline. For more information related to the infiltration of Wagner's Pentecostal influence on the movement see Jon Bialecki, "Third Wave and the Third World," 177–200.

114. Kane, *The Christian World Mission*, 212.

115. Cook, "Americanization," 24.

to its fringes . . . insisting on integration first, whether the church grows or not, is a self-defeating policy and, with rare exceptions, contrary to the will of God."[116] In other words, churches should find their homogeneous market and do whatever is necessary to bring them to church until the church has reached the fringes of the target demographic. Barna's ideas of marketing the church were simply an extension and evolution of McGavran's HUP. David Wells states:

> So when you put all of this together—acceptance of church-growth ideas, the need to grow the church by removing cultural impediments, and the growing transformation of the evangelical world into a sort of corporate understanding in which consuming has a central part—then the marketing of the church is an almost inevitable outcome.[117]

The disciple making model of Jesus was reliant upon relationships and it began with a simple invitation, "Come and see" (John 1:39). What exactly was Jesus calling these initial disciples to see? His invitation was to come and be with him because he was the attraction, and the salvation he offered and the kingdom that he inaugurated broke down all the impediments of culture, language, customs, socioeconomics, and preferences. Christ is a savior for all people, all the time, forevermore. George Hunter considered the receptivity of a culture to be, "The greatest contribution of the church growth movement to this generation's world evangelism."[118] Christ's invitation to come to Him, however, was never based on the receptivity of man, but on the receptivity of God to accept man based on the atonement of Calvary. The receptivity approach teeters on the fringe of an overly anthropocentric missiology, rather than a pneumocentric evangelism. Furthermore, it is God who calls a person to salvation through the conviction of the Holy Spirit,[119] and this spiritual process is not based upon a person's perceived receptivity to the Gospel.

The Church Growth Movement ultimately became focused on drawing the largest crowds, while Jesus focused on investing in a few who would reach the crowds. McGavran's focus on people movements and a harvest evangelistic approach would naturally lead to a highly group-oriented

---

116. McGavran, *Understanding Church Growth*, 176-177.

117. Wells, "Marketing the Church: Analysis and Assessment," excerpt from a lecture delivered at Southeastern Baptist Theological Seminary, October 27, 1994.

118. Wells, "Marketing," 188.

119. Romans 8:29–30.

approach to disciple making, rather than primarily an individualized relational approach. He states, "People become Christians by making individual decisions but collectively."[120] The risk of this type of approach to making disciples is the production of nominally committed disciples due to the lack of intentional discipling. Jesus discipled persons through intimate relationships, which were highly personalized. Is the highest calling of the church to increase attendance, and attract new members or might there be a different way of defining success in light of the Great Commission? Jesus commanded his church to go and make disciples, not to go and draw crowds or attract multitudes. The bifurcated approach of McGavran's evangelism and discipling as a mode of disciple making grew and evolved into a "one without the other" culture fostered by the later iterations of the Church Growth Movement.

The Church Growth Movement's church-centered view of the Great Commission institutionalizes disciple making. McGavran's insistence that the end result of disciple making was, "bringing people into responsible church membership"[121] is a bit short-sighted and assumes that people who are involved in the church are being trained to be disciples who are making disciples. His definition of mission and evangelism[122] ultimately lacked the discipling follow through which led to nominal biblical knowledge and fledgling commitment. McGavran was often defending church growth principles from critics who said that they led to conversions, but also immature Christians. McIntosh writes, "When people movements took place, the maturing (or *perfecting* to use Donald's terminology) usually occupied a back seat to the ingathering of new converts. Thus, these new Christians were often somewhat shallow and untrained."[123] The *perfecting* stage of the Great Commission was often assumed and overlooked in the Church Growth Movement. A good example of this assumptive mindset is stated as McGavran's view of maturing believers by McIntosh, "He felt it was best to win people to Christ and then worry later on about perfecting them. Once new believers were under the direction of a new Lord and a

---

120. Rainer, *Book of Church Growth*, 35.

121. Wagner, *Your Church Can Grow*, 14.

122. McGavran defined mission as, "An enterprise devoted to proclaiming the Good News of Jesus Christ, and to persuading men to become His disciple and dependable members of His church." Donald McGavran, *Understanding Church Growth*, 26.

123. McIntosh, "Life of Donald McGavran: Coming of Age," 161.

new book, at least they were on the right way."[124] The result of this type of thinking is intricate intentionality in evangelistic efforts to make disciples, but often a lack of intentionality in maturing disciples.

Jesus reached disciples, trained his disciples, and then commissioned them to make more disciples. Thus, the end goal of disciple making is the making of more disciples, which is much more than evangelism and dependable church membership. This assertion is not to lessen the importance of church membership, and certainly, the Great Commission was the mode in which Jesus chose to build His church. McGavran's meshing of soteriology and ecclesiology resulted in a symbiotic relationship between the two which bloomed and grew within the movement. The priority of discipling new believers to be "responsible church members" rather than multiplying disciple makers ultimately misses the mark of the commission of Christ. Church membership becomes part of the salvation process rather than a result of the salvific work of Christ in the life of a believer.

CONCLUSION

The chapter has offered criticisms of Donald McGavran's theology and its subsequent impact on the Church Growth Movement's short-sighted view of disciple making. The critiques are not intended to delegitimize McGavran's influence on missiology and American evangelicalism. Few people have made a more positive impact on world missions and American ecclesiology than Donald McGavran. His understanding of conversion, however, was at the very least unclear due to his lack of articulating a theological position related to how people experience salvation. His theology and sociology conflated into normative pragmatic methodologies which have often been misconstrued due to his lack of clear articulation. It is hard to argue against the assertion that the Church Growth Movement eventually, "stressed quantity over quality"[125] concerning disciple making. Another issue was the use of resources, finances, and personnel to attract crowds and increase church attendance, rather than the Jesus model of investing relationally in a few to produce disciples who made disciples. The morphing of the Church Growth Movement into an attractional consumeristic model usurped lasting generational results in disciple making. The evangelistic outreach to homogeneous demographic segments also limited

---

124. McIntosh, "Life of Donald McGavran: Coming of Age," 161.
125. Cook, "Americanization of the Church Growth Movement," 40.

The Age of Church Growth and Pragmatism

church growth to reaching, "our kind of people." The ecclesial version of the missiological HUP philosophy eventually caused urban churches to move to large suburban areas where programmatic changes resulted in lots of catered activities but lacked long-term transformation through disciple making. Eventually, these congregations became less than the kingdom mosaic expected as commissioned by the, *panta ta ethne* (Matt 28:19) in the Great Commission. Rainer, a product and proponent of the Church Growth Movement, writes in the postscript of his book, *The Book of Church Growth*:

> In the midst of the verbiage of concerns, however, we need to remember what the Church Growth Movement has done for evangelical Christianity. It has caused us to refocus on kingdom building, on making disciples, and on winning the lost to Jesus Christ. It has made us evaluate again the question: What is the true mission of the church? Such introspection has been healthy for evangelical Christianity.[126]

Rainer is correct in his assessment of the positive impact of the Church Growth Movement, but his assertion of the refocus of making disciples is up for debate. If McGavran's definition of making disciples is in mind, then it is a plausible conclusion. This chapter has shown, however, that McGavran's concept of making disciples offers hermeneutical inconsistency when his views of Matthew 28:19–20 are examined, which has led to confusion and misunderstanding. Making disciples is more than a conversion experience, it is a comprehensive approach that encapsulates the full measure of bringing the lost to Christ and equipping them to grow and multiply. When compared to the disciple making methods and model of Jesus, there are inadequacies in the Church Growth Movement which led to its ultimate demise in American evangelicalism. The goal of this chapter was to highlight those inadequacies while at the same time honoring the missiological legacy of Donald A. McGavran.

The next chapter will introduce the Emergent Church Movement, whose leaders sought to correct what they perceived as the negative influences of the later iterations of the Church Growth Movement including the Mega Church Movement, Attractional Church Movement, and Seeker Sensitive Movement. Brian McLaren and other leaders of the Emergent movement viewed the missiological principles of the Church Growth

---

126. Rainer, *Book of Church Growth*, 319.

Movement as containing inadequate methodologies of outreach for the growing postmodern mindset in Western cultures.

Chapter 4

An Emergent Generosity of Orthodoxy

A History and Critique of the Emergent Church Movement

> Orthodoxy must be generous, but it cannot be so generous
> that it ceases to be orthodox.[1]
>
> —Albert Mohler

IN THE LATE 1990S, a group of church leaders began to rethink their approach to reaching a new generation of postmodern thinkers, and as a result, a new iteration of Christianity began to emerge. This new emergence has become known as the Emergent Church Movement. Leaders of the movement called for a corrective response to the ecclesial consumeristic mindset that became prevalent in the waning years of the Church Growth Movement. Some church leaders became increasingly weary of the "What's in it for me?" mindset of the Western church which they saw as a product of the Church Growth Movement.[2] Emergent leaders sought to change this

---

1. Mohler, "A Generous Orthodoxy: Is It Orthodox?"

2. Emergent leaders also hoped to bring attention to the growing dissatisfaction that Americans had toward the church, which they perceived as a product of the Church Growth Movement. For example, Brian McLaren states, "The church growth movement of the 1990s was based on the assumption that people really wanted to go to church, but there were obstacles—the music wasn't good enough or the preaching wasn't good enough," he said. "I think that was true in the 90s. But today, people are saying why would I even want to be part of this thing?" Jeff Brumley, "Increasing Rejection."

monastic mindset by creating a neo-monastic movement that propelled the church back into the world as a visible presence of Christ.[3]

The following chapter will explain and examine the genesis of the emergent movement, extrapolate, and expose the theological underpinnings, or lack thereof, of the movement, and analyze its disciple making corollaries. The chapter will argue that effective disciple making could not be produced from this movement due to its opaque and faulty theological convictions particularly related to a misguided theology of evangelism.. The emergent movement relied on praxis over doctrine, and in so doing consistently offered a subjective hermeneutic. The failure of the emergent movement to establish a coherent orthodoxy due to the underpinning of postmodern philosophies led to its eventual waning from the American ecclesial scene. Whereas disciple making within the Church Growth Movement was obstructed due to an attractional consumeristic pragmatism, the Emergent Church Movement suffered from a lack of clear disciple making modalities and a flawed missional theology.

While various emergent leaders will be named, the focus of the theological discussion will be centered on the most influential leader of the movement, Brian McLaren.[4] Many of the core principles of the movement have come from the writings of McLaren, which is why Carson calls him, "the emerging church's most influential thinker."[5] Examining the Emergent Church comes with difficulties due to the amorphous and ill-defined emergent movement. Is the emergent movement a form of evangelicalism or is it a new type of Christianity? The answer to this question has been debated, but there is agreement on the eventual fragmentation of the movement into two streams: *emerging* and *emergent*.

A good clarification of the difference between the two terms is found in the writings of Scot McKnight. He believes there are two streams to the movement: *emergent* and the broader *emerging* movement. He describes *emergent* as a crystallized version found in Emergent Village with its leaders Brian McLaren, Tony Jones, and Doug Pagitt. This version is a mix of orthodox, missional, evangelical, church-centered, and social justice leaders who,

---

3. Brian McClaren articulates this consumeristic ecclesial mindset in this way, "Churches tend to become gatherings of self-interested people who gather for mutual self-interest—constantly treating the church as a purveyor of religious goods and services, constantly shopping and 'trading up' for churches that can 'meet my needs' better." Brian McLaren, *Generous Orthodoxy*, 107.

4. McKnight, "McLaren Emerging," 60.

5. Carson, *Becoming Conversant*, 35.

together with lay folk, identify with a new type of Christianity. The broader version of the *emerging* movement includes an array of authors, pastors, and even mega-church leaders who collectively are seeking to become more missional to a postmodern audience.[6] Mark DeVine refers to the entirety of the movement as *emerging* and also identifies two streams which he refers to as the "doctrine-friendly" stream and a stream that presents a range of "doctrine-averse to doctrine-wary" leaders.[7] DeVine views the "doctrine-friendly" stream as led by the Acts 29 network with Mark Driscoll and influenced by the late Redeemer Presbyterian Pastor and author Tim Keller. Similarly, as does McKnight, he views the "doctrine-wary" and "doctrine-averse" stream as led by those affiliated with the Emergent Village such as Tony Jones, and Brian McLaren, among others. For this group, he also uses the term *emergent*.[8] The popular website, however, EmergentVillage.com[9] cemented the term *emergent* as a corollary with McLaren, Jones, and other doctrine-averse leaders.

Mark Driscoll, who eventually distanced himself from the *emergent* movement, offers his reasons for remaining emergent but not affiliated with the Emergent Church. He states, "The emergent church is part of the Emerging Church Movement but does not embrace the dominant ideology of the movement."[10] He believes that the Emergent Village theology is nothing but classic liberalism. Whereas in classic liberalism accommodates modernity, the new liberalism espoused by the emergent leaders accommodates postmodernity.[11] Author Kevin DeYoung states, "Defining emerging church is like nailing Jell-O to the wall."[12] In the introduction to his book *Evangelicals Engaging Emergent*, William Henard denotes the difficulty of examining the Emergent Movement, "This book purposes to be a provocative look at the Emergent Church. The task is not a simple one. Just defining 'Emergent' provides an incredible difficulty within itself."[13]

6. Carson, *Becoming Conversant*, 35.

7. DeVine, "Emerging Church," 8–9.

8. Research for this chapter included multiple books and articles that used these two terms *emergent* and *emerging* in confusing and conflating ways. One can quickly get caught up in the milieu of the various uses of the terms.

9. This website domain is no longer affiliated with the emergent church but is now a site that is somehow related to home ownership, home maintenance, and design ideas.

10. Driscoll, *Confessions of a Reformission Rev*, 21.

11. Driscoll, *Confessions of a Reformission Rev*, 21

12. DeYoung and Kluck, *Why We're Not Emergent*, 16–17.

13. Henard, *Evangelicals Engaging Emergent*, 2.

DeYoung describes the emergent movement as less of a "movement" and more of a "conversation" about the future of Christianity.[14] The pragmatic outflow of the conversations was the desire to recreate new pockets of evangelicalism by focusing on the life of Jesus, creating authentic communities, offering spiritual atmospheres, becoming servant leaders through welcoming strangers, and being generous people.[15] Carson writes, "At the heart of the 'movement' or as some of its leaders prefer to call it, the 'conversation,' lies the conviction that changes in the culture signal that a new church is 'emerging.' Christian leaders must therefore adapt to this emerging church."[16]

The underlying question related to the movement was how to communicate the gospel with the postmodern world and postmodern thinkers. Emergent leaders are critical of evangelicals who they see as failing to emerge because they are blind to the evolving culture and hide the gospel in outdated modes and expressions. Therefore, authors like Mark DeVine refer to the movement as more of a "protest" rather than a "movement." [17] Few Christian leaders would disagree that creating an authentic community, being servants and generous people, and finding new and better ways of communicating with this new generation are admirable goals. The question, however, goes deeper than the pragmatic workings of the emergent churches and their leaders. The question to be examined in this chapter is simply, did emergent churches create biblical disciples of Jesus? Another inherent difficulty of this chapter is the fact that churches rarely define themselves as part of the Emergent Church. There is, however, an obvious flaw with church leaders who have been influenced by the original founders of this movement. At best the leading voices offer an obscurity and opaque approach to biblical doctrine, and at worst their theological ponderings equate to classic theological liberalism. DeYoung asserts, "I think it is fair to say that even for those (emergent leaders) who affirm core doctrinal beliefs, and that does not include everyone in the movement, orthodoxy as a set of immovable theological assertions is largely downplayed, if not completely rejected."[18]

---

14. DeYoung and Kluck, *Why We're Not Emergent*, 17.
15. DeYoung and Kluck, *Why We're Not Emergent*, 18.
16. Carson, *Becoming Conversant*, 12.
17. DeVine, "Emerging Church," 4.
18. DeYoung and Kluck, *Why We're Not Emergent*, 106.

An Emergent Generosity of Orthodoxy

The initial pages of the chapter will share insights into the formations of the Emergent Church Movement, its protestant nature, and its characteristics and distinctives. The concluding pages of the chapter will review, analyze, and critique Brian McLaren's theology of evangelism and offer a final evaluation of the movement's efficacy in disciple making.

THE GENESIS AND CHARACTERISTICS OF THE EMERGENT MOVEMENT

In the mid 1990s the Emergent Church Movement began in large part as a response to the growing dissatisfaction of postmoderns with the traditional established church. A group of youth pastors and college ministers organized a series of conferences, sponsored by the *Leadership Network*, geared toward an understanding of why traditional techniques were no longer effective in reaching postmoderns.[19] Over a three-year period these conversations developed into relationships centered around ministry approaches to reach the postmodern Generation X (those born between 1961-1981). These relationships and discussions would eventually become the foundation of the Emergent Church Movement. Payne states, "When the year 2000 arrived, the relationship between these leaders and the relationship with the sponsoring Leadership Network was falling apart, and an organization known as *Emergent* was created in 2001."[20] This separation and eventual creation of *Emergent* led to an Emergent Convention which was attached to the National Pastors' Convention and hosted annually by *Youth Specialties*. These conferences and conventions spawned a large number of books, articles, and blog posts which helped to inculcate church leaders from around America into this evolving emergent mindset.

The church leaders at these conventions, in large part, began conversations related to the possibility that though there had been seismic shifts in the way postmoderns see truth and the purpose of life, this was not reflected in the church's theology and practice. The lack of theological and methodological adjustments by the evangelical American church had caused a growing chasm to develop between this new cultural accretion and the church. The emerging Enlightenment mentality taking place within the postmodern American culture led to an increased focus on subjectivity, personal expression, and individualism. The embrace of personal

---

19. Burge and Djupe, "Emergent Fault Lines," 8.
20. Payne, *Kingdom Expressions*, 50.

subjectivity, particularly regarding alethiology (the study of truth) and epistemology (the study of belief), eventually caused many postmoderns to jettison modernity's espousal of objective truth. Another key component of the changing spiritual pursuits of postmoderns is related to the new influx of information and technology which gave young people unprecedented access to explore other world religions.[21] Burge and Djupe write, "Those who embrace this form of postmodern philosophy have become loosely organized under the label 'emergent church' and have begun to help push the church through what many of them believe to be the first steps that will usher in a new understanding of Christianity."[22]

Gibbs and Bolger offer a simplistic definition of emergent churches. They define them as, "communities that practice the way of Jesus within postmodern cultures."[23] They offer nine practices that are characteristic of emergent churches: Emergent churches (1) identify with the life of Jesus, (2) transform the secular realm, and (3) live highly communal lives. In response to these activities emerging churches will (4) offer hospitality and a welcoming atmosphere to strangers, (5) serve with generosity, (6) participate as producers, (7) create as created beings, (8) lead as a body, and (9) take part in spiritual activities.[24] Payne also offers a helpful description of emergent churches:

> Such churches attempt to remove the sacred and secular barrier. They desire a holistic spirituality and are ready to discard any trappings of modernity that detract from the gospel. Emerging churches focus on living life together rather than placing the focus on service. They work to form tight communities, believing that the church is a people. Rather than argue about faith, emerging churches seek to welcome, listen, and learn from those of other faith traditions. They desire to love all people without targeting them. Emerging churches serve their communities with the expectation of nothing in return. As the emerging church gathers for worship, they seek to produce expressions that are reflective of who they are ... Such churches are comfortable experimenting with ancient spiritual expressions from church history in conjunction with more modern and normative spiritual disciplines.[25]

---

21. Burge and Djupe, "Emergent Church Practices," 2.
22. Burge and Djupe, "Emergent Church Practices," 2.
23. Gibbs and Bolder, *Emerging Churches*, 44.
24. Gibbs and Bolder, *Emerging Churches*, 44–45.
25. Payne, *Kingdom Expressions*, 48.

An Emergent Generosity of Orthodoxy

Extrapolating common beliefs among emergent churches is difficult due to the amorphous nature of the movement. After all, it is enormously challenging to distill common beliefs among churches that relish obscurity. Scot McKnight, however, writes of five themes that are characteristic of the Emergent Church Movement, which he calls *five streams*. In his *Christianity Today* article, *Five Streams of the Emerging Church*, he states that all five of these streams flow into one "emerging lake."[26] Though he identifies with the Emergent Church Movement, he is also aware of the theological nebuloustic approach of its leaders and their loose commitment to the authority of Scripture. McKnight's five streams which help to identify emergent churches include provocative rhetoric, postmodern thought, and faith as praxis-oriented, post-evangelical, and politically active.

First, emergent churches are provocatively rhetoric, meaning that they must be intentionally argumentative to draw attention to their causes and concerns. This gives way to the spirit of protest that, in large part, encapsulates the etymology of the movement. Second, emergent churches have a postmodern flare about them. McKnight writes of three ways in which the emergent church attempts to reach postmoderns: ministering to postmoderns, ministering with postmoderns, and ministering as postmoderns. It is certainly the latter that draws the most err from orthodox evangelicals and ultimately became the path of the leaders of the movement. Leaders such as Brian McLaren, Tony Jones, Rob Bell, and Doug Pagitt certainly embrace the alethiology and epistemology of postmodernity. One of the over-arching characteristics of the postmodern mindset is a rejection of objective truth with the belief that truth has been historically subjectively built by cultures over the century thus it is not absolute. Payne explains the approach of those who minister as postmoderns:

> Those within this category often question the Bible, absolute/propositional truth, the exclusivity of salvation in Jesus, and other convictions that have existed for the two thousand years of church history . . . It is common for them to embrace postmodern ways of thought, such as rejecting metanarratives, and subscribe to the social construction for relativistic truth. These postmodernists are more likely to consider themselves as emergent.[27]

Third, emergent churches focus more on orthopraxis than orthodoxy. They believe that faith must be expressed and live out publicly to an unbelieving

---

26. McKnight, "Five Streams of the Emerging Church."
27. Payne, *Kingdom Expressions*, 49.

world. This is often fleshed out in their worship, lifestyles, focus on social justice issues, and missiological principles. Fourth, emergent churches are post-evangelical, meaning that they were birthed out of a protest of evangelicalism. McKnight identifies two main ways in which the movement is post-evangelical: a rejection of systematic theology, and skepticism over the exclusivity of the "in or out" mindset of evangelicals. Regarding the rejection of systematic theology he writes:

> God didn't reveal a systematic theology but a storied narrative, and no language is capable of capturing the absolute truth who alone is God. Frankly, the emerging movement loves ideas and theology. It just doesn't have an airtight system or statement of faith. We believe the great tradition offers various ways for telling the truth about God's redemption in Christ, but we don't believe any one theology gets it absolutely right.[28]

The inherent skepticism of the bifurcation of "saved and lost" or "in and out" is especially troubling to those who identify as emergent. This skepticism is the seed of universalism, which critics of the Emergent Church Movement have cited as a major concern. McKnight writes, "Even if one is an exclusivist, (believing that there is a dividing line between Christians and non-Christians), the issue of who is out pains the emerging generation."[29]

Finally, emergent churches tend to be politically active, often supportive of left-leaning social causes. McKnight would not characterize the emergent church as a friend to either political party, stating that the majority of leaders hold to a traditional view on moral issues. He states, "I don't think the Democratic Party is worth a hoot, but its historic commitment to the poor and to centralizing government for social justice is what I think government should do. I think the Religious Right doesn't see what it is doing."[30] While he doesn't show support for either political party, certainly there are political overtones in his statement. These do not indicate an apolitical view, but rather a political fluidity which sides with the political party that advances social issues through activism and justice.

---

28. McKnight, "Five Streams of the Emerging Church"
29. McKnight, "Five Streams of the Emerging Church"
30. McKnight, "Five Streams of the Emerging Church"

EMERGENT MOVEMENT AS PROTEST

Just as postmodernism is a protest of modernism, the Emergent Church Movement is a protest of conservative evangelical traditionalism. Carson agrees that the Emergent Church Movement is a protest of traditional forms of Christianity, but also states that it is a protest on three fronts. He argues, "The emerging church movement is characterized by a fair bit of protest against traditional evangelicalism and, more broadly, against all that it understands by modernism. But some of its proponents add another front of protest—namely, the seeker-sensitive church, the megachurch."[31]

He attributes this to the personal stories of the emergent leaders in which they have found some type of discontent with evangelicalism. He states, "Many of them (emergent leaders) have come from conservative, traditional, evangelical churches, sometimes with a fundamentalist streak. Thus, the reforms that the movement encourages mirror the protests of the lives of many of its leaders."[32] Carson asserts that much of these protests are crystallized in a book published in 2003 entitled, *Stories of Emergence: Moving from Absolute to Authentic*. The book shares the story of fifteen people who eventually identified with the Emergent Church Movement, most of which came out of fundamental settings. Carson asserts, "What all of these people have in common is that they began in one thing and 'emerged' into something else. This gives the book a flavor of protest, of rejection: we were where you were once, but we emerged from it into something different."[33]

DeVine describes the movement as, "A movement that seems, in significant measure, to have sprung from seeds of discontent."[34] Though part of the protest of the emergent church is against evangelicalism, many of those who would characterize themselves as emergent left established traditional churches seeking new communities of faith. Many within this movement could be categorized as white, twenty-something, technically savvy, with a postmodern view of the world. Because of their technological propensities, many of these types of thinkers found each other through blogs, social media, and chat rooms in the mid-2000s. They also found teachers, speakers, and preachers that they could relate including Brian

---

31. Carson, *Becoming Conversant*, 36.
32. Carson, *Becoming Conversant*, 14.
33. Carson, *Becoming Conversant*, 14.
34. DeVine, "Emerging Church," 4.

McLaren, Tony Jones, Doug Pagitt, and Dan Kimball among others. DeVine believes that there are four primary areas in which these emergent Christians found like-minded areas of protest: authenticity, community, mission, and mystery.[35] Each of these facets represents the foundational principles that sparked the movement.

Emergent Christians agonize over the lack of authenticity found within the traditional church and see many of the relationships within those walls to be disingenuous. Hypocritical artificiality which, in the minds of the emerging crowd, discouraged authentic relational vulnerability including doubts, brokenness, and the transparency that came with these visceral emotions. Also, emergent Christians believe that this lack of genuineness caused an inhospitable atmosphere for those who come to church seeking answers to spiritual questions. This is due, in large part, to the immediate pressure to conform to doctrinal and creedal statements without sufficient time to explore, question, and reflect on their truthfulness. Emergent churches seek to create authentic safe atmospheres for postmoderns which encourages spiritual exploration as these spiritual seekers consider the claims of Jesus, and Christianity with openness and patience. A reason why these emerging Christians believe that authenticity is lacking is due to what they perceive as a lack of cultural contextualization within the traditional congregations. When true cultural contextualization is missing, then there will be a lack of genuine communication and authenticity within relationships due to the inability to have a shared understanding between people. The emerging church sees itself as contextualized missionaries to the postmodern culture as they seek ways to best communicate the gospel, and thus protest the cultural rigidity of the traditional church.[36]

Another protest of the emergent church is against the evangelical propensity toward urgent evangelism. DeVine believes that the one stream of the emergent church, which is considerably outside of orthodoxy, displays conversion-averse tendencies which are often found in more main-line liberal forms of Christianity.[37] In their effort to encourage spiritual exploration and questions, there is often no immediate imploring to make a decision for Christ. This likely springs from the emergent reticence of labeling people as *saved* and *lost*, and the emergent distinctive of faith

---

35. DeVine, "Emerging Church," 6.
36. DeVine, "Emerging Church," 12.
37. DeVine, "Emerging Church," 22.

An Emergent Generosity of Orthodoxy

through dialogue. DeVine shares a warning from self-proclaimed emergent Scot McKnight:

> I offer here a warning to you and to the emerging movement: any movement that is not evangelistic is failing the Lord. We may be humble about what we believe, and we may be careful to make the gospel and its commitment clear, but we better have a goal in mind, the goal of summoning everyone to follow Jesus Christ and to discover the redemptive work of God in Christ through the Spirit of God.[38]

There is also inherent within emergent circles a reframing of the term *missional* as being less attractional in approach and more intentionally missional. There is an incarnational missiology associated with the emergent church in which there is a recapturing of the outward thrust of the Great Commission toward postmodern culture. This is an important aspect of the missional focus of the movement because they believe that the thirty-five and under crowd are not attracted to the programmatic models of the modern church. There is a strong emphasis on "I am the church" rather than "I am going to church."[39] Brian McLaren views the emergent mission as interacting with individuals who are not part of their religious community and see the world much differently. He states, "Living missionally gets us beyond the us-them thinking and in-grouping and out-grouping that leads to prejudice, exclusion, and ultimately to religious wars."[40]

Emergent thinkers like McLaren view missional living as constantly reassessing their role and purpose in their respective communities. McLaren and Campolo speak of this constant assessment as asking, "What am I—and what are we—supposed to be doing in this world these days, to fit in with God's creative and ongoing mission."[41] There is, perhaps, much to admire in this missional view as the church is confronted with a future of less church attendance, but an increasing cultural curiosity on spiritual matters. There are, however, two criticisms of the missional posture of the emergent movement in regard to disciple making. First, there is a difference between being conversational and missional if the dialogue doesn't have a disciple making agenda centered on the gospel message. While missional approaches must include dialogue with unbelievers, it must not be relegated to conversation

38. DeVine, "Emerging Church," 22.
39. DeVine, "Emerging Church," 23.
40. McLaren, *Generous Orthodoxy*, 109.
41. McLaren and Campolo, *Adventures in Missing the Point*, 77.

for the sole purpose of dialogue or the exchanging of ideas. What makes the dialogue missional is the message of Christ, and the eventual presentation of the tenets of the gospel message for the purpose of making a disciple.

Second, the term *missional* as used in the emergent church lacks theological clarity and doctrinal substance. In other words, emergent mission is not a result of a missional theology, but rather it is a missional approach seeking a theology. This is clearly seen in McLaren's idea of missions, "The term, as I understand it, attempts to find a generous third way beyond the conservative and liberal versions of Christianity so dominant in the Western world."[42] The key word in this statement is "find" which certainly denotes a search for a missional theology rather than a mission birthed from theology. Any mission that is not birthed from clear theological convictions is at risk of unbiblical strategies, and worse, outright heresy. McLaren also states, "Theology is the church on a mission reflecting on its message, its identity, its meaning."[43] McLaren's idea is that one does not begin with a set of theological beliefs which determines mission, but rather begins with a mission in which some sort of theology emerges in the process. At the center of the emergent mission is making the world a better place now, which is centered on the emergent utopian concept of the kingdom of God.[44] This approach is devoid of orthodox theology and places man at the center, rather than God.

DISTINCTIVES OF THE EMERGENT CHURCH

There is found within emergent writings a few distinctives that collectively share a postmodern flare in relation to how these churches approach theology, missions, and ultimately disciple making. These distinctives include relativism, inclusivism, and faith through dialogue. As stated, these distinctives are a protest against the philosophies of modernity and are often intentionally anti-modernity. Emergent distinctives are regularly drawn from a premodern renaissance of sorts which seeks to take the church back to a more sacred ecclesiology as conveyed and embraced by the early church. This premodern focus is often conflated with a postmodern theory which entirely negates and largely ignores the perceived conundrums of modernity. Saler writes:

42. McLaren, *Generous Orthodoxy*, 105.
43. McLaren, *Generous Orthodoxy*, 105.
44. DeWaay, *Emergent Church*, 51.

The impression that this language (the language of emergent theology) gives is that the theology of the emergent church represents a genuinely new phenomenon on the theological scene, one that creatively rereads the premodern sources largely disdained by the Enlightenment and much subsequent Protestant theology through the lens of postmodern thinkers, that, despite their diverse methodologies, all hold in common the contention that Enlightenment-based modernity in the West has shown itself to be deficient at best and destructive at worst.[45]

Each of these distinctives is mired in a subjectional hermeneutic in which the construction of truth becomes entirely personal. The rugged individualistic focus of postmodern theory and praxis is the underpinning for such subjectiveness.

Relativism as Emergent Distinctive

The subjective relativism which is pervasive in emergent thought is the product and symptom of an eradication of an objective truth. The leading emergent thinkers view objective truth as a product of modernity and incompatible with postmodern philosophies. An acceptable faith for the emergent church asserts that epistemology must conform to an understanding that human beings are susceptible to the environment in which they are raised. Dan Kimball, a leading emergent thinker and one of the early members of the Emergent Village, writes of truth, "Postmodernism, then, holds there is no single universal worldview. All truth is not absolute, community is valued over individualism, and thinking, learning, and beliefs can be determined nonlinearly."[46] Another emergent leader, Rob Bell, writes, "To think that I can just read the Bible without reading any of my own culture or background or issues into it and come out with a pure or exact meaning is not only untrue, but it leads to a very destructive reading of the Bible that robs it of its life and energy."[47] Foundational to these two views of faith and truth, is a subjectiveness in which situational context becomes the lens or filter in which one views Scripture and their worldview.

Ed Stetzer notes that the founding leaders of the emergent movement were heavily influenced by J. D. Caputo's "hermeneutic of deconstruction"

---

45. Saler, "Emergent Church and Liberal Theology," 114.
46. Kimball, *Emerging Church*, 49.
47. Bell, *Velvet Elvis*, 54.

which is articulated in Caputo's book, *What Would Jesus Deconstruct?* The influence of this writing caused some within the movement to turn against the institutional church for what they called the "consumer culture." They perceived that this culture had westernized the church by attaching unneeded ecclesial structures thus encumbering the gospel within the clutches of modernity. This encumbering was also perceived to be a limiting factor in outreach to postmoderns.[48] Caputo's work is intentionally provocative, especially toward conservative-minded evangelicals, and he consistently quotes Nietzsche and Derrida in making his arguments. His book is endorsed by leaders of the emergent movement such as Jones and McLaren, the latter writing the forward to the book.

Stetzer offers an appropriate summary of Caputo's book, "Caputo sought to put forth a way to retain orthodoxy while at the same time exposing the attachments and accommodations that existing forms of Christianity make to conform to the reigning plausibility structures."[49] Caputo's influential views treat deconstruction as "The hermeneutics of the kingdom of God, as an interpretive style that helps get at the prophetic spirit of Jesus—who was a surprising and sometimes strident outsider, who took a stand with the 'other.'"[50] He goes on to explain, "In my view, deconstruction is good news, because it delivers the shock of the other to the forces of the same, the shock of the good (the ought) to be forces of being (what is), which is also why I think it bears good news to the church."[51] The "other" of which Caputo regards as Jesus standing against is not the devil, or evil, rather the "other" is a figure of truth which he presents as being closeted away or repressed by the institutional modern church. This "truth" which Caputo perceives as being repressed by the modern institutional church, and encumbered with capitalistic consumerism.

Inherent within this subjectivity is a shying away from any type of absolutism, which in a postmodern mindset, is akin to pharisaical narrow-mindedness. Therefore, there is encouragement within the emergent movement to remain open to relativism. McLaren writes of the book, "Relativists are right in their denunciation of absolutism. It also affirms that absolutists are right in their denunciation of relativists. And then it suggests that they are both wrong because the answer lies beyond both absolutism

---

48. Stetzer, "Emergent/Emerging Church," 55-57.
49. Stetzer, "Emergent/Emerging Church," 56.
50. Caputo, *What Would Jesus Deconstruct?* 26.
51. Caputo, *What Would Jesus Deconstruct?* 27.

and relativism."[52] If this definition seems confusing, it might be because it is. This type of nuanced language is typical among emergent leaders. Another example of subjectiveness is found in Pagitt's response to Driscoll's orthodox views of the authority of Scripture as absolute. Pagitt states he is troubled that Driscoll's views are not, "changing or changeable."[53] In his response to Driscoll's view Pagitt argues for the right to bring in cultural accretions into biblical interpretation suggesting that people are unable to properly interpret Scripture without a cultural lens. This is not entirely an argument without some merit, but it hints at a certain subjectiveness in which the truths of Scripture are subject to the whims and cultural accretions of personal experience. This is exactly why arguments of epistemology are so important to the perpetuation of Christian orthodoxy. Humanity's ability to suppress moral truths in favor of a subjective belief that favors the whims of the individual is as ancient as Eden, therefore an objectively valid standard of truth is essential. R. Scott Smith rightly asserts, "When believers persist in embracing relativism, they end up committing adultery against God by buying into a moral philosophy that is utterly opposed to God's revealed truth."[54]

Chuck Colson's response to Brian McLaren's views of epistemology is quite helpful in giving a proper rebuttal to the emergent church leader's propensity of espousing a relativistic subjectivism. He writes to McLaren in opposition to a postmodern view of truth:

> People may think something is true, but of course truth is never determined by what people think. We might, as you put it, tell the truth as we know it and even swear to it. That happens all the time in a court room. What you're getting there is a human perception of circumstances or something that was witnessed or believed. It is a pursuit of what is true, that is a true account of things that help settle the issues in that trial. That is quite different than Truth or ultimate reality. Truth is truth and all of us are seeking it – however imperfectly we may perceive events. But our perceptions do not make it truth nor does our imperfection negate Truth.[55]

---

52. McLaren, *Generous Orthodoxy*, 38.
53. Pagitt, "Response to Mark Driscoll," 43–44.
54. Smith, *Truth and the New Kind of Christian*, 168.
55. In the article "Chuck Colson's Response," Colson responds to McLaren's critiques of an article he wrote for *Christianity Today* regarding postmodern epistemology.

Inclusivism as Emergent Distinctive

Related to the emergent understanding of epistemology is its view of the proliferation of truth into all aspects of society including other religions. As Rob Bell states, "Truth is everywhere, and is available to everyone."[56] In his book *A New Kind of Christianity*, McClaren deals with the pluralism question by offering a survey of how the Scripture views people who subscribe to other religions. For example, he uses Paul's statements in Romans 2:1–29 as a way of proving that those of other beliefs outside of Christianity are equally enjoying God's blessings and presence. He states, "Paul makes clear that people are never judged based on the knowledge they don't have, and that God will bless 'those who by patiently doing good seek for glory and honor and immortality.'"[57] He notes that in Romans 5:12–21 Paul espouses a view that the impact of Jesus' obedience overcomes Adam's disobedience so that grace can reach "all" or the "many" because "where sin increased, grace abounded all the more."[58] But, does he mean that grace has made salvation through Christ available to those of other religions, or does he mean that those faithful to other beliefs have a share in the obedience of Christ? He answers the question a few pages later in what could be akin to an inclusive universalistic view:

> We would no longer envision a day when all other religions would be abolished and only our own will remain. We would no longer consider ourselves as normative and others as "other." We would stop seeing the line that separates good and evil running between our religion and all others. We would be freed from the tendency to always think "insider/outsider" and "us/them." We would learn to discover God in the other, and we would discover a bigger "us," in which people of all faiths can be included.[59]

It is an important point that the influential McLaren sees the *missio Dei* as "A decentralized, grassroots, spiritual-social movement dedicated to plotting goodness and saving the world from human evil—both personal and systemic."[60] McLaren's religious inclusivity is envisioned as "a community dedicated to teaching the most excellent way of love, whatever the new

---

56. Bell, *Love Wins*, 78.
57. McLaren, *New Kind of Christianity*, 209.
58. McLaren, *New Kind of Christianity*, 210.
59. McLaren, *New Kind of Christianity*, 215.
60. McLaren, *New Kind of Christianity*, 216.

An Emergent Generosity of Orthodoxy

disciple's religious affiliation or lack thereof."[61] Therefore, in the emergent's economy of inclusivity a "new disciple" can continue to have whatever religious affiliation they desire, or none at all. This type of universal inclusivity envisions a day where people of all religions, regardless of faith or belief, work together in harmony to make the world a better place. McLaren and Bell espouse the view that there is some measure of truth in all religions, rather than the more biblical view that the truth of the gospel is available to people of all religions. The embodiment of this belief is seen in the ways in which the emergent church interacts with those of other faiths. For example, McLaren writes of emergent members observing the Muslim tradition of Ramadan, noting the similar fashion and dedication that Muslims and Christians share regarding religious fasting.[62]

Another example of this type of inclusivity is found in the writings of emergent leader Samir Selmanovic. He was one of the early leaders of the Emergent Village, serving on the coordinating council and the Faith and Order Commission of the National Council of Churches. In the book, *An Emergent Manifesto of Hope*, he writes a chapter on the subject of inclusivism entitled, "The Sweet Problem of Inclusiveness." He refers to Christianity as "a Christ management system" in which Christianity is seen as a hoarder of grace and intentionally exclusive. He writes:

> Christianity's idea that other religions cannot be God's carriers of grace and truth casts a large shadow over our Christian experience. Does grace, the central teaching of Christianity, permeate all of reality, or is it something that is alive only for those who possess the New Testament and the Christian tradition? Is the revelation that we have received through Jesus Christ an expression of what is everywhere at all times, or has the Christ Event emptied most of the world and time of saving grace and deposited it in one religion, namely ours? We (emergent churches) want nothing less than to reinterpret the Bible, reconstruct the theology, and reimagine the church to match the character of God that we as followers of Christ have come to know.[63]

Selmanovic's chapter could be interpreted as a manifesto of universalism as he proclaims a "kingdom of God" which encompasses those of other religions including those without any belief at all. His view of the Kingdom

---

61. McLaren, *New Kind of Christianity*, 216.
62. Burge and Djupe, "Emergent Church Practices," 4–5.
63. Selmanovic, "Sweet Problem," 191.

of God is typical of emergent authors and is ultimately the precipitator of inclusivism in emergent beliefs. He writes, "It is worth being reminded that Christ never proclaimed, 'Christianity is here. Join it.' But Christ did insist, 'The kingdom of God is here, enter it.'"[64] He views the ultimate context of spiritual aspiration for a follower of Christ not as Christianity, but the kingdom of God. He asserts, "The kingdom of God supersedes Christianity in scope, depth, and expression. Even it its best form, Christian religion is still an entity in the human realm."[65] Selmanovic continues, "There is no salvation outside of Christ, but there is salvation outside of Christianity."[66] Emergent belief does not equate Christianity with Christ, rather they view the two as variant. In this belief Jesus Christ came to offer grace to everyone through a resident kingdom of God in which all are invited as participants, and Christianity is a westernized Greco-Roman institution which falsely claims to be the arbiter of truth. The prolific use of the "other" to describe a mystic faith which is outside of the realm of Christianity seems to suggest that there is a salvific stream available through faithful belief outside of Christianity. Selmanovic summarizes his chapter on inclusivism by stating, "When we open ourselves to be taught by the 'other,' we don't become less the followers of Christ but more so."[67] Perhaps Selmanovic should be reminded of the words of Peter and John in Acts 4:12, "And there is salvation in no one else; for there is no *other* name under heave that has been given among men by which we must be saved."

Faith Through Dialogue as an Emergent Distinctive

The underlying goal of the emergent church is to reach postmodern people not through a presentation of the gospel, nor through persuasion, but through dialogue and conversation. After all, emergent leaders view their movement as one big "conversation" and "dialogue" concerning the future of the church and its praxis.[68] Part of this conversation has as its goal a missional component to reach postmoderns. Robert Webber gives clear indication of this missional purpose when he states, "People in a postmodern world are not persuaded to faith by reason as much as they are moved

64. Selmanovic, "Sweet Problem," 192.
65. Selmanovic, "Sweet Problem," 194.
66. Selmanovic, "Sweet Problem," 195.
67. Selmanovic, "Sweet Problem," 198.
68. Carson, *Becoming Conversant*, 12.

to faith by participation in God's earthly community."[69] Brian McLaren's *A New Kind of Christian* trilogy has been a major contributor to emergent theory and praxis, and it is apparent from these writings that McLaren sees the device of conversation and dialogue as a key component to emergent mission. He uses the phrase "partner in the emergent conversation" three times in the acknowledgements section of the first book. He also writes in the forward of the first book, "I am more interested in generating conversation than argument, believing that conversations have the potential to form us, inform us, and educate us far more than arguments."[70]

A few examples which they share include McLaren and Campolo's *Adventures in Missing the Point*, which covers a wide range of topics with McLaren offering his thoughts and Campolo providing a response. This certainly, and likely intentionally, gives the impression of two emergent thinkers in dialogue inviting the audience to enjoy a front-row seat to their conversation. Dan Kimball's book on the emergent church includes commentary throughout from McLaren and Rick Warren. Burge and Djupe believe that *faith through dialogue* is a major focus throughout emergent writings stating that entire books have been written in a conversant style.[71] Another example of this type of emergent writings include *The Church in Emerging Culture: Five Perspectives*, which consists of five "dialogues" with Christian thinkers offering variant views and opinions including Brian McLaren, Andy Crouch, Michael Horton, and Erwin McManus. Concerning this Burge and Djupe conclude, "While this ongoing dialogue is crucial to the formation of this new theology, it is interesting to note where the conversation falls silent."[72] One specific area in which the emergent movement does fall silent is in the arena of human sexuality. It seems emergent leaders such as McLaren would rather discourage discussions concerning divisive issues rather than give a clear answer. For example, he writes, "Perhaps we need a five-year moratorium on making pronouncements (concerning homosexuality). After all, many important issues in church history took centuries to figure out."[73] This type of evasiveness in dialogue frustrates those who seek to construct an emergent theological conception. Academic observers of the movement have noted that this conversation

---

69. Webber, *Ancient-Future Faith*, 79.
70. McLaren, *Last Word*, xxiii.
71. Burge and Djupe, "Emergent Church Practices," 6.
72. Burge and Djupe, "Emergent Church Practices," 7.
73. McLaren, *Brian McLaren on the homosexual question*.

is not always coming from a myriad of sources. The most influential contributors to emergent theories are mostly well educated, white males in the Western world.[74]

BRIAN MCLAREN'S THEOLOGY OF EVANGELISM

The impact of Brian McLaren on the emergent movement cannot be overstated. His books have been highly influential in emergent thinking, and one can hardly read emergent material without noticing his prominence. With McLaren's influence on the movement, it is entirely appropriate to spend the remaining portion of the chapter reviewing and analyzing his theology of evangelism. In reviewing McLaren's, *A New Kind of Christianity*, Scot McKnight writes:

> Unfortunately, this book lacks the "generosity" of genuine orthodoxy and, frankly, I find little space in it for orthodoxy itself. Orthodoxy for too many today means little more than the absence of denying what's in the creeds. But a robust orthodoxy means that orthodoxy itself is the lens through which we see theology. One thing about this book is clear: Orthodoxy is not central.[75]

Though McLaren seeks to espouse new emergent thoughts on orthodoxy, McKnight finds his theology to be archaic. He writes, "It may be new for Brian, but it's a rehash of ideas that grew into fruition with Adolf von Harnack and now find iterations in folks like Harvey Cox and Marcus Borg. Brian's new kind of Christianity is quite old."[76] Douglas Blount agrees that McLaren's hermeneutics are anything but orthodox and run contrary to the orthodox faith. He states, "I argue that McLaren's interpretive starting point, and, consequently, both his interpretive approach and the readings it generates cannot be properly called Christian."[77]

In order to properly evaluate the Emergent Church Movement's disciple making foci, McLaren's theology of evangelism will be given careful examination. For the purpose of this evaluation, four areas of Brian McLaren's theology worthy of consideration are his thoughts on the mission of the church, his view of Scripture, the ministry of Jesus, and the kingdom

---

74. Burge and Djupe, "Emergent Church Practices," 7.
75. McKnight, "Review: Brian McLaren's 'New Kind of Christianity.'"
76. McKnight, "Review: Brian McLaren's 'New Kind of Christianity'"
77. Blount, "New Kind of Interpretation," 110.

of God. All four of these areas offer collectively a comprehensive view of his theology of evangelism. His views were formative to the theology of the Emergent Movement, though, like much of the emergent thinkers, his theology has a fluidic tone. McLaren often works things out in front of his readers thus his writings are an outward expressive processing of theological concepts in front of an audience.[78]

Formative to McLaren's understanding of the missional purpose of the church was the work of Lesslie Newbigin, David Bosch, and Vincent Donovan. These missiologists, especially Newbigin and Bosch,[79] were influencers on what became to be, the Missional Church Movement. McLaren was impacted greatly by Newbigin's work in reassessing the West as a mission field, particularly related to the post-Enlightenment culture which became pervasive in the twentieth century. In the process of searching to define the term *missional*, McLaren states:

> The term, as I understand it, attempts to find a generous third way beyond the conservative and liberal versions of Christianity so dominant in the Western world. The conservative version is preoccupied with the "personal Savior" gospel, and the liberal version has lost something vitally important in their engagement with modernity.[80]

McLaren defines his missional understanding in this way, "To be and make disciples of Jesus Christ in authentic community for the good of the world."[81] What, however, does he mean by, "for the good of the world?" He asserts that "for the good of the world" a new missional understanding will stop the exclusionary mentality of what McLaren calls a "hell-oriented gospel."[82] He explains:

> Missional Christian faith asserts that Jesus did not come to make some people saved and others condemned. Jesus did not come to

---

78. In his book, *Generous Orthodoxy*, 21, McLaren writes, "Writing for me has always been a way of discovery and questioning."

79. McLaren, *Generous Orthodoxy*, 105. A clear influence on McLaren from Newbigin and Bosch is seen in his statement, "Now every Christian is a missionary, and every place is a mission field," 109.

80. What McLaren perceives as lost in liberal Christianity is the fostering of individual commitments and discipleship. Interestingly, in his view, liberals focused on social issues such as women's rights, caring for the poor, and the environment to the detriment of personal discipleship. McLaren, *Generous Orthodoxy.*, 138–139.

81. McLaren, *Generous Orthodoxy*, 107.

82. McLaren, *Generous Orthodoxy*, 109.

help some people be right while leaving everyone else to be wrong. Jesus did not come to create another exclusive religion—Judaism having been exclusive based on genetics and Christianity being exclusive based on belief. Missional faith asserts that Jesus came to preach the good news of the kingdom of God to everyone, especially the poor. He came to seek and save the lost. He came on behalf of the sick. He came to save the world. His gospel, and therefore the Christian message, is Good News for the whole world.[83]

As part of this "Good News for the whole world," he explains that the message of Jesus was good news for the saved and the unsaved. In McLaren's view, it is wrong to promote the gospel through what he calls an "offer/threat combination"[84] where people come to faith out of fear. He explains, "I think that the missional way is better: the gospel brings blessing to all, adherents and nonadherents alike."[85] By this he means that the end result of gospel influence is the correction of injustice, feeding of the hungry, and clothing the naked. Yet, what is missing from McLaren's chapter on mission is a biblical understanding of the eternal death from which the gospel ultimately saves people. He distills his missional understanding into the statement, "blessed in this life to be a blessing to everyone on earth."[86] McLaren asks a rhetorical question, "But what about heaven and hell? Is everybody in?" His response, "Why do you consider me qualified to make this pronouncement? Isn't this God's business? Isn't it clear that I do not believe this is the right question for a missional Christian to ask?"[87]

The gospel mission, according to McLaren, is to be a blessing to the whole world, while this view sounds attractive, it is short sighted when held against the preaching of Jesus in the Gospels The parable of the sheep and the goats in Matthew 25:31-46, the parable of the good fish and the bad fish in Matthew 13:47-50, and the parable of the wheat and the tares in Matthew 13:36-43, all point to a poignant point regarding the coming judgment. Regardless of McLaren's desires to change the kingdom narrative of Jesus, there is coming an eternal separation between those who have been dressed in the righteousness of Christ, and those who have not. Clearly

---

83. McLaren, *Generous Orthodoxy*, 109–110.
84. McLaren, *Generous Orthodoxy*, 111.
85. McLaren, *Generous Orthodoxy*, 111.
86. McLaren, *Generous Orthodoxy*, 113.
87. McLaren, *Generous Orthodoxy*, 112.

An Emergent Generosity of Orthodoxy

McLaren's missional formations are much different than the gospel of the kingdom which Christ preached and the eternal urgency for which the Great Commission exists. It is hard to imagine that the Emergent Church Movement could produce long-term disciple making impact without a clearly articulated biblical gospel.

McLaren's misinterpretation of the gospel mission is likely related to his theological and hermeneutical interpretations on the canon of Scripture. Primary to this analysis is his retort of the meta-narrative and repudiation of the plenary-verbal inerrancy of Scripture. He asserts that proposing a Christian meta-narrative is inviting people into the Bible's story line, which, according to McLaren, smacks of Greco-Roman propaganda and absolutism. Like most emergent thinkers, McLaren prefers a deconstructionist approach of absolutism (objective truth) which he finds as endemic in Western confessionalism.[88]

McLaren offers his view of doctrinal orthodoxy in his book, *A Generous Orthodoxy*. He states, "Let me go on record as saying that I believe sound doctrine is very, very, very important, and that bad doctrine, while not the root of all evil, is a despicable accomplice to a good bit of the evil in this world."[89] There is, however, a discrepancy in his writings with his view of Scripture and orthodox doctrine. In his book, *A New Kind of Christianity*, McLaren rejects the orthodox view regarding the importance of the meta-story of the Bible. He states, "To be a Christian—in the West at least, since the fifth or sixth century or so—has required one to believe that the Bible presents one very specific storyline, a story line by which we assess all of history, all of human experience, all of our own experience."[90] He continues, "We begin our quest for a new kind of Christian faith by questioning this storyline."[91]. He states in *Generous Orthodoxy*, "Orthodoxy in this book is seen as a kind of internalized belief, tacit and personal, that becomes part of you to such a degree that once assimilated, you hardly need to think of it. We enter it, indwell it, live, and love through it."[92] There is a conflation in McLaren's view of orthodoxy and orthopraxy. His writings offer the impression that McLaren's orthodoxy is based more on human

---

88. Carson, *Becoming Conversant*, 32.
89. McLaren, *Generous Orthodoxy*, 32.
90. McLaren, *New Kind of Christianity*, 35.
91. McLaren, *New Kind of Christianity*, 35
92. McLaren, *Generous Orthodoxy*, 33.

experience than the sacredness of Scripture so that one's orthopraxy shapes orthodoxy leading to subjectivism.

Inherent in McLaren's writings is a rejection of plenary verbal inspiration of Scripture. He sees the Bible, not as a meta-story, but as a collection of narratives written by men and approved by God rather than written by God through men. He states, "Remember, the Bible is not a constitution. It is like the library of math texts that show the history of the development of mathematical reasoning among human beings."[93] He understands the Bible to be a slowly evolving human understanding of God, where, ironically, the biblical writers are much like him, developing their theologies as they write. He states, "Scripture faithfully reveals the evolution of our ancestors' best attempts to communicate their successive best understandings of God. As human capacity grows to conceive of a higher and wiser view of God, each new vision is faithfully preserved in Scripture like fossils in layers of sediment."[94] He continues, "The Bible is a story and just because it recounts what happened, that doesn't mean it tells what should always happen or even what should have happened."[95] McLaren's statements display a limited hermeneutic, which offers no continuity to present-day application other than a few moral lessons.

McLaren's views of the mission and ministry of Christ, the gospel, and the kingdom all conflate into a call to social action and good Christian citizenry. McLaren writes of how Roman Catholic missionary Vincent Donovan influenced his concept of the mission of Christ:

> I was to learn that any theology or theory that makes no reference to previous missionary experience, which does not take that experience into account, is a dead and useless thing. Praxis must be prior to theology. In my work (theology would have to proceed) from practice to theory. If a theology did emerge from my work, it would have to be a theology growing out of the life and experience of the pagan peoples of the savannahs of East Africa.[96]

McLaren espouses a view of Jesus Christ as a social justice revolutionary and His gospel as social liberation in the here and now, rather than on eternal eschatological realities and the redemption of man. In his view, the gospel is not a message about salvation from God's wrath against sin

93. McLaren, *New Kind of Christianity*, 106.
94. Challies, "The False Teachers: Brian McLaren."
95. McLaren, *Generous Orthodoxy*, 167.
96. McLaren, *Generous Orthodoxy*, 92.

and spending eternity with Christ. Greg Gilbert shares McLaren's gospel view as, "The good news that God has invaded this dark world and, in the face of its exclusionary systems and cruel powers, has called out a people who will lead lives marked by love, compassion, and acceptance. Most Christians have made the gospel into a religion when Jesus meant it to be a revolution."[97] McLaren writes, "What if he didn't come to start a new religion—but rather came to start a political, social, religious, artistic, economic, intellectual, and spiritual revolution that would give birth to a new world?"[98] He espouses a liberation gospel that frees people not from the wrath of God or eternal separation, but rather from societal wrongs and oppression such as poverty and injustice through social justice.

In McLaren's liberation soteriology the gospel is not primarily about the forgiveness of a person's sin, but rather how the kingdom of God can save the world in the here and now.[99] When asked about his view of the Great Commission of Jesus Christ in Matthew 28:19–20, McLaren responded with the following statement:

> I believe in and am committed to the Great Commission, but I wouldn't define it as "converting people to the Christian religion." I would define it as making disciples of Jesus (or learners of the way of Jesus) by proclaiming his good news of the commonwealth of God. Sadly, sometimes "converting people to the Christian religion" can make them even more hostile than they were before now with God "on their side," intensifying their pre-existing fears and hostilities. But there are other ways – in my mind, more faithful, more Spirit-empowered ways – to be Christian, just as there are more faithful, more Spirit-empowered ways to be Muslim, Hindu, Jewish, atheist, Buddhist, etc.[100]

In McLaren's soteriology, there is no radical change from wrath to righteousness or from death to life, but only the hope of a more Spirit-empowered way to exist in the here and now. McLaren's view of salvation rests on the immediate more than the eternal as he asserts, "Salvation means being rescued from fruitless ways of life here and now, to share in God's saving love for all creation, in an adventure called the kingdom of God."[101] This

---

97. Greg Gilbert, "Brian McLaren and the Gospel of Here & Now."
98. McLaren, *Secret Message of Jesus*, 4.
99. Shogren, "Wicked Will Not Inherit the Kingdom of God," 105.
100. McLaren's response to the question, "What about trying to convert people?"
101. Campolo and McLaren, *Adventures in Missing the Point*, 19.

idea is further reflected in his statement of frustration which mocks the gospel outreach of the evangelical church. He states:

> Is it any surprise that it's stinking hard to convince churches that they have a mission to the world when most Christians equate 'personal salvation' of individual 'souls' with the ultimate aim of Jesus? Is it any wonder that people feel like victims of a bait and switch when they are lured with personal salvation and then hooked with church commitment and world mission?[102]

This statement gives a clear indication of McLaren's rejection of the gospel as a way of personal salvation as the ultimate aim of Jesus. In McLaren's view salvation and gospel transformation, related to the Great Commission, is relegated to a change in ethical behavior where one becomes a kingdom citizen whose sole purpose is to liberate the poor, distressed, and those suffering injustice. While these are all important, it is worth noting that McLaren and other emergent leaders offer little to no focus on eschatological judgment, heaven, hell, or eternity. The doctrine of eternity is de-emphasized within McLaren's theology of evangelism, and discipleship becomes more about shaping a person to become a better global citizen than a disciple maker equipped to hold forth the truths and doctrine of Scripture.

Critique of Brian McLaren's Theology of Evangelism

In critiquing McLaren's theology of evangelism, it is worth mentioning that he believes the word *evangelism* has been "bastardized" and today has a dirty reputation.[103] While there are some who seek to evangelize postmoderns, others try to reach this generation with postmodernist beliefs. This becomes problematic when one considers that postmodernism rejects many of the foundational orthodox beliefs of Christianity including the possibility of the transcendent. The deconstructionism found in the writings of philosophers like Jacques Derrida is inherent within the postmodern mindset. Postmodern thinkers believe that epistemology is intensely personal as they see truth as dependent upon a person's judgment. Grenz summarizes Derrida's views, "Nothing transcendent inheres in reality, he argues, all that emerges in the knowing process is the perspective of the

---

102. McLaren, *Generous Orthodoxy*, 107.
103. McLaren, *New Kind of Christianity*, 12.

An Emergent Generosity of Orthodoxy

self who interprets reality."[104] Grenz explains, "This means that there is no one meaning of the world, no transcendent center to reality as a whole."[105] Therefore, embracing a postmodern view of epistemology to evangelize postmoderns, one would have to reject the meta-narrative of Scripture as transcendent and objective. This explains McLaren's lack of orthodox views of Scripture. In an effort to present Christ and the gospel to postmoderns, he has embraced postmodern epistemology in questioning the veracity of the canon, absolute and propositional truth and the exclusivity of salvation in Jesus Christ.[106] A proper critique of McLaren's orthodoxy begins with his view of the missiology of Jesus.

McKenzie summarizes McLaren's view of the missiology of Jesus, "McLaren's vision of Jesus—welcoming all without judgement or hostility—grounds his approach to mission and inter-faith relationships. Mission carried out in the 'way of Jesus' will be mission that is inclusive of all and open to the 'other', even those within other religious traditions."[107] McLaren's soteriology is more closely related to universalism than orthodox Christology. The conventional view is that Jesus preached a message of the need for individuals to repent and believe in His propitiation so that they would not spend eternity separated from God. Jesus solved the problem of original sin and its decaying implications on humanity. McLaren sees Jesus as a "medicinal cure to a lethal infection that plagues humanity."[108] What does he mean by "lethal infection?" Consider his statement in *A New Kind of Christianity*, "What if there really is a great and good and kind God, and we humans really are God's creatures, though we lose our way sometimes."[109] Certainly, humanity's central problem is more than "losing our way sometimes." Scripture reveals the human problem as more than an occasional loss of moral consciousness and more of a loss of spiritual life and entrance into spiritual depravity. Consider Paul's words in Romans 5:12, "Therefore, just as through one man sin entered the world, and death through sin, and thus death spread to all men, because all sinned."[110]

---

104. Grenz, *Primer on Postmodernism*, 6.
105. Grenz, *Primer on Postmodernism*, 6.
106. Payne, *Kingdom Expressions*, 49.
107. Mackenzie, "Mission and the Inclusive Kingdom," 260.
108. McLaren, *Everything Must Change*, 81.
109. McLaren, *New Kind of Christianity*, 13.
110. See also Genesis 3:17–19.

McKenzie states, "McLaren argues that churches have neglected Jesus' life and ministry by over-emphasizing Jesus as Savior and calls Christians to follow Jesus as Lord by following his teaching and example."[111] According to McLaren a proper view of Jesus begins with seeing him through a Jewish context rather than a Greco-Roman context. In this view, Jesus is seen as one with a generous offer to all, even to those of other faiths. McLaren asks how Jesus would respond if he encountered leaders of other religions. He proposes that Jesus "would embrace them with open arms and without hesitation, proving himself over time to be the best friend they ever had."[112] There is within these statements no expectation of a person repenting of sin, confessing Christ as Lord, and turning from their previous beliefs. His view of Jesus as one who can change a person's ethics, making them a better person for society, rather than one saved from eternal judgment is problematic. Emergent thought is praxis driven; therefore, McLaren focuses more on Jesus making a person a better member of society and citizen while deemphasizing the propitiating ministry of Christ on the cross. Surely the emphasis of Jesus as the way, the truth, the life, and the only way to the Father is the central message of the gospel, rather than a universal sociopolitical code.

A critique of McLaren's theology of evangelism and doctrinal views must also include his statement in *A New Kind of Christianity*: "There will be no new kind of Christian faith without a new approach to the Bible because we've gotten ourselves into a mess with the Bible."[113] His postmodern view of epistemology is clearly seen in how he encourages people to approach Scripture. In an effort to make the Bible more appealing and to reach postmodern thinkers, Emergent Church leaders like McLaren espouse Scripture as narrative while rejecting a grammatical-historical hermeneutic. McLaren believes that truth is not inherent within Scripture as if God were writing it as objective, but rather truth is found through a person's wrestling with Scripture. In this view, the person is the ultimate determiner of truth, instead of the words of God. He states, "To say that the Word (the message, meaning, or revelation) of God is in the biblical text, then, does not mean that you can extract verses or statements from the text at will and call them 'God's words.'" He continues, "It means that if we enter the text together and feel the flow of its arguments, get stuck in its points of

---

111. McKenzie, "Mission and the Inclusive Kingdom," 259.
112. McLaren, *Why Did Jesus?* 4.
113. McLaren, *New Kind of Christianity*, 67–68.

tension, and struggle with its unfolding plot in all its twists and turns, God's revelation can happen to us."[114] In *A New Kind of Christianity*, McLaren passionately argues that the Bible be seen not as a "legal constitution" but rather a "community library" which evolves in meaning as human cognition develops over time. He characterizes the flood account of Genesis as the story of "a god who mandates an intentional supernatural disaster leading to unparalleled genocide."[115] He subverts the authority of Scripture by dismissing the more difficult passages as authoritative, while embracing the more palatable as God's Word. In McLaren's biblical economy, there are pericopes that should be reframed or dismissed.

Finally, McLaren's view of the kingdom of God is far from orthodox. The New Testament clearly reveals that the kingdom of God is both a present reality and a future hope. Jesus prayed, "Your kingdom come, your will be done on earth as it is in heaven."[116] In this prayer, Jesus offers a view of the kingdom as an already/not yet eschatological reality. McLaren and the emergent view of the kingdom of God shapes this movement's missiology. As they identify with Jesus and his gospel of the kingdom it is not about spreading the good news of salvation in Christ to prepare people for a new eschatological kingdom reality, rather it is much more about the kingdom of the here and now. McLaren states, "I see the kingdom as primarily being about God's will being done on earth, in history, with a forward light cast beyond this life."[117] His missiology and evangelism is not as much about preparing people for the kingdom to come as it is about bringing God's kingdom to earth through changing people to be more sensitive to justice, poverty and social transformation. Gilbert asserts, "The fact is that the kind of kingdom McLaren wants Jesus to have preached doesn't have any real use for a cross, for it is but a superfluous illustration of the kind of life the kingdom would call us to live."[118]

As the American evangelical church seeks to make disciples who are faithfully committed to the whole counsel of God, it will be critical to ground these believers in a firm belief in the plenary verbal inspiration of the Bible. Christian praxis without a strong biblical mooring in traditional orthodox beliefs is surely to fail because it has no foundation from which

---

114. McLaren, *New Kind of Christianity*, 91.
115. McLaren, *New Kind of Christianity*, 109.
116. Luke 11:2.
117. Streett, "Interview with Brian McLaren," 7.
118. Gilbert, "Brian McLaren and the Gospel of Here & Now."

to build. The Psalmist agrees, "Your word is a lamp to my feet and a light to my path" (Ps. 119:105). For the disciple of Jesus, the Bible is not a book of stories worthy of consideration, nor is it a collection of moral encouragements, rather it is the living Word of God on every page, in every pericope, and through every literary biblical genre. It will also be critical to articulate the lost condition of the human soul and the propitiatory ministry of the cross of Christ with a view of an already, not yet kingdom of God.

DISCIPLE MAKING IN THE EMERGENT CHURCH MOVEMENT

Brian McLaren writes, "It (the gospel) was a summons to rethink everything and enter a life of retraining as disciples or learners of a new way of life, citizens of a new kingdom."[119] McLaren asks the question, "What is the gospel?" In answering the question, he denies Pauline influence on the definition not allowing Paul's theological contributions in Romans or elsewhere to give weight to the discussion.[120] Most emergent leaders downplay Paul's letters, especially concerning their theological constructions. Nowhere in McLaren's chapter on the gospel in *A New Kind of Christianity* does one find a clear soteriological argument regarding substitutionary atonement or even a mention of the cross or resurrection of Jesus. In discussing the gospel, its impact is relegated to social and relational changes instead of spiritual regeneration. McLaren states, "The time has come today to cancel debts, to forgive, to treat enemies as neighbors, to share your bread with the hungry and your clothes with the naked, to invite the outcasts over for dinner, to confront oppressors not with sharp knives but with kindness."[121] McLaren also questions the authority of Scripture, "There will be no new kind of Christian faith without a new approach to the Bible."[122] Perhaps McLaren would be wise to hear Timothy George's critique of the Emergent Movement. George states:

---

119. McLaren, *New Kind of Christianity*, 139.

120. McLaren spends the bulk of chapter 14 in *A New Kind of Christianity* breaking down the long-held theological truths found in the book of Romans, relegating its chapters as mere anecdotes for a sick and divided church. He describes the book of Romans as "not a premeditated work of scholarly theology." McLaren, *New Kind of Christianity*, 146.

121. McLaren, *New Kind of Christianity*, 140.

122. McLaren, *New Kind of Christianity*, 66–67.

An Emergent Generosity of Orthodoxy

> A church which cannot distinguish heresy from truth, or no longer thinks this is an important thing to do, has lost its right to bear witness to the transforming gospel of Jesus Christ who declared Himself to be not only the Way and the Life, but also the only Truth which leads to the Father.[123]

There is within emergent circles a focus on practice over orthodox theology. A de-emphasis of doctrine and a stronger focus on making the most out of life has led to a view of Jesus which emphasizes his ethical lessons more than his resurrection and his redemptive purpose.[124] Ambiguity in doctrine and theology with emergent leaders has led to a focus on Jesus as a way of life rather than Jesus as the giver of life. Without a strong focus on orthodoxy, it is hard to imagine that the Emergent Church Movement could train, equip, and disciple new believers on their new identity as being "in Christ." Any movement that focuses on changing the world, more than Christ changing the person from being dead to being alive can never lead to effective disciple making. Van Hoozer states, "Pastors have the great privilege and responsibility of helping disciples to get real, as they become more like Christ. The primary way we get real and become more like Christ, is through Scripture and doctrine."[125] The universalist underpinnings of McLaren's theology of evangelism have also diluted any efficacy for making disciples who make disciples. The emergent church's response to the perceived failures of the modern church is flawed due to its proclamation of truth as propositional. Included in this is the reticence of emergent leaders to proclaim the inherent sinful condition of humankind, the reality of eternal judgment, and the New Testament's theology of evangelism. When compared to the disciple making model and methods of Jesus, which had as its core thrust of redemptive component, the emergent movement falls short due to its lack of orthodoxy.

CONCLUSION

One of the great mysteries of researching the Emergent Church Movement is determining where the emergent stream is today. Though the leaders of

---

123. George, "The Future for Theological Education Among Southern Baptists," presented to the Southeast regional meeting of the *National Association of Baptists Professors of Religion*, 18.

124. DeYoung and Kluck, *Why We're Not Emergent*, 113.

125. Van Hoozer, *Hearers and Doers*, 238.

the emergent movement continue to write, their influence on American evangelical ecclesiology has all but vanished. Even the infamous Emergent Village is nowhere to be found in Google searches and present-day writings. All of this leads me to conclude that the emergent stream has dried up, while the emerging stream continues to influence due to the work of those who, with inspiring courage, continue to reach postmoderns. The difference is, that they are reaching postmoderns without buying into postmodern thinking. These leaders continue to have a substantial influence on Christian thinking and represent a group that regularly engages with postmoderns through apologetics and dialogue. And herein lies perhaps the greatest disciple making hope for the American church and its disciple making effectiveness. Emergent leaders such as McLaren, Pagitt, Bell, and Kimball offer ideas without substance, and missions without a coherent orthodox theology. Their emptying of the gospel message and subsequent focus on humanitarian justice over the coming judgment in the eschaton has placed these leaders outside of doctrinal norms, and into heretical lanes. Carson summarizes his critique of the emergent church in this way:

> If emerging church leaders wish to become a long-term prophetic voice that produces enduring fruit and that does not drift off toward progressive sectarianism and even, in the worst instances, outright heresy, they must listen carefully to criticisms of their movement as they transparently want others to listen to them . . . And above all, they need to embrace all the categories of the Scriptures, with the Scriptures' balance and cohesion—including what the Bible says about truth, human knowing, and related matters.[126]

All evidence points to the fact that the emergent leaders did not take Carson's advice, nor did they make the needed theological corrections. A true disciple making movement will have a mission that proceeds from the redemptive purpose of the biblical *missio Dei*, orthodox doctrine, sufficiency of Christ as the only way to heaven, and an urgency to make disciples who make disciples.

On his blog, McLaren was asked the question, "Is the Emergent Church Movement Fizzling Out?" His answer gives the impression that McLaren views the Missional Church Movement as a continuation of the Emergent Church Movement, or at least a companion movement:

> My sense is that more and more of us who are deeply involved with emergence Christianity are simply talking about God, Jesus,

126. Carson, *Becoming Conversant*, 234.

the Bible, mission, faith, spirituality, and life . . . and doing so from a new and fresh perspective, but not using the "e" word so much. Sometimes it's the word "missional" that works, sometimes it's "progressive," sometimes it's "new kind of"—it goes under lots of labels.[127]

McLaren calls Lesslie Newbigin, "One of the theologians who have helped me the most."[128] There is little doubt that McLaren and other Emergent leaders would consider themselves in step with much of the missiology espoused by Newbigin, Guder, the *Gospel and Our Culture* network, and the Missional Church Movement. It is to this movement that chapter five will give insights and analysis.

---

127. McLaren, "Is the Emerging Church Movement Fizzling Out?"
128. McLaren, *Generous Orthodoxy*, 110.

Chapter 5

If Everything is Missional, Is Anything Truly Missional?

A History and Critique of the Missional Church Movement

> If everything that the church does is to be classed as "mission," we shall have to find another term for the church's particular responsibility for the heathen, those who have never yet heard the name of Christ.[1]
>
> —Stephen Neill

Since the end of the twentieth century, the American evangelical church has been heavily influenced by a new paradigm related to its focus and mission. The Missional Church Movement began in Europe through the influential writings of Lesslie Newbigin and was embraced and significantly shaped by such people as Darrell Guder, Craig Van Gelder, Dwight J. Zscheile, George Hunsberger, David Bosch, and others. Though evangelicals were slow to embrace this new way of thinking, once embraced through the writings of Ed Stetzer and Alan Hirsch they were enthusiastic about re-envisioning the purpose of the church.[2]

All the ecclesial movements studied so far in this book have had their genesis from an influential thinker, missiologist, and eventually a seminal writing. Donald McGavran's *The Bridges of God* was the catapult from

---

1. Neill, *Creative Tension*, 81–82.
2. Payne, *Kingdom Expressions*, 83.

which the Church Growth Movement sprang, and Brian McLaren's *A New Kind of Christianity* was integral in the formation of the Emergent Church Movement. The roots of the Missional Church Movement in America can be traced back to a similar genesis. Newbigin's seminal book, *The Other Side of 1984, Questions for the Churches*, in which he analyzed the challenges facing the western church as the culture moved to a more secular position, was the most important influence of the formation of the Missional Church Movement.[3] Whereas McGavran sought to create church growth through missional bridges and McLaren urged contextualized missional conversations, Newbigin desired a missional awakening to take place within congregations as they began to understand the new world in which they served. Newbigin and his wife served as missionaries to India from 1936 to 1974. Upon returning to Britain Newbigin was shocked to see how the West had drifted from its Christian roots while he served on the mission field.[4] Newbigin eventually realized that just as India was a mission field to be reached, now too was his own country, which had essentially become a place to be reached for Christ again. In the late 1990s a group of mainline leaders, who were heavily impacted by Newbigin's writings, formed *The Gospel and Our Culture* network for the purpose of discussing the theological and ecclesiological foci and its implications on the American church. These discussions have been crystallized in the formative and influential book, *Missional Church, A Vision for the Sending of the Church in North America*, edited by Darrell Guder.

Following the publication of Guder's book, the word *missional* became a proliferated term in books, articles, and by churches and denominations in describing their vision and purpose. Even today it is not uncommon for seminaries to offer courses with the term *missional* in the title.[5] Each of these various publications, curriculums, and entities are seeking a common refocusing of the ecclesial *missio Dei* to the Western church to help Christians see themselves as missionaries and churches as missionary-sending organizations. The Missional Church Movement has similarities to the previously studied movements. First, its most influential thinkers within the movements write to correct perceived missiological and ecclesiological drifts within the Western church. Second, each of the movements sought a redefining or readjustment of the purpose of the church as a response to the

---

3. Guder, *Missional Church*, 3.
4. Guder, *Missional Church*, 1.
5. Prebble, "Missional Church," 224.

declining influence of Christianity in the Western world. Third, each of the movements resulted in a large quantity of publications and literature for the purpose of ecclesial missiological redeployment. Fourth, the missiological principles of each movement have been espoused by people from a variety of denominational, political, and theological positions with concepts that have impacted both the church and the academy. The Missional Church Movement, like the Emergent Church Movement, views social action as part of kingdom work and important to its evangelistic outreach while the Church Growth Movement has historically held evangelism as an ecclesial priority over social action in a local congregation.[6] Also, Donald McGavran and Lesslie Newbigin served as missionaries in India, and both grew disgruntled regarding traditional missiological approaches.[7]

Newbigin shares his deep appreciation for McGavran's missiological principles in his writing *Signs Amid the Rubble*, "When McGavran and I were both serving as missionaries in India, his books came to me as illuminating my situation. I find marks of approval in the margins of my copies of his earliest works."[8] Both the Emergent Church Movement and the Missional Church Movement share similarities related to the formational writings of Barth and Newbigin regarding the *missio Dei*. As with the Missional Church Movement, this doctrine created the foundations for the Emergent Church Movement and was formational on Brian McLaren's missiological principles.[9]

The word *missional* was first used in the 1883 book, *The Heroes of African Discovery and Adventure, from the Death of Livingstone to the Year 1882*, but had largely been unused until the writings of Newbigin and the

---

6. McIntosh, "Church Movements," 46.

7. In his book, *Open Secret*, Newbigin spent a portion of chapter nine offering an overview and critique of McGavran and the Institute of Church Growth. He affirms McGavran's missiological impact, "Dr. Donald McGavran has forced missionary agencies in the many parts of the world to ask why churches do not grow and to plan deliberately for church growth and expect it as the normal experience of missions" (p. 122). While he does affirm McGavran's criticism of the old mission station approach, Newbigin does express his opinion regarding the over emphasis of numerical growth within Church Growth ideology. He also takes issue with McGavran's separation of "discipling" and "perfecting." He states, "Can 'discipling' and 'perfecting' be separated even for a moment?" (p. 135). Lesslie Newbigin, *The Open Secret*.

8. Newbigin, *Signs Amid the Rubble*, 84–86.

9. Brian McLaren lists Newbigin's books *Open Secret*, and *Proper Confidence* as being a major influencer on his postmodern views.

If Everything is Missional, Is Anything Truly Missional?

theological discussions that ensued by the World Council of Churches.[10] Beginning in the 1990s many writings were produced which used the term *missional* either in the title or as a major theme. Van Gelder and Zscheile offer a concise overview of the major themes that eventually dominated the literary corpus of the Missional Church Movement. The themes of these writings within the North American ecclesial culture would have a major impact on the way churches, denominations, and Christian organizations viewed their mission. These themes include (1) God as a missionary God who sends the church into the world. (2) God's mission in the world as related to the reign (kingdom) of God. (3) The missional church as an incarnational (verses an attractional) ministry sent to engage a postmodern, post-Christendom, globalized context. (4) The internal life of the missional church focuses on every believer living as a disciple engaging in mission.[11]

The word *missional* has been used so often since the refocused efforts of Newbigin and Guder that it became over-saturated and at times devoid of theological meaning. The over-saturation of the term eventually watered down the original intent of the movement to refocus the church on its *missio Dei*, thus its ecclesial mission, and is largely why the movement eventually waned. The term came to lack theological meaning and eventually became a descriptive term synonymous with programming rather than tied to the theological purpose of the church. The term *missional* cannot be only about social action or something the church does, but rather it must contain a robust theology in which the church recognizes the significance of the mission of God to save people by the gospel of Jesus Christ. The church must embrace a missional focus in which its missional theology includes a comprehensive doctrine of conversion, thoroughly pneumatological and trinitarian in its self-understanding and practice.[12]

The over-proliferation and lack of clarity in the theological and ecclesiological meaning of the word *missional* eventually caused the movement to shift away from the original vision of Newbigin, Barth, Guder, and others. Roxburgh states, "The word 'missional' seems to have traveled the remarkable path of going from obscurity to banality in only one decade."[13] To Roxburgh's point, much of the missional church literature focused too much on what the church was supposed to do (*missio ecclesia*) rather than

---

10. Payne, *Kingdom Expressions*, 84.
11. Van Gelder and Zscheile, *Missional Church*, 4.
12. Franklin, "Missionaries in Our Own Back Yard," 190.
13. Van Gelder and Zscheile, *Missional Church*, 1.

what the church is (*missio Dei*). A key missional church attribute includes the *missio Dei* as formational to the *missio ecclesia* so that the true missional purpose of the church is not lost due to purposeless activity. As seen in the Emergent Movement, a mission without the right theology eventually devolves into a group of people doing random acts of kindness.

THE HISTORY AND FOUNDATIONS OF THE MISSIONAL MOVEMENT

Since the Reformation of the sixteenth century, the new protestant congregations, and denominations, which formed as a result, have been concerned with the clarification of the true purpose of the church. The theological processes that resulted from this clarification brought major confessional statements regarding the purpose and praxis of the church.[14] From these various confessional statements, the doctrine of the mission of God (*missio Dei*) was developed as the purpose of the church to serve the world as bearers of their God-given mission. Bosch states, "Until the sixteenth century the term *mission* was used exclusively with reference to the doctrine of the Trinity, that is, of the sending of the Son by the Father and of the Holy Spirit by the Father and the Son."[15] As the Protestant churches came to understand their mission to the world, various mission societies were created to engage in global outreach which often resulted in the church outsourcing its missional purpose. There came to be a dichotomous approach to church and mission, which ultimately needed to be corrected.

The Tambaram and Willingen Conferences of the IMC

There were significant theological concepts that developed in the twentieth century that reoriented church and mission, not as dichotomous theologies, but rather into a comprehensive missional approach. The result was a shift from "a theology of missions" to "a missional theology" for the church. Theologians began to argue for a "theocentric" (God-centered) approach

---

14. Van Gelder and Zscheile list several confessional statements which resulted in this search for understanding concerning the purpose of the church. These include the Augsburg Confession (1530), the Belgic Confession (1561), the Heidelberg Catechism (1563), the Dordrecht Confession (1632), and the Westminster Confession (1646).

15. Bosch, *Transforming Mission*, 1.

rather than an "ecclesiocentric" (church-centered) approach.[16] At the beginning of the twentieth century, however, mission had primarily been relegated to an expansion of the Christian enterprise which spread from the West to the various parts of the world. The mission of the church was carried out by societies supported by the church, but not actually within or through the church. Goheen and Sheriden write of the situation:

> There are serious problems with this notion of mission. And it is precisely these problems that stand in the way of a thoroughly missionary understanding of the church. As these assumptions were dismantled in the next quarter of a century, the biblical notion of a missionary church emerged.[17]

Denominationalism spread throughout the Western world in the years following the Protestant Reformation and with the surge in the newly founded ecclesial segments, missionary organizations resulted.[18] A dichotomy developed, particularly in the United States in the nineteenth Century, between missiology and ecclesiology. Mission became a task carried out by missionary societies, supported by the church but separate from it. Goheen and Sheriden call this development a "scandal" as the primary role of the church had been contracted *extra-ecclesia* (external of the church). Lesslie Newbigin saw this dichotomy as, "one of the biggest calamities of missionary history."[19]

Goheen and Sheriden view the 1938 meeting of the International Missionary Council conference in Tambaram, India as a watershed moment in forming a "theologically rich notion of a missionary church."[20] The work of the council at Tambaram, in Newbigin's view, rescued the missional purpose of the church from two equally dangerous errors: the liberal social gospel and the individualistic gospel of evangelical pietism. The emphasis on continuing the mission of Christ in the church is replete within the doctrines of the final documents of the Tambaram meeting. There is also a strong emphasis on the nature and function of the Church as an "active witness bearer"[21] to the world. The final report of the conference highlights six primary missional purposes of the church. (1) The plea to recognize

16. Payne, *Kingdom Expressions*, 84.
17. Goheen and Sheriden, *Becoming a Missionary Church*, 21.
18. Marty, *Righteous Empire*, 67-68.
19. Goheen and Sheriden, *Becoming a Missionary Church*, 21.
20. Goheen and Sheriden, *Becoming a Missionary Church*, 19.
21. Goheen and Sheriden, *Becoming a Missionary Church*, 25.

evangelism as a God-given task inherent in the nature of the church. (2) The witness of the church to non-Christian religions. (3) An emphasis on the inner life of the church stressing the importance of worship, fellowship, sacraments, preaching, teaching, and reading the Word, prayer, and music for the church in its mission. (4) The mission of the church in society—the healing, economic, social, international, and political calling of the church. (5) The unity of the church and its importance for mission. (6) The unfinished evangelistic task to unreached parts of the world.[22] Though this conference was only the infancy of ecclesial missional thinking, it proved to have a great influence on Lesslie Newbigin, and eventually, the Missional Church Movement. The resurgent missional thinking within the American ecclesial structure eventually developed into two strains of evangelicalism. One strain originated out of Donald McGavran's missiological principles, which focused primarily on getting the church back to its evangelistic mission within the North American context. The other strain came from the Billy Graham Association which focused on world evangelization and eventually morphed into the Lausanne Committee for World Evangelization.[23] Each of these strains became heavily influential to the church in America as it sought missional purpose.

Swiss theologian Karl Barth's influence on the missionary nature of the church played a significant role in influencing local churches to examine their missionary nature in the 1930s. Barth espoused a theological understanding of God's trinitarian mission in the face of the demise of classical liberalism's assault on the infrastructure of Christendom within Western culture. Van Gelder and Zscheile explain:

> Barth, in developing his doctrine of the Word of God, utilized a Western trinitarian understanding to reframe discussion of God theologically. This tradition focused on the essential unity within the divine community and then proceeded to elucidate the distinct roles of the three persons of God. In returning to this Western trinitarian tradition, Barth reclaimed the classical meaning of "mission" within the interrelations of God as that of sending—the Father sent the Son, and the Father and the Son sent the Spirit.[24]

---

22. These points are taken from Goheen and Sheriden (pages 24-28) as found in *World Mission of the Church*.

23. Van Gelder and Zscheile, *Missional Church*, 25.

24. Van Gelder and Zscheile, 26. It should be noted that Barth was the one who originally used the phrase "the Father sent the Son, and the Father and the Son sent the Spirit." The quote was from his address to the Bradenburg Mission Conference in 1932 as found

If Everything is Missional, Is Anything Truly Missional?

Barth became one of the first theologians to articulate mission as an activity of God himself as seen through the trinitarian nature. He stressed that the term *missio* in the ancient church was an expression of trinitarian activity and connected this activity to the gathering, forming, and sending of the church into the world. In other words, there is an intrinsic *missio* for the church because God is a sending God, as displayed in his trinitarian activity. Bosch writes of Barth's influence on missional theology:

> Barth may be called the first clear exponent of a new theological paradigm which broke radically with an Enlightenment approach to theology. His influence on missionary thinking reached a peak at the Willingen Conference of the IMC (International Missions Council) in 1952. It was here that the idea (not the exact term) *missio Dei* first surfaced clearly. Mission was understood as being derived from the very nature of God. It was thus put in the context of the doctrine of the Trinity, not of ecclesiology or soteriology.[25]

Barth, along with Karl Hartenstein,[26] caused the church to rethink its theological position regarding its mission. The church could no longer be the starting point for mission, rather it was the result of God's mission. This seismic shift in theological philosophy informed the Missional Church Movement particularly as it related to the writings of Lesslie Newbigin. The shift was entirely appropriate as the church in North America was still functioning missionally from the European model rather than as an outworking of the mission of God handed down to the church. Christendom as the driving force of culture in the Western world had disappeared yet the church was still attempting to operate as if nothing culturally had shifted. It should be clearly stated that the theological formations of the missional church conversations are trinitarian in large part due to the influence of Barth. Also significant to the development of missional ecclesial thinking was the Willingen Conference, of which Barth's writings would have a seismic impact.

---

in *Classic Texts*, Thomas, 106.

25. Bosch, *Transforming Mission*, 390.

26. Goheen and Sheriden point to Hartenstein as the first to use the term *missio Dei* in 1934 prior to the Tambaram Conference. "Hartenstein's voice was a lonely voice, especially in the 1930's. His insights likely influenced Tambaram, but it would not be until Willingen that much of his theological work would bear fruit. It would be then that a theological framework would be established that would incorporate both the growing insights about church and mission since Tambaram and the new experiences of the world church." 31.

Repairing the Missional Breach

The Willingen Conference of the International Missions Council in 1952 had a profound impact on the American ecclesial mission as it introduced the idea of *missio Dei* and in so doing moved the church from mission as a function of the church to mission as an agency of God's activity in the church for the benefit of the world. The Willingen meeting was a pivotal moment for the Church as it brought together the budding missionary theologies of Emil Brunner, Karl Barth, Karl Hartenstein, and Hendrikus Berkhof into one coherent missional vision. Though the conference attendees did not recognize it at the time, the results of the meeting would define a missional ecclesiology for decades to come. Goheen and Sheriden state, "It was the time when the scattered bricks from the global church, from missionary theology, and from biblical and theological studies were gathered and built into a unified framework."[27] Perhaps the most quoted words of the Willingen conference are taken from the section entitled, "The Missionary Calling of the Church." It states, "There is no participation in Christ without participation in his mission to the world. That by which the Church receives its existence is that by which it is also given its world-mission. 'As the Father has sent Me so send I you.'"[28]

Georg F. Vicedom's book, *The Mission of God: An Introduction to the Theology of Mission*, thrusted the conception of the *missio Dei* as the primary function of the church. He states, "The mission, and with it the church, is God's very own work. Both the church's mission and the church are only tools of God, instruments through which God carries out his mission."[29] The discussion of the missionary nature of the church would continue well after Tambaram and Willingen. Questions regarding the missionary nature of the church continued to be discussed within the World Council of Churches (WCC). Should the *missio Dei* be understood primarily within God's ongoing work of redemption and the church as the primary way in which God works in the world? Others considered the *missio Dei* in more general terms as God's continuing care of creation. The focus of the WCC became the clarification of the *missio Dei* in which it extrapolated its findings in a publication entitled, *The Church for Others*,[30] in 1967. The findings of this council were that the *missio Dei* could be identified with a process of historical transformation whereby humankind would gradually achieve the

---

27. Goheen and Sheriden, *Becoming a Missionary Church*, 33.
28. Blaxall, "Willingen, 1952," 2.
29. Ficedom, *Mission of God*, 5–6.
30. World Council of Churches, *Church for Others*.

goals of the messianic kingdom through the processes of secular history. The findings of the WCC would eventually lead some of the younger churches to no longer relate to the WCC, and this crisis had a causal effect in creating a merger between the WCC and the International Missionary Council.

The reorganization would be known as the Commission on World Mission and Evangelism (CWME). Lesslie Newbigin would serve as the first director of the newly formed CWME.[31] Also significant to the development of missional thinking was Vatican II in which Hans Kung's theological and ecclesiological influence was substantial. The results of Kung's work would eventually be articulated in his seminal work, *The Church*, written in 1967. Kung argues that the kingdom of God is a larger framework for understanding the church, one in which the church is sent as missionaries into the world by a missionary God. While the work of Vatican II was obviously Roman Catholic in focus, the implications of Kung's theology did have an impact on the way evangelical theologians thought about mission.

Barth's influence continued to shape the ecclesiological mission. The ecclesial mission was now seen as preceding the church, and mission was to be understood as God's mission. The church was missionary by nature because its founder was intrinsically missional. Barth's influence was seen in both Roman Catholic and evangelical circles. While many in the evangelical world took exception to the more generalized view of the *missio Dei* as produced by the WCC, the work of the WCC and Vatican II provided some of the theological underpinnings of what would eventually become the Missional Church Movement. Donald McGavran's missiological principles also brought a new perspective on the missionary nature of the church in America.[32] He confronted the more generalized view of the *missio Dei* produced by the WCC at the Uppsala assembly of the council in 1968. At the meeting, McGavran pushed back on the secular understanding of the WCC as he asked, "Will Uppsala betray the two billion?"[33] Meaning, of course, the two billion people living in the world that had not heard the gospel. It is important to note that though Donald McGavran's legacy is tied to the Church Growth Movement, his passion was relentlessly focused on global missiological evangelism. Toward the end of his life, McGavran reiterated the importance of missional focus as the Great Commission as

---

31. Van Gelder and Zscheile, *Missional Church*, 31–33.

32. Payne, *Kingdom Expressions*, 85.

33. McGavran, "Will Uppsala Betray the Two Billion?" 149–153.

he wrote to the Chair of Missions at Trinity Evangelical, David Hesselgrave, "What is needed in North America and indeed around the world is a society of missiology that says quite frankly that the purpose of missiology is to carry out the Great Commission. Anything other than that may be a good thing to do, but it is not missiology."[34] Though McGavran was the primary influencer on the Church Growth Movement,[35] his comments at the Uppsala meeting would also lend influence on the formational understanding of a missional church and his missiological impact remains enormous. All these theological conclusions led to a new way of how a local church viewed its mission. Van Gelder and Zscheile state, "With this shift in perspective, the primary agency for mission moves to divine initiative through the ministry of the Spirit as the larger framework within which our human responses take place."[36] With this new shift the church recognized that God was at work in calling people to salvation and the church was to join him in that mission.

The real thrust of the Missional Church Movement in America was initiated from the work of the *Gospel and Our Culture* network. The network was heavily influenced by the principles that emanated from both the Tambaram and Willingen conferences as articulated through Newbigin.[37] It was created in the late 1980s to introduce an American ecclesial audience to Newbigin's philosophy as outlined in his book, *The Other Side of 1984*.[38] The network brought Newbigin's discussions from Great Britain to America in order to assist the American ecclesial scene to understand the paradigm shift needed within the local church as the nation entered into a post-Christian era. The *magnum opus* of this network was Guder's book entitled *The Missional Church*, which articulated the network's beliefs and presented Newbigin's philosophies to the American scene. Guder summarizes the network's findings as a new paradigm as the church hears from God concerning the mission of the church in "fresh ways":

---

34. Hesselgrave, *Paradigms in Conflict*, 316.

35. Charles Van Engen's chapter in *Evaluating the Church Growth Movement*, offers the following criticism of McGavran and the Church Growth Movement in light of Newbigin's concerns, "Much CG theory has fueled a functional view of the church, to the extent that churches (and congregations) are only significant as they are useful tools to achieve some other goal." Charles Van Engen, "Centrist View" in *Evaluating the Church Growth Movement,* Engle and McIntosh, 104.

36. Van Gelder and Zscheile, *Missional Church,* 8.

37. Goheen and Sheriden, *Becoming a Missionary Church* 19.

38. Guder, *Missional Church,* 3.

If Everything is Missional, Is Anything Truly Missional?

> We have learned to speak of God as a "missionary God." Thus, we have learned to understand the church as a "sent people." "As the Father has sent me, so I send you" (John 20:21). This missional reorientation of our theology is the result of a broad biblical and theological awakening that has begun to hear the gospel in fresh ways. God's character and purpose as a sending or missionary God redefines our understanding of the Trinity.[39]

The definition of a missional church as stated in Guder's book was widely distributed and codified the trinitarian missiology which resulted from Barth, Hartenstein, Newbigin, and the Willingen Conference into the movement.

THE INFLUENCE OF LESSLIE NEWBIGIN

The influence of Lesslie Newbigin on missional thinking in Western ecclesial culture is significant. The clarity with which Newbigin analyzed Western post-Enlightenment culture and the challenges involved in reaching it, was monumental in its influence on missional thinking within the American ecclesial culture. Guder writes:

> Newbigin brought into public discussion a theological consensus that had long been forming among missiologists and theologians. He then focused that consensus on the concrete reality of Western society, as it has taken shape in the century. His conclusions have mobilized Christian thinkers and leaders on both sides of the Atlantic.[40]

Lesslie Newbigin became a Christian in his first year of school at Queens College in Cambridge, and this conversion had a profound impact on his life. His conversion came through the influence of the Student Christian Movement (SCM) at Queens and through his volunteer efforts at a Quaker Center in South Wales. He had volunteered to assist unemployed miners in the area but felt as though he really could not give them what they needed beyond menial recreation and supplies. He felt that the miners needed, "Some kind of faith that would fortify them for today and tomorrow against apathy and despair."[41] He concluded that this faith was

---

39. Guder, *Missional Church*, 4.
40. Guder, *Missional Church*, 3.
41. Newbigin, *Unfinished Agenda*, 11.

the Christian faith but knew that he too needed this same fortifying faith. One evening at the Quaker Center, after an especially troubling day, he laid in his bed feeling empty knowing that he could not give to others what he did not have himself. He had a vision that evening of the cross of Christ and later wrote of his conversion:

> I was sure that night in a way that I had never been before, that this was the clue that I must follow if I were to make any kind of sense of the world. From that moment I would always know how to begin again when I had come to the end of all my own resources of understanding and courage.[42]

He would soon become a leader in the SCM, which dedicated itself to equipping students with a strong sense of Christian vocation. In a time in Western culture when society was still trying to rebuild from the Great War, Newbigin learned to be attentive to the human needs around him and, in cooperation with his experience at the Quaker Center, saw this response as an essential aspect of Christian discipleship. He was heavily impacted by the many distinguished guest speakers brought to the university by the SCM. These speakers included John R. Mott, J. H. Oldham, William Paton, and William Temple.[43] The recurrent theme that influential students such as Newbigin heard was the challenge to be responsible Christians who impacted the world and made a difference in the lives of others. With Britain still under the shadow of the doldrums of The Great War, this type of impact was needed. The ethnic diversity of the SCM made an indelible impact on Newbigin's missiology and gave him a greater appreciation for those of other backgrounds. Through SCM, he became acquainted with students from various parts of Africa and Asia and created life-long friendships with these students experiencing the struggles of their nations in living under the weight of colonial powers.[44]

In the summer of 1936, Newbigin completed his theological studies at Westminster Theological College in Cambridge. He was ordained by the Church of Scotland for missionary service and married Helen Henderson whom he had met through SCM. Together they responded to the call to serve in India and set sail in 1936 arriving in Madras in October of that year. Upon arriving Newbigin experienced the static contentment of the

---

42. Newbigin, *Unfinished Agenda*, 11–12.
43. Shenk, "Newbigin in His Time," 30.
44. Shenk, "Newbigin in His Time," 32.

If Everything is Missional, Is Anything Truly Missional?

missionaries who were serving.[45] He became frustrated at the lack of passion the missionaries had for sharing the news of Christ. He wrote in his diary concerning this frustration:

> I must say I couldn't help being horrified by the sort of relation that seems to exist between the missionaries and the people. It seems so utterly remote from the New Testament. There seems to be no question of getting alongside them and sharing their troubles and helping them spiritually. We drive up like lords in a car, soaking everybody else with mud on the way, and then carry on a sort of inspection. They all sort of stand at attention and say "sir." It is awful, but one thing is as sure as death: surely, they won't stand this sort of thing from the white man much longer.[46]

Newbigin's frustrations would eventually lead him to reimagine missional approaches and by the 1940s he had developed a proper critique and response.[47]

In 1945, the editor of the *International Review of Missions* asked Newbigin to write an article expressing his thoughts on the current missionary situation in India. The article was published as "The Ordained Foreign Missionary in the Indian Church."[48] In the article, Newbigin offered an overview of the evolution of the British missionary role in India and how the missionary eventually served as an administrator over the process. In this role, the missionary controlled the entirety of the enterprise including the finances giving little to no leadership to the indigenous people reached by the missionary efforts. Newbigin argued that this pyramid structure of power had led to the static position of the missional efforts because the Indian people were never given administrative responsibilities making the efforts purely a white man's enterprise. He asserted that the missionaries must give up administrative positions equipping through discipleship the nationals that had been reached. His suggested paradigm shifts eventually raised the question as to what the missionary would be left to do. Newbigin's suggestions caused a stir among missionary leaders as he viewed the missionary role as one of service to the church and the Indian people.[49] He, along with two other Scottish missionaries, embodied the new roles as

---

45. Newbigin, *Unfinished Agenda*, 37.
46. Newbigin, *Unfinished Agenda*, 39.
47. Shenk, "Newbigin in His Time," 35.
48. Newbigin, "Ordained Foreign Missionary," 86–94.
49. Newbigin, "Ordained Foreign Missionary," 86–94.

suggested in his article as they placed themselves under the administrative authority of the locals, rather than the mission society.[50] His new way of missional approach would stay with him for the rest of his life and, in large part, would eventually shape his view of missional approaches in reaching Western culture.

Newbigin would attain global attention due to his influence on the founding of the Church of South India in 1947. The newfound prominence assured that he would be present at most major ecumenical events in the decades to come and would eventually lead to his appointment as director of the World Council of Churches, in which he managed the merger between the International Missionary Council and the World Council of Churches.[51] Though serving in a prominent role, Newbigin found himself missing the mission field, and in 1965 he was called back to India to serve as bishop of the Madras diocese. He would later retire in 1974, at age sixty-five, returning to Birmingham, England where he would lecture at Selly Oak College for five years. At the age of seventy-two, he began pastoring a small, struggling inner-city church affiliated with the United Reformed Church.[52] Though retired, he would continue to have a major influence on an emerging refocusing of Western ecclesiology.

In the early 1980s, Newbigin's life took a remarkable turn. He was invited to participate in a committee convened by the British Council of Churches to prepare for a major conference on *Church and Society* planned for 1984.[53] Frustrated by the increasing secularism of the West, Newbigin felt that the initial proposals for the conference did not adequately address the pervasive post-Christian mindset and the eradication of Christendom in his country. He asked that the conference be postponed in order to think carefully and prepare thoughtfully about the fundamental issues faced by the churches. The committee agreed to postpone the conference and asked Newbigin to write down his thoughts regarding the challenges faced by the churches to serve as a discussion document, offering the questions that needed to be considered by the conference.[54] The result of Newbigin's writing was a small booklet entitled, *The Other Side of 1984*, which addressed the missional challenges faced in a post-Enlightenment and post-Christian

50. Shenk, "Newbigin in His Time," 36.
51. Shenk, "Newbigin in His Time," 43.
52. Shenk, "Newbigin in His Time," 43.
53. Westin, *Lesslie Newbigin*, 13.
54. Westin, *Lesslie Newbigin*, 13.

society. The ongoing iteration of the discussion of Newbigin's questions became known as the *Gospel and Our Culture* program. The largest of these gatherings happened in 1992 at the international conference in Swanwick.[55] The discussions on the re-focusing of the mission of the church eventually made their way to America with the proliferation of Newbigin's theories through Guder's book and the eventual Missional Church Movement.

The emerging refocusing and reframing on ecclesiology in the twentieth century brought about changes, specifically in how the church carried out its mission. The younger churches within evangelical Protestantism saw that the theological relationship between mission and church not only needed to be revitalized but rehabilitated. New paradigms were demanded that reflected a recovered biblical understanding of the mission of the church considering the changing global situation.[56] Newbigin had a major influence on this changing paradigm as he articulated the breakdown of Christendom and informed church leaders on how Western culture and the Gospel could find a greater synthesis.

He attributed the breakdown to three causes: first was the failure of the Western church in its apostolic mission. He states, "Missions were conceived of as the extension of the frontiers of Christendom and the conveyance of the blessings of Christian civilization to those who had hitherto been with them."[57] In other words, the church had become much more about codifying its presence and maintaining its buildings than in its salvific purpose. Second, having lost its missional purpose, the church was even more susceptible to cultural attacks upon its ethical traditions. This problem is related to the loss of apostolic ministry as the church saw fewer and fewer people converted and discipled, which led to a growing Enlightenment secularism that inundated Western culture. Third, the consequences of the Industrial Revolution caused society to divide into a mechanized division of labor. Newbigin explains, "I detect a sort of atomizing process, in which the individual is more and more set free from his natural setting in family and neighborhood and becomes a sort of replaceable unit in the social machine."[58] In essence, men became slaves to the industry, often forfeiting their familial roles. In response to Newbigin's reflections, Laing writes, "When faced with such major theological challenges in its heartland, the

55. Westin, *Lesslie Newbigin*, 13.
56. Laing, *From Crisis to Creation*, 33–34.
57. Newbigin, *Household of God*, 12.
58. Newbigin, *Foolishness to the Greeks*, 34.

inadequacy of the church's ecclesiology was exposed, and it was forced to re-examine its essential nature. The Western church was in decline and lacked the theological resources to counter the challenges."[59]

What was needed was a reinvention and intentionality of the *missio Dei* as the true mission of the church. Newbigin states:

> I do not think we will recover the true form of the parish until we recover a truly missionary approach to our culture. I don't think we will achieve a truly missionary encounter with our culture without recovering the true form of the parish. These two tasks are reciprocally related to each other, and we have to work together on them both.[60]

Newbigin would publish fifteen more books and over one hundred and sixty smaller works during his retirement years. The works written in this phase of his life became instrumental to missional thinking in the West as they focused on ecclesiology, ecumenism, and mission, which had been the culmination of his life's work. His later works, in large part, galvanized the future focus of the Missional Church Movement as a new congregational contextualization began to take shape. His insistence on churches understanding the missional challenge facing the church in the West would lead to a new cultural contextualization that focused the church more on their "sending" than on their "coming."[61] Newbigin insisted on a theology of cultural plurality. To describe this cultural theology, he deployed a "three-cornered relationship" which consisted of the gospel, culture, and the church. He proposes under *the gospel as communicated* a "challenging relevance" in which the gospel is embodied in such a way that people of the culture can properly understand it.[62] Once the gospel is taken to a culture there must be a "radical discontinuity," or a break into a new direction. The culture or community's understanding of the Bible is dependent upon its own traditions, which Newbigin calls the "hermeneutical circle."[63] The church's commitment to the Bible's authority, embodied through discipleship, enables the hermeneutical circle between the Bible and the church to become the hermeneutic of the gospel in a particular culture. The third part of the triangular relationship is between the missionary church and the

59. Laing, *From Crisis to Creation*, 36.
60. Newbigin, *Mission in Christ's Way*, 65.
61. Westin, *Lesslie Newbigin*, 13.
62. Newbigin, *Open Secret*, 165-172.
63. Newbigin, *Foolishness to the Greeks*, 62.

culture as the church's outreach becomes a missionary dialogue.[64] The quest for this refocusing contextualization, with all the theological underpinnings of Newbigin and Barth, led to the proliferation of missional material and a new ecclesiology for the American church in the later twentieth century.

DISTINCTIVES OF THE MISSIONAL CHURCH MOVEMENT

Since the middle of the twentieth century, the Christian church in Western culture, particularly in North America, has found itself in unfamiliar territory. For generations, the church functioned in a comfortable and familiar environment where the basic beliefs of Christendom were widely accepted and rarely questioned. With the increasing postmodern secularization of North American culture, churches have struggled with how they should relate to culture, and how they should try to engage their new world. Much of the decline in modern church attendance is due to a maintenance mentality that has been widely embraced. Milfred Minatrea defines this maintenance mentality:

> Not surprisingly, churches find themselves increasingly out of touch with the rapids of cultural change and the real world in which their neighbors lived. Most cared about those on the outside, but they felt impotent to connect and share with unchurched persons in any significant way. Consequently, their churches no longer anticipated having a major impact upon society and hoped only to reach enough people to help the church survive.[65]

The Congregation as Missional

The overarching goal of the Missional Church Movement was to create causal motion away from this maintenance mindset and to refocus the church toward its original purpose. Congregations were encouraged to see themselves as missionary in nature and overcome the historical dichotomy of church and missions/mission by connecting ecclesiology and missiology.[66] A missional ecclesiology sees mission as not merely an activ-

---

64. Hunsberger, "The Newbigin Gauntlet," 11.
65. Minatrea, *Shaped by God's Heart*, 7.
66. Van Gelder and Zscheile, *Missional Church*, 6.

ity of the church, nor only an activity embraced by mission agencies, but the sole purpose of the church's existence. Guder states, "Rather, mission is the result of God's initiative, rooted in God's purposes to restore and heal creation. *Mission* means *sending*, and it is the central biblical theme describing the purpose of God's action in human history."[67] The *Gospel and Our Culture* network espoused the idea that mission is not just something the church does, rather it defines the church as God's sent people. Either the church is defined by mission, or there will be a reductionist approach to the gospel and the mission of the church. Thus, the challenge is the move from a church with a mission to a missional church.[68]

Van Gelder and Zscheile discouraged the use of the term *Missional Church Movement* because to label the missional church would be to add it to a long list of previously attempted strategies to help congregations become relevant. The missional leaders saw their writings as much more than prompting another movement and viewed their missional understandings as drawing on a different biblical understanding of God and God's mission from previous movements.[69] Leaders saw previous attempts as inadequate as they focused too readily on the purpose/mission of the church without first attending to the reality of God's being and agency. Van Gelder and Zscheile explain, "God's being, and agency require us to attend first to the identity/nature of the church before seeking to address its purpose/mission—what the church is prior to what the church does."[70]

The authors argue for a biblical view of the nature of the church, believing if the *missio Dei* is not the origin and identity of all ecclesial practice, then all activities are subject to error. They continue, "Thus, the missional church conversation presents an alternative way to think about the church, one that focuses on God's mission as determinative for understanding the mission of the church."[71] In this sense, every member of a congregation is seen as a missionary, and missions are not perceived as an expression of the missional church but as the essence of the church.[72] This type of thinking roots the theological foundations of the movement as the church being the *imago Dei* (image of God) bearers, existing for the *gloria Dei* (glory of

---

67. Guder, *Missional Church*, 4.
68. Guder, *Missional Church*, 6.
69. Van Gelder and Zscheile, *Missional Church*, 8.
70. Van Gelder and Zscheile, *Missional Church*, 9.
71. Van Gelder and Zscheile, *Missional Church*, 9.
72. Minatrea, *Shaped by God's Heart*, 11.

God). As Minatrea summarizes, "God desires His church to relish in His glory, share His glory among the nations, and reflect His glory in word and deed. The church is a body made in His image, sent on His mission, to be to His glory."[73] Much of the effectiveness of the missionary congregation will depend upon the contextualization of cultural analysis as the Western church sees itself as missionaries to an unreached population.

The Apostolic Congregation in Postmodern Context

The leaders of the *Gospel and Our Culture* network in their *magnum opus*, *Missional Church*, defined the distinctives of what would become known as the Missional Church Movement. The first of these distinctives is the realization that the church in North America is now set within a dramatically changing postmodern context. Collectively they call for a new vision of ministry for the North American church, due to the crisis of churches functioning as modern within the changing culture of postmodernity. They write, "The churches have become so accommodated to the American way of life that they are now domesticated, and it is no longer obvious what justifies their existence as particular communities."[74] In response to the lack of intentional disciple making, they note, "The religious loyalties that churches seem to claim and the social functions that they actually perform are at odds with each other. Discipleship has been absorbed into citizenship."[75] Heavily influenced by missiologist David Bosch, the leaders of the network ultimately saw the loss of the disciple making purpose of the church as a result of a communal mindset. The risk of a communal mindset is the church seeing itself as a place where Christians gather and a place where the Christian character of a society is fostered. The natural outflow of this mindset is the church's identity being mostly in organizational form with its clergy being the professional authorities. Deploying Barth and Newbigin's philosophies, the key distinctive was to be mission as founded on the mission of God in the world, rather than the church's efforts to extend itself. This theocentric missional approach embodied the thoughts of the trinitarian thinkers such as Newbigin, Barth, and Bosch.

A second distinctive of the Missional Church Movement is the need for the gospel of Jesus as the main influencer of the missional church as

73. Minatrea, *Shaped by God's Heart*, 9.
74. Hunsberger, "Missional Vocation," 78.
75. Hunsberger, "Missional Vocation," 78.

it returns to an apostolic mission rooted in the reign of God. Though trinitarian theocratic missiology had been deployed into the American ecclesial culture, what had yet to be articulated was how these philosophies impacted ecclesiological approaches. What does it mean that the church bears the stamp of the trinitarian eternal community, and how does that affect the eventual sending that characterizes that eternal communion? The writers of *Missional Church* point readers to the gospel account of Jesus Christ as sending out his disciples as one who was Spirit-filled. They state, "Jesus proclaimed that this Spirit rested on him and anointed him to preach good news (Luke 4:17–21). This mutuality in sending marks the divine communion as a communion of mission, and this in turn leaves its mark on the church."[76] Thus, the imperative takes the American church back to the Nicene-Constantinopolitan Creed, "One, holy, catholic, and apostolic church." The term apostolic denotes both the foundation of the church and its mission.[77] Robert Scudieri concludes, "The church is apostolic not just because it represents the apostles' teaching, but because it represents Christ."[78] The loss of apostolic function is in large part, due to the proliferation of consumeristic mentalities found within the American church culture, exacerbated by the later iterations of the Church Growth Movement. There has been a societal expectation that the church is a vendor of religious services and goods, and those who attend are the consumers. In this view, the clergy are the church's sales representatives, religious doctrines its products, and evangelization practices its marketing techniques.[79] Missional church leaders sought to correct this consumeristic model.

To correct the loss of apostolic function missional church leaders, call for a "rehearing of the gospel." In this rehearing, there is a fresh hearing of the gospel as an effort to get back to its roots to be clear about the essence of what it means to be the church.[80] George Hunsberger articulates this thought:

> The gospel, centered profoundly for Jesus in the announcement that the reign of God is at hand, is eschatological in character. It pulls back the veil on the coming reign of God, thereby revealing

---

76. Hunsberger, "Missional Vocation," 82.
77. Moltmann, *Church in the Power*, 358.
78. Scudieri, *Apostolic Church*, 28.
79. Finke and Stark, *Churching of America*, 17.
80. Hunsberger, "Missional Vocation," 86.

> the horizon of the world's future. The gospel portrays the coming of Jesus, and particularly his death and resurrection, as the decisive, truly eschatological event in the world's history. Therefore, a community with origins in the gospel is an eschatological community of salvation . . . The church is defined by its origins in a gospel that casts a vision of its destiny that always draws it forward.[81]

When the mission of the church is absent of the gospel of Jesus Christ it becomes woefully impoverished, and it loses its real sense of mission. A fresh missional approach to the gospel involves the church paying special attention to the announcement of Jesus regarding the reign of God. The reign of God is seen in the gospel of Christ and the church must embody the reign of God in its evangelistic outreach as a way of understanding its missionary role in the world. Hunsburger writes, "Evangelism would move from an act of recruiting or co-opting those outside the church to an invitation of companionship."[82] Van Gelder summarizes this embodying of the reign of God as evangelism, "In being missional by nature, local congregations seek to reach beyond themselves into their local areas of bear witness to the reign of God and to invite others into the community of faith."[83]

A third distinctive of the Missional Church Movement is equipping church members as missionaries to their communities. Lois Barrett writes, "The church is that gathering of the reign of God assembled to be a sign of that reign, to proclaim the reign of God in word and deed, to make decisions, and to give allegiance to their ruler."[84] MacIlvaine's definition of the Missional Church Movement also gives a strong indication of the missionary nature of church membership. He states, "A missional church is a unified body of believers, intent on being God's missionary presence to the indigenous community that surrounds them, recognizing that God is already at work."[85] Missional churches seek to equip their membership to display an interest in the society and culture in which they exist, first through generous acts of service but also through various artistic outlets.[86] At times these missional members will seek leadership positions in their communities to better connect and more intentionally live out a missional

---

81. Hunsberger, "Missional Vocation," 86.
82. Hunsberger, "Missional Vocation," 97.
83. Van Gelder, *Essence of the Church*, 168.
84. Barrett, "Missional Witness," 113.
85. MacIlvaine III, "What is the Missional Church Movement?" 91.
86. An example of this is found in Andy Crouch's article, "Creating Culture," 25–29.

lifestyle. After earning the right to be heard they intentionally and lovingly invest in relationships for the purpose of inviting friends to a different way of life found in Christ to be lived out in a missional community of believers.[87] Part of the missionary experience of church members is to recognize that God is already at work in offering common grace, and God, through His Spirit, is actively convicting unbelievers of their need for saving grace. Missionary members are equipped by missional churches to have confidence as gospel messengers knowing that God has preceded them in mission.[88] In other words, God is inviting people to join Him in his missional enterprise. Furthermore, the missional theology emboldens the members to be missionaries to their community by rooting them in God, who in His very essence, is missional. If God is continually extending grace to the world, then missionary members can extend themselves to others as an agent of this common grace as they seek to fulfill the Great Commission. Alan J. Roxburgh summarizes the goal of equipping missionary church members:

> Missional leadership will require skills in evoking a language about the church that reshapes its understanding of its purpose and practices. The practices of a disciple community will require a language different from that of a voluntary society. The practices of missional life call forth a people who live by standards of judgement and action quite different from those of the culture in which they are set. Leaders will enable God's people to give voice to this language of the reign of God as a way of living into such practices.[89]

The Structure of Missional Churches

A fourth distinctive of the Missional Church Movement is the development of structures for shaping its ministry and practice in a way that connects it within the larger church. When considering the structures of the missional church, the leaders of the movement sought to apply the theological understandings rooted in the *missio Dei* to the structures. Organizational formation must translate the witness of the church tangibly to its culture. Guder suggests three foundational principles for the structuring of the missional

---

87. Crouch, "Creating Culture," 92.
88. Crouch, "Creating Culture," 103.
89. Roxburgh, "Equipping God's People for Mission," 214.

church in America.⁹⁰ First, the Scriptures function authoritatively in the formation of the churches' structures. In the formation of missional ecclesial structures, leaders deploy a specific hermeneutic, missional in essence, which enables churches to recognize the content of the message, and the way it should be made known. This missional hermeneutic recognizes the authority of Scripture as the Bible serves as the warrant for the church's mission, instructing and guiding missional communities to engage their situations. Guder states, "Scripture is the Holy Spirit's powerful tool to guide our formation in the mission community that God has called us to be."⁹¹

Second, contrary to McGavran's Homogenous Unit Principle, missional church leaders believed the church's catholicity demands a necessary cultural diversity for its structures. From its very beginning, the church was founded and mandated to be multicultural, and this informs the present-day membership.⁹² The Spirit was given to the apostolic band for the purpose of translating the gospel into different languages to engage and reach varied communities. Leaders teach that the New Testament does not prescribe a certain organizational structure in order to keep it flexible to better engage within the culture it is set. Thus, the church's task within these cultures is to find the visible organizational form that is worthy of its calling to be a witness to Christ in its cultural context. Culture shapes the visible church, rather than the visible church shaping its culture which does not mean cultural values, but cultural organization structures. The resulting organizational diversity powerfully demonstrates the gospel as a witness to the world and its inherent catholicity.⁹³

Third, the local particular community is the basic missional structure of the church. The New Testament view of koinonia defines the Christian church as a company of followers of Jesus called by God's Spirit and joined together as God's people in a particular place for a particular purpose. Guder writes, "The primary organizational challenge for the church is to find ways to structure the life of the particular communities so that they can carry out faithful witness in their places, always in responsible connection to the entire church around the world."⁹⁴ As the local church is shaped

---

90. Guder, "Missionary Structures," 222.
91. Guder, "Missionary Structures," 223.
92. Acts 1:8.
93. Guder, "Missionary Structures," 233.
94. Guder, "Missionary Structures," 234.

by Scripture it must creatively translate its gospel presence and witness to a growing multicultural American audience. The traditional church models must emerge as true missional communities resisting the urge to galvanize and remain flexible in structure to be a visible authentic community of the reign of God.

How do these missional distinctives practically express themselves in a local church? Milfred Minatrea notes the following areas of praxis which typify missional churches and delineate missional thought.[95] (1) Missional churches have a high threshold for membership and offer clear expectations for being a part of a missional community. (2) Missional churches are real, but not real religious, meaning that relationships between members are authentic and not superficial. (3) Missional churches teach to obey, rather than to know as they emphasize practical implications of faith and how to apply them to everyday life. (4) Missional churches practice a content-driven worship without being bound to form and often rewrite worship every week. (5) Missional churches have members that live apostolically as sent missionaries to their world. (6) Missional churches expect to change the world through authentic relationships, which they see as the key to transformation. (7) Missional church's praxis flows from their missional purpose as they give specific reasons which guide their labors. (8) Missional churches measure growth by capacity to release, not simply by retaining members as they work to equip and send. (9) Missional churches place kingdom concerns first which they see as superseding denominational loyalties.

DISCIPLE MAKING IN THE MISSIONAL CHURCH MOVEMENT

Perhaps the most important contribution of the Missional Church Movement was the reframing and refocusing of the church to its missionary purpose as the visible presence of Christ to a post-Christendom society. Disciple making will not occur unless there is an outward missional approach among God's people. The Missional Church Movement espouses mission as the heart of the church, and the reason for its very existence. As Newbigin states, "Mission is not just church extension."[96] Yet, the question

---

95. Minatrea, *Shaped by God's Heart*. These nine points of practical application make up the chapters of Milfred Minatrea's book.

96. Newbigin, *Open Secret*, 59.

If Everything is Missional, Is Anything Truly Missional?

that must be asked to analyze disciple making within the movement is, what is mission, and did it lead to disciple making in the Missional Church Movement? As seen previously, the moorings spring forth from the *missio Dei* and are lived out through a Spirit-filled community engaging their culture as God's agents incarnationally living out the reign of God.

The nebulous nature of exactly what is meant by *mission* within the movement springs from the lofty theologizing and theorizing of its leaders. The frustration in examining the Missional Church Movement comes from the mainline leader's lack of attention on equipping members of the missional community to be disciple makers. There is a general lack of attention given to the Great Commission of Christ to His church for the purpose of making disciples by going, baptizing, and teaching. A good example of this is found in Newbigin's view of mission as an explosion of joy. In his writings, mission is the outflowing result of an explosion of joy within ecclesial structures, which overflows to the world.[97] As the church embodies this explosion of joy it is transformed into a living testimony of the gospel and expresses this joy through selfless and sacrificial love which represents Christ. This embodying serves to live out the love of Christ for the sake of neighbors and as a sign of the reign of God.[98] Newbigin's explosion of joy as mission creates a missional purpose that is not necessarily launched from the Great Commission, but rather as a natural expression of a salvific ethos.

According to Newbigin, missional motivation cannot come from a command because a command, "... tends to make mission a burden rather than a joy, to make it part of the law rather than part of the gospel."[99] Yet, the command of Jesus to His disciples, and ultimately to His church, is one of disciple making as the church goes into the world for the purpose of making new disciples, who will in turn, replicate. While all commands and commissions come with particular burdens associated with them, those burdens are not necessarily bad, but rather ought to be motivating. The church living out a joyous presence certainly is part of the mission, but it is not the crux of the disciple making mission that has been handed down to the church. The mission is much more granular as Christians are called to have gospel conversations for the purpose of winning men and women to Christ and discipling them to full maturity.

97. Newbigin, *Gospel in a Pluralist Society*, 116.
98. Newbigin, *Gospel in a Pluralist Society*, 229.
99. Newbigin, *Gospel in a Pluralist Society*, 116.

Repairing the Missional Breach

Part of the esoteric nature of the word *missional* has to do with the fundamental question as to what the church is on mission to do. Certainly, the Great Commission of Christ in Matthew 28:19-20 commands the church to be bearers of the gospel presenting Jesus as the source of salvation. Newbigin and other missional leaders see the nature of salvation as bringing relational wholeness as believers become missional agents incarnationally living out the reign of God as members of an eschatological kingdom. Newbigin states, "Salvation means wholeness, which must include the restoration of social justice and interpersonal relationships."[100] Without question, salvation does bring wholeness and this change does find its way into every crevice of the new believer's life, including relationships. The change, however, is much more than a new relational wholeness or change in the way a person sees their world and is ultimately expressed within relationships. It is much deeper, much more personal, as the regenerated person is raised to life from the doldrums of eternal death to a reinvigorated sanctification.[101] This evangelical view of mission is often criticized by mainline proponents within the missional church. Patrick Franklin, for example, criticizes conservative evangelicals' view of the gospel as a "form of reductionism." He states, "Conservative evangelicals have sometimes reduced the gospel to the forgiveness of sin and the salvation of the soul."[102] In support of his view he uses Newbigin's description of the gospel as personal in nature, a revelation of God Himself, and not, "The revelation of a timeless truth, namely, that God forgives sin."[103] This macro-gospel view discourages an individualistic disciple making gospel, which emphasizes one's relationship with God as the crux of the gospel while considering a relationship with others and social justice action as being primary. Some mainline theologians see this individualistic view of the gospel as too narrow because it makes matters of social action and relationships superfluous. Franklin is working from Newbigin's corporate election view of missiology. He states, "If such an individualistic view of humanity were true, election would not be necessary. God would then approach each person as an isolated individual outside of a community context to reconcile that individual to Himself."[104]

---

100. Hunsberger, *Bearing the Witness of the Spirit*, 103.
101. Ephesians 2:1–10.
102. Franklin, "Missionaries in Our Own Back Yard," 173.
103. Franklin quotes Newbigin from *The Open Secret*, 48.
104. Franklin, "Missionaries in Our Own Back Yard," 174.

If Everything is Missional, Is Anything Truly Missional?

God, however, is inviting people individually to follow Him, and following the positive response of the person, he sends the redeemed as agents of redemption, i.e., as disciple makers. Hull reminds the church, "Making disciples begins with introducing men and women to Christ."[105] God is a sending God calling believers to be active participants of the *Missio Dei*. But how is this to be lived out? What makes the Christian's mission different than a charitable secular organization or loftier than only social action? The difference is found in recognizing and responding to the calling to be in Christ, and secondly recognizing and responding to the missional calling to the world as redeemed, Spirit-filled disciple makers. The believer is called to Christ as new disciples, (Christocentric calling) and sent to the world as disciple makers, (Missiocentric calling). The Christian's calling is first, Christocentric as they respond to the invitation of Jesus to "follow me."[106] Gordon T. Smith writes:

> There is a sense that our work is but an echo of the work of God who has created all things but who now, in Christ Jesus, is redeeming all things. In Christ, God is bringing about the fulfillment of his reign, His Kingdom. And for the Christian, our work is necessarily a participation in the reign of Christ and the purposes of Christ in the world. The Christian's missional calling is always "In Christ." A disciple's life is marked by the life, death, resurrection and ascension of Christ Jesus and the outpouring of the gift of the Spirit.[107]

A Christian's missional work is done in response to Christ's internal work in the believer. In redeeming disciples, they become part of the Holy proclamation exalting Christ through their work, whatever that might be, and in this existence, all work is essentially missional because it has as its end, the making of disciples. The disciple's first calling is to Christ because they are in Christ. Consider the invitation of Jesus to His disciples in John 1:43, and Mark 1:16–20. The final words of John's gospel record Jesus issuing the same invitation again in John 21:18–22. On thirteen occasions Jesus uses the same simple invitation, *follow me*. Yet, those two words are loaded with expectations, exhilaration, and adventure. Contrary to Franklin's views, this is not a reductionist understanding of the gospel mission, rather it lies at the very heart of the Great Commission of Christ.

---

105. Hull, *Disciple-Making Church*, 43.
106. Mark 1:16–20
107. Smith, *Consider your Calling*, 27.

The model of disciple making as presented in the Gospels by Jesus is one of calling men and women to follow him through a personal, salvific decision, which substantially changes the very essence of their existence. The following precedes the sending, and in the process of the missional sending there is an expectation that the disciple will pursue relational connections which honor God and offer a hermeneutically accurate gospel.[108]

Newbigin also saw discipleship as essential to mission. He states, "Ministerial leadership is, first and finally, discipleship."[109] He goes on to say, "A preaching of the gospel that calls men and women to accept Jesus as Savior but does not make it clear that discipleship means a commitment to a vision of society radically different from that which controls our public life today must be condemned as false."[110] In Newbigin's view, the end goal of discipleship was to challenge the reigning plausibility structures of the surrounding culture. This could be accomplished by learning a different set of priorities, ethical standards, and societal convictions which enabled Christians to challenge sinful and oppressive elements in culture. Newbigin states:

> Jesus' ministry entailed the calling of individual men and women to personal and costly discipleship, but at the same time it challenged the principalities and powers, the ruler of this world, and the cross was the price paid for that challenge. Christian discipleship today cannot mean less than that.[111]

Essentially, missional leaders such as Newbigin view discipleship as creating, equipping, and nurturing believers to live out the reign of God in their community. Faithful discipleship in missional churches resists the temptation to define success only through church growth, rather success is defined by inviting people to become Christ's disciples and join the community in its continuing apostolate mission. A mission-driven community of discipleship lives out the gospel internally as the church enjoys a *koinonia*

---

108. Newbigin does believe that personal conversion is at the very heart of mission. He states, "The calling of men and women to be converted, to follow Jesus, and to be part of his community is and must always be at the center of mission." *Open Secret*, 121. While Newbigin believes and promotes personal conversion, this emphasis is often diminished as many authors choose to focus on Newbigin's view of corporate election more than personal conversion. This may explain why the call to make disciples is nebulous in missional thinking.

109. Newbigin, *Gospel in a Pluralist Society*, 241.

110. Newbigin, *Foolishness to the Greeks*, 132.

111. Newbigin, *Gospel in a Pluralist Society*, 220.

If Everything is Missional, Is Anything Truly Missional?

community, but also opens the gospel externally by the way it lives, so that others may see and respond. Guder states, "The process of movement toward the missional church will be rooted and shaped by intense engagement with Scripture. It will confront the forms of cultural captivity that mark our conformity to this world in North America."[112]

Hauerwas and Willimon propose a similar mindset, "We argue that the political task of Christians is to be the church rather than to transform the world."[113] The Great Commission of Jesus, however, inaugurates a much more intentional mission interaction with the lost world. The result of Christian discipleship must accomplish more than merely reflecting Christ, although this is important, but also intentionally engaging the lost in gospel conversations which leads to spiritual transformation. In the Great Commission of Jesus for his church, disciple making embodies an indoctrination of biblical truths not only for the benefit of the one being discipled but also for those to whom the disciple is commissioned to reach.

The contribution to the ecclesial mission of the American church through the influential thinkers of the Missional Church Movement has been substantial. The re-focusing of the church to recognize and rediscover its important role within the *missio Dei* continues to serve as a wake-up call to shake loose of the program-driven mentality of the Church Growth Movement and to embrace its role as agents of God's kingdom reign within its culture. Not only for the sake of growing church kingdoms through membership and attendance, but as an incarnational presence that offers love, hope, and forgiveness to a watching world. Unlike the Emergent Church Movement, there is a high value of theology, doctrine, and Scripture within missional thinking in which the Holy Spirit transforms the believer through the living Word.

Ultimately, the nebulous and opaque use of the term *missional*, caused the movement to lose the momentum it had gained following the release of *Missional Church* and the influential work of the *Gospel and Our Culture* network. As the Missional Church Movement focused on returning the church back to the mission, rather than seeing mission merely as a program the church seeks to accomplish, ultimately mission became everything. The movement failed to make a long-term impact on the American evangelical church, as everything the church did became *missional* while at the same time, perhaps nothing really was *missional* when compared to the Great

---

112. Guder, "Missionary Structures," 247.
113. Hauerwas and Willimon, *Resident Aliens*, 38.

Commission of Christ to make disciples who make disciples. If mission is everything, the inherent risk is that the particulars of the disciple making mission are lost in the greater macro-missional view. Stephen Neill agrees:

> There is a great deal of talk today about the theology of mission. This may be a good thing, but I apprehend certain dangers in both of two contrary directions. The first is that we may cast our net too wide and so make the enquiry almost meaningless. If everything is mission, nothing is mission. If everything that the church does is to be classed as "mission," we shall have to find another term for the church's particular responsibility for the heathen, those who have never yet heard the name of Christ.[114]

Keith Ferdinando suggests three reasons why the term mission has come to take on obscurity.[115] First, there has been the recognition that communicating the gospel is not the only thing Christians are sent into the world to do. Second, increasingly widespread pluralist and inclusivist approaches to non-Christian religions imply that evangelism is not a necessary, perhaps not even desirable, function of the church. Third, the increasing secular use of the term within organizational mission statements. David Bosch's seminal work, *Transforming Mission*, offers a pessimism related to a widely accepted definition of the term. He states, "Ultimately, mission remains indefinable. The most we can hope for is to formulate some approximations of what mission is all about."[116] Concerning Bosch's impact on modern missional thought Ferdinando concludes, "Consequently, he suggests that it is impossible to construct a single biblical theology of mission on which to base contemporary practice." Though Bosch's work is considered one of the most important scholarly missiological writings in decades, his inability to offer a concise missional hermeneutic has led to the continued opaqueness of the term.

A future faithful *missio ecclesia* will not be possible without a return to the Great Commission as the *missio Dei* of the church, thus it becomes the focus upon which all other ministry foci ultimately become subservient. The American evangelical church must avoid three temptations related to this preferred *missio ecclesia*: first, the temptation to define mission too broadly as to miss the micro-contours of how it is to be lived out. While the *missio Dei* is the very nature of God as a missional God, the risk becomes

---

114. Neill, *Creative Tension*, 81–82.
115. Ferdinando, "Mission: Problem of Definition," 46–47.
116. Bosch, *Transforming Mission*, 9.

that it is only a doctrine of which theologians research, write, and theologize. If this is the case it loses its practical implications not only for the church but also in the lives of those who make up the membership of the church. Second, the temptation to view mission too narrowly. The mission of the church is not to be outsourced to programmatic models, agencies, denominations, or offerings sent to missionaries serving on the fringes of the globe. This approach is devoid of personal responsibility regarding the church equipping its members to be active disciple makers, who by their Christ-centered followship become sent ambassadors through a mission-centered commission.

Finally, mission cannot be only regarded as thoughtful social actions in which the church responds to social justice issues such as caring for the poor, disenfranchised, underserved, and correcting societal wrongs. If the mission of the church is only to clothe the naked, feed the hungry, and assist the downtrodden, what makes it any different from charitable organizations? Nothing the church does can be called missional without the gospel. Carson calls for a return to a faithful gospel mission:

> At one time, "holistic ministry" was an expression intended to move Christians beyond proclamation to include deeds of mercy. Increasingly, however, "holistic ministry" refers to deeds of mercy *without* any proclamation of the gospel—and that is not holistic. It is not even halfistic, since the deeds of mercy are not the gospel: they are entailments of the gospel. Although I know many Christians who happily combine fidelity to the gospel, evangelism, church planting, and energetic service to the needy, and although I know some who call themselves Christians who formally espouse the gospel but who live out few of its entailments, I also know Christians who, in the name of a "holistic" gospel, focus all their energy on presence, wells in the Sahel, fighting disease, and distributing food to the poor, but who never, or only very rarely, articulate the gospel, preach the gospel, announce the gospel, to anyone. Judging by the distribution of American mission dollars, the biggest hole in our gospel is the gospel itself.[117]

This type of myopic non-gospel missional view embodies a liberation philosophy devoid of the gospel. Chris Sugden asserts that the result of mission ought to be, "God at work in society beyond the church applying the effects of Christ's victory on the cross through social change."[118] Part of

---

117. D. A. Carson quoted in Justin Taylor's, "Biggest Hole in the Gospel."
118. Chris Sugden quoted in Melvin Tinter, "Reversal or Betrayal?" 266.

the mission of the church as disciple makers surely will lead to social change and the betterment of life for many, but the heart of the *missio ecclesia* is not social change, but soul change through a gospel-centered disciple making mission.

CONCLUSION

Much like the Church Growth Movement, and the Emergent Church Movement, the Missional Church Movement sought to correct perceived evangelistic drifts within the local church in America. Within each movement, there is a distinct call for recalibrating the mission of the church to look beyond the stained-glass windows and practice missional outreach to its community and the broader culture in general. The Church Growth Movement morphed into a much more attractional mindset regarding evangelism, while the Emergent Church Movement and Missional Church Movement sought to move members out of the church buildings and into postmodern cultures for the purpose of growing and expressing the kingdom of God. The Missional Church Movement was begun within mainline denominational circles, and only later embraced by evangelicals within the American ecclesial landscape. The over-saturation of the term *missional* and the residual ubiquitous nature of the term ultimately failed to keep the focus of American evangelicalism, particularly as many congregations became insular in fighting for survival. Also impactful was the lofty theologizing of missional leaders which led to an opaque understanding, meaning that generally, the orthodoxy expressed failed to reach a granular long-term impact within American evangelical churches. Much of the missional writings did not articulate a practical expression of the Great Commission as the *missio Dei* mandate of the church, which ultimately failed to lead to multiplying missional people and churches. The call of Christ places an indebtedness in the life of a disciple to embrace a missional disciple making mission. The mission ought to be embraced both individually and institutionally within ecclesial structures if the postmodern, post-Christian America is to be reached for Christ. As Lewis reminds the church:

> It is easy to think that the Church has a lot of different objects—education, building, missions, holding services . . . The Church exists for nothing else but to draw men into Christ, to make them little Christs. If they are not doing that, all the cathedrals, clergy, missions, sermons, even the Bible itself, are simply a waste of time.

If Everything is Missional, Is Anything Truly Missional?

> God became man for no other purpose. It is even doubtful, you know, whether the whole universe was created for any other purpose. It says in the Bible that the whole universe was made for Christ and that everything is to be gathered together for Him.[119]

What is mission? As Lewis states, it is the drawing of people into Christ, the making of disciples, who are equipped and sent out to make more "little Christ." Hirsch reminds the church of its eternal mission, "Disciple making lies at the core of the Church's mission; it is not an optional extra. Discipleship is adherence to Jesus and the process by which we are formed in Him. His life ministry is embedded in and through His people."[120]

As the Christian global community continues to seek a consensus definition of mission, Stetzer argues that a shared definition is not nearly as important as obedience to the Great Commission. He states:

> With our working definitions in order, the inevitable question is "now what?" What do we do with our language so that we might understand how to live on mission with Jesus to reach the lost? Central to our calling as followers of the King is our call to display the glory of God through the redemption of those who are far from Him.[121]

How well and how often the Church understands its commission and responds to the "now what?" will ultimately determine whether the Bride of Christ has been obedient to its redeemer and has been truly missional.

---

119. Lewis, *Mere Christianity*, 171.
120. Hirsch, *Disciplism*, 31.
121. Ed Stetzer, "Missional and Missions."

Chapter 6

Toward A Faithful Missional Future
Ministry Shifts Needed to Repair the Breach

> No one creates a discipling culture, modeled on the life and ministry of Jesus, by accident.[1]
>
> —Mike Breen

It is not a reach to assert that each Christian generation is in earnest search of a new and better missional future. With each new generation comes an attempt to create a more faithful iteration of the church to better evangelize the current culture and increase church involvement. These attempts will ultimately be recorded by church historians as movements, but movements by their very nature have beginnings and endings, thus the American evangelical church continually finds itself in a state of recovery and discovery. Yet, the American evangelical church does not need a new missional discovery, but rather a re-discovery of the disciple making model and methods of Jesus Christ as revealed in the Gospels. The church should not yearn for a new movement but rather return to an ancient movement, method, and model as its mission. Jesus began a movement of disciple making which was carried on by subsequent generations, and the church in America should renew its commitment, not as a new movement or iteration, but as its perpetual mission. Steve Addison writes of movements:

---

1. Breen, *Building a Discipling Culture*, 17.

Toward a Faithful Missional Future

> Movements are characterized by discontent, vision, and action. Discontent unfreezes people from their commitment to the way things are. Movements emerge when people feel something needs to change. If the vacuum created by discontent is filled with a vision of a different future and action to bring change, then a movement is born. Movements change people, and changed people change the world.[2]

Movements are born in a vacuum of discontent, fueled by vision, and brought to life through the actions of people committed to a common cause.[3] The American evangelical church must first have discontent at its current state and then embrace the disciple making example of Jesus as its strategy for future effectiveness. Jesus did not come to start a religion; he came to redeem humankind and to start a movement that would spread the good news of his redemptive mission from person to person. While methodological approaches might vary as the church attempts to find a more effective and faithful way of making disciples within each generation, the original movement of missional disciple making in the New Testament is to be perpetual. The Tambaram report titled, *The World Mission of the Church* taps into the essence of this truth. It states, "The church exists to continue the work Christ began."[4] This work of which Christ began is the winning of the world through the making of disciples. The church is sent to the world as a "message" and a "movement."[5] With this in mind, the church isn't looking to begin a new movement, it is in essence the movement which Jesus created, redeemed, and sent to make disciples of all nations.

The leaders of the Church Growth, Emergent Church, and Missional Church movements all have sought to offer a more faithful missionary approach, and each offered a missional hermeneutic unique in orthodoxy and orthopraxy. I have sought to reveal the strengths and weaknesses of each of these movements and ultimately why they are referred to as past

---

2. Addison, *Movements*, 12.

3. McIntosh also contributed to the definition of a movement in his 1994 address to the *American Society for Church Growth* in 1994. He defines a movement to be "a self-perpetuating company of people who are united by a common cause and committed to having a significant impact on their social environment." He also notes three dimensions of a movement: it must have people, particularly a leader, a common cause, and a commitment to impact the social environment. Rainer, "Church Growth," 60.

4. *World Mission of the Church: Findings and Recommendations of the Internal Missionary Council, Tambaram, Madras, India, December 12 to December 29, 1938*, 79.

5. Goheen and Sheriden, *Becoming a Missionary Church*, 13.

movements and not present movements. The Church Growth Movement, through the influence of Donald McGavran and later iterations, taught new and better evangelism approaches to attract people back to church. The Emergent Church Movement, through the influence of Brian McLaren, sought to make the gospel more palatable and the church more relevant to the postmodern culture, all the while bringing attention to human suffering and social justice. The Missional Church Movement, through the influence of Lesslie Newbigin and the *Gospel and Our Culture* network, sought to remind the Western church of its trinitarian *missio Dei* and to see itself as missionaries in a foreign land. Each offered new evangelism approaches, ecclesiological structures, or church growth ideologies.

It should also be noted that each of these movements had missional aspects, influence, and left positive impacts on the American evangelical church. The Church Growth Movement has had its critics, (including me), however, one cannot deny that the movement did accomplish the seminal task of calling the Western church back to gospel proclamation. The movement restored hope and vitality to church leaders and was a significant catalyst for church renewal in American evangelicalism.[6] McGavran's principles have left an indelible mark on the church, especially in discerning the social and behavioral tendencies of a culture. Understanding these tendencies, once discovered, serves as a useful tool for developing disciple making approaches. The Church Growth Movement's use of social sciences to discern ways to evangelize cultures has encountered significant backlash over the decades, however, if the church is going to effectively reach a postmodern audience it will necessitate such tools as cultural exegetical discoveries. Finally, the Church Growth Movement, within the framework of the Lausanne Covenant, rescued vast pockets of American evangelicalism from liberal theological drifts. McGavran, and others within the movement, espoused a high belief in Scripture as divinely inspired, truthful, and pregnant with authority.[7]

McGavran's key missiological questions as seen in *The Bridges of God*, once applied to the church, did catapult the church in an outward direction as the church was reminded of its evangelistic mission. As with Newbigin and McLaren, McGavran's principles brought to the church a missiological focus, which had been greatly neglected during the early part of the twentieth century. The Emergent Church Movement also sought to turn the

---

6. Hull, "Is the Church Growth Movement Really Working?" 147.
7. Rainer, *Book of Church Growth*, 74–76.

focus of the church toward missional encounters, and while orthodoxy was lacking, the intentions of its leaders to begin a new conversation with postmoderns are admirable. While I have found points of critique within each movement, it should be noted that each offered valid missiological principles that should continue to inform the present mission. A biblically faithful mission, however, is far more than making ministry adjustments, having conversations with postmoderns, and making the church more attractive to each generation. Jesus is the attraction; he is the mission; this is his church, and the members therein are his members. Thus, members of the body of Christ are to be missional disciple makers who seek those who need to be discipled into the likeness of Christ. In this mindset, regenerated disciples are collectively as the church, the true Great Commission movement envisioned by Christ and empowered by the Spirit. It is my prayer that we will soon see a great rediscovery of this truth.

As seen in the previous chapter, the word *missional* has ultimately suffered from an opaque ubiquitousness, and thus the question remains, is the term missional too co-opted, and is it the best term to describe the missionary nature of the church? Goheen and Sheriden write of this word, "And so it could be said, echoing a British newspaper's editorial quip about the word postmodern, 'The word missional has no meaning; use as often as possible.'"[8] The church must recapture the biblical meaning of the word. The true missional approach of the church is not found in pragmatic strategies, nor in the whims of the latest so-called movement, but rather in recovering its missional purpose to make disciples within the cultural context it finds itself in. For clarity's sake, it is vital that the American evangelical church recover and rehabilitate the word *missional* from the doldrums of obscurity and properly marry it again, to its original disciple making etymology. The following chapter will offer a view of the postmodern cultural context in America, its implications on the church, and missional shifts needed to better engage culture as disciple makers who are actively engaged in a biblically faithful missional focus.

THE END OF CHRISTENDOM IN AMERICA

In his book, *Meet Generation Z: Understanding and Reaching the New Post-Christian World*, James Emery White writes of the new reality that is prevalent in American culture:

8. Rainer, *Book of Church Growth*, 74–76.

A recent survey of thirty-five thousand Americans by the Pew Research Center found that the rise of the "nones" has grown to encompass 23% of America's adults. This means that nearly one out of every four adults in the United States when asked about their religious identity, would say "nothing." Further, many who were once in the church are now leaving it. About 19% of Americans would call themselves "former" Christians.[9]

According to White, Generation Z will be the first generation to grow up in a post-Christian society and eventually, it might be said that they were the most secular generation in American history. Statistics reveal alarming realities as to the rise of secularism in the United States while the Christian church in America continues to decline. The data shows that just like rates of religious affiliation, rates of religious attendance are declining as well. Over the last decade, the share of Americans who say they attend religious services at least once or twice a month dropped by 7 percentage points, while the share of those who say they attend religious services less often (or at all) has risen by the same degree. In 2009, regular worship attendees outnumbered those who attended services only occasionally or not at all by a 52 percent to 47 percent margin. Today those figures have flip-flopped; more Americans now say they attend religious services a few times a year or less (54 percent) than say they attend at least monthly (45 percent).[10] These trends reveal that a change in ministry approach is needed within the local church to reach a culture that James Emery White titles, "post-Christian." Other scholars such as Russell Moore disagree with the title of "post-Christian" as it relates to current American culture. Moore asserts that this title began to be used in response to a survey performed and subsequent article published by the Pew Research Center in 2012 entitled, *Nones on the Rise*. The article states:

> The number of Americans who do not identify with any religion continues to grow at a rapid pace. One-fifth of the U.S. public – and a third of adults under 30 – are religiously unaffiliated today, the highest percentages ever in Pew Research Center polling. In the last five years alone, the unaffiliated have increased from just over 15% to just under 20% of all U.S. adults.[11]

---

9. White, *Meet Generation Z*, 11.
10. "In US Decline of Christianity Continues at a Rapid Pace," *Pew Research Center*.
11. "Nones on the Rise," *Pew Research Center*.

Toward a Faithful Missional Future

Shortly after the results of this survey were published White wrote a book entitled, *The Rise of the Nones* in which he used the cultural descriptor "post-Christian" prolifically and the title began to be widely distributed in the years following. In response to the title of "post-Christian" Moore states that, surprisingly, the term began to be used by two distinct groups: progressive secularists and American evangelicals. The secularists used the term as a moniker of celebration as they saw the negative impacts of religious quarrels and religious belief as stifling human ingenuity. The use of the term by American evangelicals was especially troubling to Moore as he writes:

> I'm more concerned, though, with the other circle using the frame of a "post-Christian" America, the circle identified with the church itself. In this reading, the "post-Christian" nature of America is not to be celebrated but lamented. The language used is one of decline and of loss. The same people who not long ago trumpeted "reclaiming America for Christ" are now some of the same who speak of America in dire "post-Christian" terms. This isn't accurate either.[12]

Moore surmises that America cannot be "post-Christian" because it was never really "Christian."[13]

In light of this discussion, perhaps it is best to refer to the current American culture as being postmodern, rather than post-Christian. The reality is clear, the evangelical church in America finds itself in a skeptical, religiously unaffiliated place and while this is a threat, it can also be an opportunity. Hirsch states:

> The result of the Enlightenment period, among many other things, was the secularization of society and the subsequent marginalization of the church and its message. We who have lived in the twentieth century know this experientially all too well. The problem we face is that while as a sociopolitical-cultural force Christendom is dead, and we now live in what has been aptly called

---

12. Moore, "Is America Post-Christian?"

13. Ed Stetzer agrees with Moore's interpretation on the cultural title of post-Christian. Referring to Christianity in America, Stetzer writes, "Christendom has come to an end. No longer is Christianity the chaplain to the broader culture. Christianity was universally assumed as the American religion even though it was not widely embraced. It was once perceived as part of our national ethos. No longer can that claim be made. The humiliation of Christendom has been underway for two centuries. It is no longer appropriate, if it ever was, to speak of "Christian America." Stetzer, *Planting New Churches*, 14.

the post-Christendom era, the church still operates in exactly the same mode. In terms of how we understand and "do" church, little has changed for seventeen centuries.[14]

To Hirsch's point, the end of Christendom in America could possibly be the door to a new and better missional approach if only the church would accept the new cultural order and adjust its disciple making approaches in response. Hauerwas and Willimon argue in their book, *Resident Aliens*, that while Christendom has ended and culture is changing, the real change came to the world in Jesus Christ and the church has struggled for centuries to grasp the cultural implications of his coming. Much like Hirsch, Hauerwas and Willimon see the end of Christendom as an opportunity for Christians to see their world as it always was. They state, "We have an opportunity to discover what has and always is the case—that the church, as those called out by God, embodies a social alternative that the world cannot on its own terms know."[15] Hauerwas and Willimon celebrate the demise of what they refer to as, "Constantinianism"[16] in American society as it gives way to a better and more faithful expression of Christian belief. They state, "The gradual decline of the notion that the church needs some sort of surrounding 'Christian' culture to prop it up and mold its young, is not a death to lament. It is an opportunity to celebrate."[17]

If the church can accept the demise of Christendom in American culture, then it can more faithfully engage with the reality of being a missional force in an alien society. As Jesus began his ministry, he entered a world not much different than twenty-first-century America in terms of its spiritual landscape. Reggie McNeal explains the religious world of Jesus:

> Institutional religion had collapsed. No one really believed in the Greek or Roman pantheon of gods. People knew these beings were mere projections embodying human traits. Judaism was also exhausted. The Sadducees had sold out to materialism and ritual. The Pharisees had produced a dead religion in search of the moral high ground with God . . . . This is why they flocked to John the Baptist and to Jesus. The collapse of institutional religion in the first century was accompanied by an upsurge in personal

---

14. Hirsch, *Forgotten Ways*, 61.
15. Hauerwas and Willimon, *Resident Aliens*, 18–19.
16. Hauerwas and Willimon use this term to describe the conflation of Christianity and culture which was initiated in 313 with Constantine's Edict of Milan. Hauerwas and Willimon, *Resident Aliens*, 17–18.
17. Hauerwas and Willimon, *Resident Aliens*, 19.

spiritual search for God and salvation . . . . Jesus tapped into this widespread disillusionment with religion but hunger for God with his teaching about the kingdom of God and how people could become a part of it.[18]

McNeal views the collapse of Christendom as an opportunity to re-calibrate its mission in North America. He calls for a missional rather than a methodological fix in which the church commits to, "A radical obedience to an ancient command, a loss of self rather than self-preoccupation, concern about service and sacrifice rather than concern about style."[19]

Like the previously mentioned theologians, Karl Barth was also concerned with the demise of the church culture and dedicated much time to writing of the new missionary reality for the Western church.[20] In Barth's mind, the issue wasn't the need to change culture, but rather of theologically re-creating a new and better church.[21] The first advent was the change needed for every culture in every generation and the responsibility of the church is to embrace the missionary role of being disciple makers and introduce the culture to the opportunity to be friends of God provided by the incarnation of Christ. This ultimately is the missional challenge given to the American evangelical Church. Disciple making in America will not take place unless the church sees itself as engaging in spiritual battles rather than cultural wars.

MISSIONAL DISCIPLE MAKING IN POSTMODERN AMERICAN CULTURE

"Can the West be converted?"[22] This was the question on the mind of Lesslie Newbigin upon his return to Britain in 1974 after serving forty years in India. He found a church that had accommodated itself to its culture at the expense of its role as missionaries.[23] Perhaps the same question should

---

18. McNeal, *Present Future*, 16–17.
19. McNeal, *Present Future*, 18.
20. Karl Hartenstein was also a key figure in the refocusing of missional ecclesiology. Flett sates that his "work in the early thirties reoriented mission thinking for the next twenty-five years." Flett, *Witness of God*, 130. Hartenstein was heavily influenced by Barth's missional ecclesiology and the recovery of the *missio Dei*.
21. Flett, *Witness of God*, 24.
22. Newbigin, "Can the West Be Converted," 2–7.
23. Goheen and Sheridan, *Becoming a Missionary Church*, 68.

be asked today in postmodern America. To effectively reach any culture for Christ, particularly a postmodern America, there must be an understanding that being missional, is by its very essence, disciple making. No church can be truly mission-driven without making disciples. Thus, this final chapter calls for a more specific term than just *missional*, but rather *missional disciple making*. Conjoining the two terms eliminates the ubiquitous nature of the term *missional* by giving it a distinctive descriptor. In other words, the true mission of the church needed for the current cultural context is making disciples as mission. David M. Gustafson defines *missional disciple making*:

> Our task is to make disciples on the pattern of Jesus Christ; he sent them out as missionaries while forming them spiritually. He prepared them in a high-discipleship, high-mission culture. He formed and equipped them for a sustainable mission. Similarly, we are called to makes disciples that function like missionaries.[24]

For this to take place there must be an understanding of the cultural ethos in which the American evangelical church exists. For missional disciple making clarity two definitions will be examined: What is postmodernism? What is culture and how can it be defined?

The cultural ethos that now exists in America (and the West more generally) has fundamentally shifted beginning in the later parts of the twentieth century and now well into the twenty-first century. The emerging landscape has become known as the postmodern condition. Van Gelder explains, "In simple terms, the postmodern condition is that which replaces what came to be known as modernity over the past several centuries."[25] Postmodernism refers to an era that followed modernity and much of what defines postmodernism is a response to the belief system found in modern thought. Beginning in the late 1990s a new vocabulary emerged which was a product of this new postmodern enlightenment in Western culture. Words such as indeterminacy, deconstruction, diversity, decentering, and the aestheticization of all of life. These words are a direct affront to the distinctives of modernity which emphasize certainty, absolutes, centers, and prediction.[26] Millard Erickson offers a few ways in which postmodernity challenges the previously held tenets of modernity.

---

24. Gustafson, "What is Missional Disciple Making?"
25. Van Gelder, "Mission in the Emerging," 113.
26. Van Gelder, "Mission in the Emerging," 114.

Erickson lists the following philosophical values of postmodern thought: A denial of personal objectivity, the uncertainty of knowledge, the end of any all-inclusive explanation, the denial of the inherent goodness of knowledge, the rejection of progress, the supremacy of community-based knowledge, and the disbelief in objective inquiry.[27]

A good summarization of postmodern thought would best be termed in this way; all people have a right to their own point of view and all views are of equal validity. In light of the growing influence of postmodern thought on American culture, the challenges of reaching a postmodern America are immense and intimidating. Speaking of America Richard Mouw states, "We are in a missionary location in North America which needs to be considered a mission field in the same way we once considered the underdeveloped world."[28] The continuing decline of the evangelical church is indicative of the fact that many church leaders have not grasped this current reality. Without an accurate comprehension of the view of America as an underdeveloped missionary field, church leaders will not respond to the changing culture and will not effectively equip their congregation to reach their communities through missional disciple making.

What is culture and how can it be defined? White defines culture this way, "Culture is the comprehensive, penetrating context that encompasses life and thought, art and speech, entertainment and sensibility, values, and faith. It cannot be reduced to that which is simply economic or political, demographic, or technological."[29] Niebuhr speaks of culture as the "Artificial, secondary environment which man superimposes on the natural. It comprises language, habits, ideas, beliefs, customs, social organization, inherited artifacts, technical processes, and values."[30] Hunter asserts that the church has viewed culture too simplistically, and thus it has failed to understand the layered complexities that exist. He states, "Culture is a knotty, difficult, complex, perhaps impossible puzzle . . . The idea that changing a culture mainly by changing the hearts and minds of ordinary people is looking less and less plausible."[31] Hunter's point is that Christian idealism will never truly penetrate the heart of culture, and the only real change will come from its faithful presence to bear witness to and to be the

---

27. Erickson, *Postmodernizing the Faith*, 19.
28. Mouw, "Missionary Location," 4.
29. White, *Meet Generation Z*, 80.
30. Niebuhr, *Christ & Culture*, 32.
31. Hunter, *To Change the World*, 40.

embodiment of the coming kingdom of God. Hunter is correct in his assertion that the church must exist as a faithful presence, living out the faith espoused in Scripture as an authentic witness. Engaging with postmodernism, however, must couple faithful presence with intentional relational investment, which is why the church must faithfully exegete Scripture, but also faithfully exegete the accretions of postmodern culture. The success of any church in missional disciple making will be found in how well it exegetes' culture and how effectively the church responds. The statistical realities facing the American church reveal that many congregations have not responded well to the shifting paradigm of North American postmodern thought and culture.

Paul offers a great example of cultural exegesis as he travels to Athens in Acts 17. In Athens, he reasoned with the Epicurean and Stoic philosophers challenging the foundational beliefs of their worldviews. The philosophies coming out of the Areopagus greatly influenced Roman thought and Paul took the gospel message directly to the epicenter of cultural beliefs. Paul's persuasive passion created a curiosity that led some of the leading thinkers of his day to ask, "May we know what this new doctrine is of which you speak?" (Acts 17:19). Ultimately, the church in America must decide to follow the example of Paul by engaging culture and winsomely challenging the tenets of postmodern thought. The alternative is to disengage from culture and retreat to stain-glassed sanctuaries as safe havens of a false Christian utopia.

Current studies reveal that the American church is not reaching postmodern culture. In his book *Comeback Churches*, Ed Stetzer offers a sobering picture of the current state of North American churches. Stetzer's research revealed that 70 percent to 80 percent of churches are stagnant or declining with thirty-five hundred to four thousand churches closing their doors each year.[32] Thom Rainer writes that approximately one hundred thousand churches are on the verge of death.[33] While there are various reasons for the decline of religious affiliation in America, it would be wrong to neglect the growing skepticism in postmodern American culture as a key factor. One of the major issues facing American evangelical churches has been their inability to consistently and accurately exegete and respond to cultural trends. There has been efficiency in scriptural exegesis, but not in cultural exegesis. If things are going to turn toward a missional disciple

---

32. Stetzer and Dodson. *Comeback Churches*, 19.
33. Rainer, *Autopsy*, 6.

making trajectory in the American church, it must start with having a better grasp of the culture to which God has called the church to serve. Stetzer warns of the rigidity of the church, "The approach of established churches will be difficult to change; the North American church is deeply rooted in modernity."[34]

The postmodern mindset is drastically different to the mindset of the modern age. Author Sam Chan describes the shift from modernity to postmodernity in this way:

> At some stage in the last few decades, we moved away from foundationalist reasoning. And we became suspicious of metanarratives and claims of ultimate truth. We moved away from the age of modernity into the age of postmodernity. The methods of evangelism that once worked so well in the 1980s no longer had the same appeal in the 2000s.[35]

The postmodern thinker seems infatuated with epistemology, particularly in relation to what is true and what is not. Gen-Xers and Millennials are the two generations that are most saturated in postmodern philosophical thought. Sociologists have a difficult time defining these generations because their views are so fluid. Postmoderns do not share a common worldview but embrace certain elements of a diversity of worldviews. Their search for truth has caused them to find nuggets of truth in a plurality of views.

As the church seeks to reach a new generation, it is best to assume that the people who need to be reached have no belief in absolute truth therefore, they will desire evidence before moving toward belief. While this is a recent trend in America, it is ultimately a product of the Enlightenment thinkers such as Rene Descartes. His famous statement, "I think, therefore I am" moved generations to a belief that truth and knowledge do not begin with God, but rather with the individual. In this transition in thinking the individual becomes the empirical judge of what is true and what is not. Postmodern thinkers pride themselves on being freely detached from underlying biases and influences. The Postmodern mantra is "question everything" which means there must be a wholesale rejection of all sources of knowledge including church, authority, traditions, and family with the burden of proof being on the source. Inherent within the

---

34. Stetzer, *Planting New Churches*, 112.
35. Chan, *Evangelism in a Skeptical World*, 102.

postmodern mindset is a strong desire for authenticity before belief.[36] Postmoderns are generally seeking the answer to two questions: What is true about themselves? What is true about the world around them? There is a deep yearning from which both questions spring, which is based on a more existential pragmatic approach. There is engrained within a postmodern mindset a longing for a truth that works; a truth that answers the deeper, more grandiose, and perplexing questions surrounding existence.

For decades the American evangelical church has based its missional approach on two assumptions: first, the person to be reached has at the very least, a belief in God. Second, the person holds the Bible and the church in high regard. Both assumptions are not true today for a large percentage of people. Will McRainey asserts, "The assumptions from the 1950s are not valid today. People know less about God the Father, Christ, the local church, and the teachings of the Bible than ever before in American history. Is it possible that our assumptions about our listeners' backgrounds should change based on these changes?"[37] The shift in how people view truth, and how they view God, has presented a great challenge to churches and missional disciple making in America today. A wholesale rejection of absolute truth by proxy eliminates belief in the sufficiency of Christ as the only way to heaven, the Bible as authoritative, the reliability of the resurrection story, and the creation narrative as historical fact.

Stetzer believes that the American church should strive to reach postmoderns but warns not to give in to this type of postmodern thinking. He states, "The church wants to reach and should reach postmoderns. However, the church must not adopt postmodernism. Postmodernism comes up short; its basic presuppositions are antithetical to the gospel at times. We cannot 'move with the times' and embrace postmodernity without strong discernment."[38] The shifting views of truth presented by postmodernism might tempt some Christian leaders to water down or minimize the truths of Scripture, such was the case with the Emergent Church Movement, but the proper future mission for the church in America is truth with authenticity. The need is not only to tell the current audience what is true about Jesus but also to show them what is true about Jesus through authentic relationships. Postmodern thinkers might reject absolute truth, but they are likely open to authentic truth. A gospel witness to this generation must carry an

---

36. Carson, *Gagging of God*, 57–58.
37. McRainey, *Art of Personal Evangelism*, 124.
38. Stetzer, *Planting New Churches*, 113.

authentic incarnational example of the truth of Christ working in the life of the believer. Postmoderns desire an authentic spirituality, sincerely held and humbly displayed. The authenticity of the faith is equally as important to postmoderns as the epistemological basis of the faith. Ross Rohde writes on the necessary approach to reaching postmoderns:

> The postmodern model starts with relationship. The postmodernist sees spirituality lived out in the life of someone he trusts. He is invited by his friend to explore spirituality with him. He learns that spirituality is really a personal relationship with Jesus Christ. He is invited to explore this relationship not only individually but also in the community of others who are seeking relationship with Jesus. As he encounters spirituality in the form of the fruit of the Spirit in the lives of his friends, in their love for him and one another and in the beauty of artistically corporate worship, he decides to believe and follow Jesus.[39]

The gospel must be shared through words, yet words alone will not communicate to this new generation of thinkers. How it is communicated is just as important as what is communicated. In other words, the message of the gospel must become incarnational in a sense as Christians embody biblical truth through authentic living. A good example is found in how Paul reached the Thessalonians, "Our gospel came to you not simply with words but also with power, with the Holy Spirit and deep conviction. You know how we lived among you for your sake" (1 Thess 1:5). As the gospel penetrated the hearts of the Thessalonians, Paul states it was a combination of spiritual and relational impact that made the difference. Spiritually, it was made possible through the power of the Holy Spirit. Relationally, it was the authentic way in which Paul and others lived out the truth of this power that greatly impacted this region. If this worked in a pre-Christian world, it is hard to imagine that it could not also be effective in a post-Christian world. The postmodern age is similar to the first-century biblical world: people of different backgrounds, cultures, languages, and beliefs living among one another. Just as Paul stood on Mars Hill and challenged the Athenian philosophers, Christianity has always been counterculture to the pluralistic beliefs of the world. Though this is true, it does not mean that Christian thought must be changed or evolve to reach new generations. The unchanging truth of Scripture has withstood the cultural tests throughout the millenniums. Rohde states:

39. Rohde "Practical Considerations."

> Christianity was extremely successful in the ancient worldview as it spread rapidly through the Greco-Roman world. It was able to express itself very well in the Renaissance through Protestantism and in the Enlightenment with Modern Evangelicalism. Now as the worldview has changed around us, biblical Christianity again finds itself needing to develop ways to culturally express itself without losing its fundamental truths.[40]

The Church of Jesus Christ does not have to depend on novelties and gadget approaches to reach this new world for Christ; the ancient truths of God's Word are still relevant and powerful enough, we just need to rediscover them. Every Christian and every church are called to be missional disciple makers to reach the world for Christ, but it must start in reaching the culture in which the Christian and the church reside. White's definition of culture is correct in stating that culture is comprehensive and as the church seeks to reach this culture, it must have a comprehensive plan.

How can the church today take the Great Commission and contextualize the mission to this current postmodern culture? The Great Commission of Christ is not a call to change culture, it is a commission to change people through missional disciple making. The need to reach this nation is immense and the number of lost people is overwhelming. There are one hundred and forty-three million unchurched people in the United States, of which one hundred and ten million are adults. To put that number in perspective, if the unchurched formed their own country, it would be the tenth-largest nation on earth.[41] While it is true that the number of non-Christians in America is growing, it should not be inferred that America is growing "anti-Christian." Spiritual curiosity certainly exists in postmodern America, and this necessitates a methodical approach in disciple making. A gradual approach will be needed in which the person views authenticity in the life of the disciple and receptivity increases as a result.[42] There is still hope and the church should not believe in a false narrative, which states that this nation is beyond the reach of Christ. Rick Richardson states:

> At the end of the day, the main problem with the church reaching new people, developing reproducers who advocate for faith and invite others into congregations, and then influencing communities

---

40. Rohde, "Practical Considerations."
41. Richardson, *You Found Me*, 37.
42. Hecht, "Faithfully Relating," 247.

Toward a Faithful Missional Future

for good is . . . the church! The biggest challenge congregations need to overcome is our own mindset and not the hostility or apathy of the larger culture."[43]

Hope will not come in the form of more ideas or a new and better iteration of previous ecclesial movements, rather it will come from intentional ministry shifts, a robust theology of evangelism, ecclesiology, and discipleship as well as a rediscovery of the methods and model of Jesus in making disciples.

MINISTRY ADJUSTMENTS FOR POSTMODERN MISSIONAL DISCIPLE MAKING

It is easy to blame postmodern culture as being too difficult to reach and too open to other religious ideologies, but the ineffectiveness of the church's outreach for the past five decades is based more on internal insufficiencies than external threats. The problem is not the culture, the problem is ineffective and antiquated models of ministry which lack intentionality and are mostly pragmatic. The early church flourished in a difficult and hostile culture, and even today the fastest-growing churches in the world are effective even though they face persecution, and resistance and are very much counterculture. The problem for the American evangelical church is that it has neglected its intended purpose as a multiplying, disciple making entity of the Lord Jesus Christ. As seen in this book, many models of ministry have been used by the American church over the years, but the church should first be mindful of the invitation of Jesus to his disciples. "Follow me," was the simple invitation from Jesus, and today, the church is called to the same purpose. Jesus Christ is the only suitable model of ministry and by following his methods and model of missional disciple making, the church will be better positioned to reach a postmodern culture. Hirsch writes of the missional disciple making goal of offering an incarnational ministry, "If the heart of discipleship is to become like Jesus, then . . . we see that Jesus' strategy is to get a whole lot of little versions of him infiltrating every nook and cranny of society by reproducing himself in and through his people."[44]

A common objection to this idea from contemporary church leaders is that modern-day culture will not respond to such an anachronistic

---

43. Hecht, "Faithfully Relating," 49.
44. Hirsch, *Forgotten Ways*, 113.

approach. There is a belief that the church needs cutting-edge methodologies which include better buildings, technology, sophisticated strategies, and creative programs, however, these methods alone will not produce more disciples. As shown in chapter three, this was ultimately the failure within the later iterations of the Church Growth Movement. The eventual attractional church model which evolved from church growth principles focused primarily on attracting as many people as possible to programs and events, however, this approach ultimately failed to keep the interest of a growing consumeristic culture. The church-centric attractional model suffered from the fatal flaw of personalities and programs becoming the draw rather than the resurrected Christ. How a church reaches people will ultimately determine how they keep them. Inherent in this attractional approach is the desire to draw large crowds, but Jesus was never interested in drawing crowds, his focus was on drawing people to himself. The central focus of the church is to engage its community for the purpose of making disciples and training them to be more like Christ. C. S. Lewis understood this when he said, "If the church is not doing this, then all the cathedrals, clergy, missions, sermons, even the Bible, are a waste of time."[45]

The missional disciple making process of Jesus is not a quick solution for declining churches or a way to increase attendance in a short amount of time, rather it is a slow organic movement that yields fruit over time. The goal of the church should not be to attract crowds, build better church members or more committed church members, but to make disciples and place them on a path toward spiritual maturity and multiplication. As believers are equipped to follow Jesus, they become more like him. A missional disciple making focus is centered on a process to lead people toward this direction. For this to take place there must be distinct shifts in method and practice so the church is in the best possible position to reach the fertile mission field which is postmodern America. The church will not reach this generation by merely placing a sign by the road inviting people to come to church, or by offering a multiplicity of programs. A much more intentional plan must be utilized to reach postmodern Americans and it will begin with a renewal in the commitment to personal, relationship-driven missional disciple making as the primary mission.

---

45. Vaus, *Mere Theology*, 167.

Shift From Programmatic Paradigms to Disciple Making Processes

Platt says, "The plan of Christ is not dependent on having the right programs or hiring the right professionals, but on building and being the right people—a community of people— who realize that we are all enabled and equipped to carry out the purpose of God for our lives."[46] Knowing the complexities of the new generation, outdated programs are simply not suited for effectiveness today. Quick-result programs are a thing of the past and the sooner the church accepts this reality the better positioned it will be to make an impact. Often, programs are preferred over processes because they are quick, pre-packaged plans that offer convenience and make less demand of schedules. The missional disciple making model of Jesus reveals a long methodical process, that involves years, not months, and involves people, not programs. Jesus' process for making disciples who would reach their world was not a sophisticated plan of intricate strategies, but rather a simple, intentional, and organic process that involved years of relational investment. Church leaders who shift toward a missional disciple making process should be prepared that it takes much time and involves entering authentic life-on-life ministry which will create periods of great complexity. Platt states:

> Making disciples is not an easy process. It is trying. It is messy. It is slow, tedious, even painful at times. It is all these things because it is relational. Jesus has not given us an effortless step-by-step formula for impacting nations for his glory. He has given us people, and he has said, "Live for them. Love them, serve them, and lead them. Lead them to follow me and lead them to lead others to follow me. In the process you will multiply the gospel to the ends of the earth."[47]

As seen in the critique of the Church Growth Movement, just because churches are successful in getting people into small groups may not necessarily mean the church is producing disciple making disciples. Success has been wrongly defined by how many people are involved in long-running programs with little thought as to what is being produced through these programs. These long running programs, over time, become stagnate ponds. Large numbers may not equate to successful ministry and much of it depends on how a church defines success. Is success found only in how

---

46. Platt, *Radical*, 92.
47. Platt, *Radical*, 93.

many people the church attracts or is it found in the type of disciple the church is producing? How would Jesus define success for his church? One doesn't have to ponder on this question for very long, because the answer is found in the Great Commission of Jesus in Matthew 28:18–20:

> And Jesus came and spoke to them saying, "All authority has been given to me in heaven and on earth. Go therefore and make disciples of all the nations, baptizing them in the name of the Father and the Son and the Holy Spirit, teaching them to observe all that I commanded you; and lo, I am with you always, even to the end of the age."

Success should be defined by how faithful a church is to the Great Commission of Christ. As seen in chapter two, the Great Commission of Jesus is a command to replicate what he had equipped his disciples to do. The plan of Christ was to give this commission to the disciples who would pass it to every subsequent generation to follow promising his authority (v. 18) and his presence and power (v. 20). Hull states, "We can and often do make evangelism the centerpiece. But apart from a vibrant culture of discipleship, we get sputtering, inconsistent, non-incarnational, and programmed evangelism. Such evangelism doesn't multiply disciples."[48] True obedience to the Great Commission of Jesus not only involves the "go and baptize," but also to "teach them to observe all things I have commanded you." Jesus calls the church to "make disciples," not merely to baptize new converts. The command to "make disciples" denotes a process because Jesus uses the phrase "make disciples" rather than "create disciples."

Before the church makes disciples, it must embrace a "come and see"[49] missional disciple making vision. There are clear implications of this statement on the outreach of the local church. Postmodernism and the rise of the *nones*[50] is certainly a threat to the American church, but often lost in the disillusionment is the fact that many postmoderns are on a journey for truth. Michael P. Murphy writes of the postmodern *nones*:

> As good postmodernists, nones are suspicious of claims made regarding absolute truth—and even more reticent about making such claims themselves. This often frustrates those who prize conviction and certitude above all else. Still, in matters of faith, such

---

48. Hull, *Conversion and Discipleship*, 58–59.

49. See chapter two for a full description of "come and see" (John 1:39) as part of the model of Jesus in making disciples.

50. Describes people who claim no religious affiliation.

Toward A Faithful Missional Future

a posture is ostensibly one of openness and receptivity, and nones are nothing if not open and receptive.[51]

Murphy offers a good reminder that while postmodern *nones* are skeptical by nature, they are open to engaging in conversation about faith. They prize authentic relationships and the exchanging of ideas, which presents the church with an opportunity to offer a "come and see" invitation. As believers go through the ebb and flow of their days, perhaps sharing a testimony of personal faith will go a long way in revealing to postmoderns a faith that works. Outreach will involve not only asking postmoderns to believe that Jesus is the Son of God, but most importantly, reasoning with them in the scriptures. Part of this reasoning will involve an apologetical approach. Ryan Van Der Avoort writes, "If apologetics is to stand in the lifegiving flow of God's work through the message of his Son, it must always fit under the broader category of Christian discipleship. In other words: if apologetics is to be Christian, it should be a subset of both making and maturing disciples."[52]

The best opportunity to reach postmoderns to believe in Jesus begins with the simple invitation, "Come and see." There is inherent with postmoderns a search for authentic community. A unified worshiping community of believers offers an incarnational apologetic to a skeptical postmodern culture. A community of worshiping believers binds the hearts of the diversity of culture, the diversity of education, backgrounds, and socioeconomic categories into one corporate authentic expression. Jonathan Leeman suggests that a unified worshiping community plays an apologetic role as the local church offers a glimpse of Christ's rule in the here and now. This apologetic role gives authenticity to the message of the church as the local congregation serves as eschatological embassies filled with authentic ambassadors of the gospel. He states, "Churches possess an ambassadorial message: "be reconciled to God' (2 Cor 5:20). And that message should be matched by a counter-cultural community: "go out from their midst and be separated from them . . . bringing holiness to completion (2 Cor 6:17, 7:1)."[53] Thus, one of the most powerful missional outreach appeals

---

51. Murphy *"Suspicious Minds."*

52. Van Der Avoort, "Don't Divorce."

53. Leeman, "We Come in Peace!" Leeman also states, "The gospel does not just create individual Christians. It creates a community, a family, a body. The gospel is church-shaped." 7.

to the postmodern mind is a worshiping community.⁵⁴ An invitation to an authentic worshiping community would be a great start and could supernaturally lead to a conversion experience for the one being invited. According to a survey from LifeWay Research, 51 percent of unchurched people say a personal invitation from a friend or neighbor would be effective in getting them to visit a church.

After the command to "go," Jesus gives a clear indication that a conversion experience is expected by the verb βαπτίζω, "baptize". The new disciple is expected to identify with the work of Jesus and a local church through the public action of baptism. Historically, the church has been effective in the first part of the commission, it is verse twenty that has often been overlooked. Spader states, "Jesus gives more than 400 commands and more than half of them are disciple making commands. Becoming a disciple of Jesus does not mean completing a curriculum or attending a church activity. It is a lifestyle of becoming more like Jesus."⁵⁵ The command is clear, the church must move from programmatic discipleship to intentional authentic "life on life" missional disciple making. The Great Commission is incomplete unless the church teaches new believers to "observe" or "obey." The word Jesus uses is τηρέω meaning that new disciples are to be taught to "guard" or "watch over" his teachings. This is deeper than mere knowledge; Jesus expects his church to disciple new believers so deeply that they are trained to obey and guard over doctrine.

Paul understood this call as he urged Timothy, "And the things that you have heard from me among many witnesses, commit these to faithful men who will be able to teach others also" (2 Tim 2:2). Casual discipleship programs often miss the mark on this type of intentionality. When churches enact a process of disciple making and train disciple makers, this type of authentic relational community becomes second nature as it is embedded in the DNA of the body of believers. In order for this to take place, the church will need to reassess its missional understanding of discipleship within the context of the Great Commission. The bifurcation of evangelism and discipleship within ecclesial circles in the twentieth century must be eradicated so that a full hermeneutic of the Great Commission can be embraced.

---

54. Zaharias, "Ancient Message," 27.
55. Spader, *4 Chair Discipling*, 37.

Toward A Faithful Missional Future

Shift From Programmatic Discipleship to Missional Disciple Making

The title of this section of the chapter should naturally lend itself to criticism of the pragmatic approaches of the Church Growth Movement and their lasting impact on the church. It is important to note, however, that Rainer's address to the American Society for Church Growth in 1994 and his subsequent paper published in the ASCG journal one year later, recognized that criticisms of the movement were fair due to the proliferation of the movement. In his address entitled, "Recovering Our Purpose," Rainer recognizes that the purpose of the Church Growth Movement wasn't to create a plethora of orthopraxical ideas, but rather to promote evangelism and the Great Commission. He notes that Gary McIntosh's address to the Society of Church Growth in 1994 listed the following items as identifiable within the Church Growth Movement:

> Church growth today may be identified with church planting, marketing, seeker sensitive methodologies, cell groups, meta-churches, prayer, spiritual warfare, generational studies, church renewal, church leadership, conflict management, change agency, or megachurches.[56]

Rainer notes, "While we church growth leaders understand that the movement is an expression to fulfill the Great Commission, we often fail to acknowledge or emphasize the key element of the Great Commission in evangelism.[57] Rainer would continue to articulate the need to keep the Great Commission as the central focus of church growth, and not allow the pragmatic foci to overwhelm the key component. Herein lies the reason for the anathematizing of the movement in the minds of many critics; it fails to extend a robust theological and ecclesiological expression without swerving into pragmatic lanes. Rainer states:

> Many of us have been pleading for years for more foundational theological works in church growth. But in reality, most of the work has already been done. Numerous theologies of evangelism have been written by able scholars. But most of these theologies of evangelism are incomplete in that they fail to include an ecclesiological component. We should write theologies of church growth that begin with a theology of evangelism and conclude

---

56. Rainer, "Church Growth," 61.
57. Rainer, "Church Growth," 61.

with ecclesiology. In other words, we will advocate that the work of effective evangelism (McGavran's term) is not complete until a person becomes a fruit-bearing disciple in a local church.[58]

Rainer's words, not intentionally, negated the very movement itself as he distilled everything about church growth back to the Great Commission of Jesus to make disciples. He rightly points out that church growth theologies were robust in evangelism but lacking in ecclesiological discipleship as a key indicator that a disciple has been made. Though McGavran consistently advocated for a homogenization of evangelism and ecclesiology, later iterations of the movement were largely pragmatic as displayed in McIntosh's identifiable church growth markers. How does the church recover an equally robust theology of evangelism and ecclesiology in light of the Great Commission as it refocuses its efforts toward a mission for postmodern times?

A helpful resource in answering this question is Alan Hirsch's *Disciplism: Reimagining Evangelism through the Lens of Discipleship*. Hirsch believes that almost all of the problems in the church can be linked to the lack of a clear idea and practice of an effective theology of ecclesial discipleship.[59] The dissection of discipleship from the Great Commission begins when congregations view discipleship as an introduction to the theology and culture of the local church or denominational distinctives. This type of approach minimizes discipleship to a church membership class or a "fast-tracked catechism for unchurch new believers."[60] Other iterations of discipleship include programmatic pathways toward Christian maturity in which the spiritual disciplines are taught, which is certainly needed, but Hirsch asks, "What is the point of it all?" He states, "If the mission of God is to sum up all things in Himself in Christ Jesus (Eph 1:10), then we will have to go beyond church attendance, quiet times, and random voluntarism to help align the church around that purpose."[61] In looking at past highly transformative movements in Christian history Hirsch has found that "discipleship as a means through which Jesus works through his people" has been the critical component for key catalytic change.[62] Hirsch surmises that "The key to the health, the maintenance, the extension and the renewal

58. Rainer, "Church Growth," 69.
59. Hirsch, *Disciplism*, 2.
60. Hirsch, *Disciplism*, 3.
61. Hirsch, *Disciplism*, 3.
62. Hirsch, *Disciplism*, 4.

of the Church is not more evangelism, but more discipleship."[63] He calls for a reframing of disciple making as evangelism within discipleship:

> If we persist at aiming at evangelism, we seldom, if ever, get to discipleship. History provides more than ample proof of this outcome. But at no time has this been more evident than in this age of mass consumption. Making more disciples is the real solution. I suggest that we need to refocus our efforts on discipleship and do whatever evangelism we can in that context. We need to reframe evangelism within the context of discipleship.[64]

To Hirsch's point, the Church Growth Movement produced a definition of a Great Commission church as one that commits to regular outreach and evangelism. He, however, suggests that using the Great Commission as a synonym for evangelism is a huge categorical error. Where does the church find evangelism in the Great Commission? He states, "There is no overt mention of it at all. In fact, the text explicitly binds us to the practices of discipleship and disciple making. It turns out that the Great Commission is not actually about evangelism."[65] Evangelism then is implied within the process of disciple making and is not the total summation of the Great Commission. Herein lies one of the critical errors of the Church Growth Movement's missional philosophies: it was largely built on a reductionist interpretation of Matthew 28:19 as evangelism to the exclusion of discipleship. The outflow of Church Growth praxis was the substitution of disciple making with attractional program-based events and altar calls. These methods of evangelism have resulted in a generation of saved people, but not necessarily discipled people. Ultimately, Hirsch's view of reframing evangelism within the context of discipleship is the cumulative summation of the Great Commission of missional disciple making. This idea of pre-conversion discipleship offers a new and exciting missional approach to reaching postmoderns. As the church engages postmodern seekers with winsome apologetic "come and see" methods as displayed in the disciple making methods and model of Jesus, discipleship starts even before conversion, and continues through a salvific moment toward Christian maturity and eventually, multiplication.

Informed by Hirsch's view, a new missional disciple making mission begins with believers who have been well equipped to offer a simple

---

63. Hirsch, *Disciplism*, 5.
64. Hirsch, *Disciplism*, 5.
65. Hirsch, *Disciplism*, 7.

invitation of "come and see." Once a person trusts in Christ and is baptized, then churches must have disciples who are trained to equip new believers to follow Jesus through a life of committed discipleship, which in its very essence is the process of being conformed to the image of Jesus.[66] Hunter speaks of the critical component of spiritual formation, "Beyond the worship of God and the proclamation of his word, the central ministry of the church is one of formation; of making disciples."[67] Hunter continues, "It is the church's task of teaching, admonishing, and encouraging believers over the course of their lives in order to present them 'as complete in Christ,' 'fit for any calling.'"[68] The moments following conversion are critical in developing life-long followers of Christ who are equipped to thrive in their new reality.

Not to be overlooked is the need for churches to equip parents to disciple children on what it means to follow Jesus long before they decide to follow Christ. The formation that Hunter mentions is most critical in the young influential minds of the new generations. Perhaps parents can guard their children from misguided postmodern views if they will simply train and disciple them regarding Scriptural truth. Parents need a distinct disciple making plan for their own families so that they can produce fishers of men and multiplying fruit bearers. Goheen and Sheriden state, "If the church in North America is doing everything right in terms of its own communal life—missionary structures, leadership, worship, discipleship—but is not training parents to form the next generation in faithfulness to the gospel, it will continue on its path toward demise."[69]

As churches make disciples, they are in essence commissioning them to go out into the world, including their workspaces, families, neighborhoods, and communities with a life-changing message. Once postmoderns "come and see" and trust in Christ, churches must have an answer to the "now what?" The moments after conversion are critical in developing a lifelong disciple. Coleman states, "Unless new Christians have parents or friends who will fill the gap in a real way, they are left entirely on their own to find the solutions to innumerable practical problems confronting their lives, any one of which could mean disaster to their new faith." He continues, "It is no wonder that about half of those who make professions and join

---

66. Romans 8:29–30.
67. Hunter, *To Change the World*, 236-237.
68. Hunter, *To Change the World*, 236-237.
69. Goheen and Sheridan, *Becoming a Missionary Church*, 119.

the church eventually fall away or lose the glow of a Christian experience."[70] A hermeneutically comprehensive Great Commission approach will ensure that the maturing of disciples through life-on-life teaching is as vital to the fulfillment of the command as the "go" and "baptize."

Shift From Inviting Crowds to Investing in Disciples

The word that seems most appropriate to churches in postmodern America is the word *invest*. Just as Jesus invested three years of his life into his small circle of disciples it is wise for the church today to begin investing in people, rather than programs. It would also be wise to spend more time building disciples than trying to draw people into our buildings. The American evangelical church cannot be faithful to its mission unless it re-commits to relational investment both before and after the conversion encounter. Programs do not disciple people; people disciple people. Investing in small groups rather than large audiences is often not the way of the contemporary church, but it is the way of Jesus in making disciples. Platt states it this way:

> The plan seems so counterintuitive to our way of thinking. In a culture where bigger is always better and flashy is always more effective, Jesus beckons each of us to focus our lives plainly, humbly, and quietly on people. The reality is, you can't share life like this with masses and multitudes. Jesus didn't. If the Son of God thought it necessary to focus his life on a small group of men, we are fooling ourselves into thinking we can mass-produce disciples today. God's design for taking the gospel to the world is a slow, intentional, simple process that involves every one of his people sacrificing every facet of their lives to multiply the life of Christ in others.[71]

> We are to go and make disciples of all nations. Then we are to baptize them in the name of the Father, Son, and Holy Spirit. And we are to teach them to obey everything Jesus commanded. All this adds up to the means to multiply people who enjoy God's grace and extend his glory around the world.[72]

McNeal believes that the lack of spiritual formation in the American evangelical church can be traced to a false assumption. The assumption is

---

70. Coleman, *Master Plan*, 47.
71. Platt, *Radical*, 103–104.
72. Platt, *Radical*, 93–34.

that if church leaders can simply get people to come to church often enough, they will grow. The method and model of Jesus for his church in making disciples, however, is much more intentional and relational. Past models have depended upon church activities to draw crowds and by proxy, grow people spiritually, but the example of Jesus is much different. For Jesus, it was never about religious activity, and his plan for building his church was relational rather than attractional. Mike Breen warns that a missional movement without a distinct relational discipleship plan will surely fail:

> If you make disciples, you will always get the church, but if you try and build the church you will rarely get disciples. Most of us have become quite good at the church thing. And yet, disciples are the only thing Jesus cares about, and it's the only number Jesus is counting. Not our attendance or budget or buildings. He wants to know if we are making disciples.[73]

Ministry success is never found in the size of the crowd, but rather in the number of disciples produced. The disciple making movement of Jesus depended upon relational investment in a few, rather than attracting the many. The central task on which Jesus focused his efforts and gave most of his time and energy was the selection and equipping of a small band of disciples. Hirsch states,

> "The founding of the whole Christian movement, the most significant religious movement in history, one that has extended itself through the ages, and into the twenty-first century, was initiated through the simple acts of Jesus investing his life and teachings in his disciples."[74]

Disciple making is nothing more or less than relational investment. It seems too simplistic and uncomplicated to be true, yet Jesus based his entire ministry on this very concept. Relational investment for the purpose of disciple making was the very essence of Christ's mission to propagate the gospel. Hirsch asserts that the one common factor of all phenomenal movements in the history of Christendom is the relational disciple making systems that catapulted them. He points out that the movements never get beyond the very essence of disciple making, "This is because it is at once the starting point, the abiding strategic practice, as well as the key to all lasting

---

73. Breen, *Building a Discipling Culture*, 5.
74. Hirsch, *Forgotten Ways*, 102.

missional impact in and through movements."[75] A good example of this type of commitment to relational disciple making is found in John Wesley's methods[76] in the spread of Methodism in Britain. Wesley's relational investment in the people of Britain and the high level of commitment expected from them was the reason why in a generation one in thirty people in Britain became Methodists.[77] The essence of disciple making is not found in a curriculum, programs, or activities, it is primarily found in relationships as seen in the second phase of Jesus's disciple making model, *come and follow me*.[78] Stop trying to draw big crowds, and start working to build big people.

Shift Toward Disciple Making Multiplication

The missional goal of the life of Jesus was to redeem humankind and start a movement of multiplication, and ultimately this was the will of his Father.[79] His model and process were so successful that in a very short period, his message spread from 120 believers in Jerusalem to a worldwide multiplying movement. His mandate was the Great Commission, his model was investing in people and his method was producing multiplying disciple makers. Within two years these disciples filled Jerusalem with his message (Acts 5:28) and in four years they were multiplying churches (Acts 9:31). In nineteen years, they had turned the world upside down (Acts 17:6) and within thirty years Paul tells the Colossians that the message of Jesus had not only spread to them, but to the whole world bringing forth fruit (Colossians 1:6).[80] Spader summarizes, "From beginning to end, scripture is clear that God's strategy for world impact is multiplication."[81] He states:

---

75. Hirsch, *Forgotten Ways*, 103.

76. Malcom Gladwell summarizes John Wesley's focus on this type of intentional discipleship, "If you want to bring fundamental change to people's lives and behavior, a change that will persist and influence others, you will need to create a community around them (new believers) where those new beliefs could be practiced, expressed and nurtured." Gladwell, *Tipping Point*, 173.

77. Gladwell, *Tipping Point*, 173.

78. Chapter two explains how Jesus invested relationally in his disciples during this important phase.

79. John 17:4.

80. Spader, *Walking as Jesus Walked*, 168.

81. Spader, *Walking as Jesus Walked*, 168.

> How long would it take to win the world for Christ if just one person could lead 1,000 people to Him every day? If you do the math, it would take over 17,500 years, and it is if no one else was born in that time. By contrast, how long would it take you to win the world to Christ if you follow Jesus' pattern of multiplication? What would happen if you win one person to Christ every six months and disciple him or her to lead someone else to Christ and then repeat the process with others? The answer is staggering. The disciplemaking Christ followers would win the world to Christ in seventeen years through the power of multiplication.[82]

The illustration of the vine and the branches in John 15 indicates that Jesus expected multiplication from his disciples, and if he expected it from his disciples then it is reasonable to believe he expects it from his church. The highest level of fruit-bearing found in John 15 is in verse five and it clearly speaks of the expectation of being a multiplying fruit-bearing believer, "I am the vine, you are the branches. He who abides in me, and I in him, bears much fruit; for without me you can do nothing." In a time where churches are hoping for a few additions each year, Jesus is calling his church to multiply. Are those whom the church has led to Christ now leading others to "come and see", investing in new disciples, training, and teaching them to be fishers of men and experiencing multiplication and replication? Every church should evaluate its ministries primarily regarding what it is producing for the glory of God and for the purpose of making disciples who make disciples.

Rainer and Stetzer's definition of a *Transformational Church* embodies this type of "new scorecard." They define a successful church as, "A congregation that joins God's mission of sharing the gospel and making disciples. Those disciples become more like Jesus, and the church thus acts as the body of Christ transforming their communities and the world for the kingdom of God."[83] In sharing this new definition of what encompasses a successful church, the authors prioritize the importance of creating a multiplying missional disciple making ministry. They state, "Churches must continuously engage in the ministry of making new disciples. And it is more than that, it is disciples changed by Jesus that change their church that changes the world."[84] This is the essence of the Great Commission and

---

82. Spader, *Walking as Jesus Walked*, 169.
83. Rainer and Stetzer, *Transformational Church*, 42.
84. Rainer and Stetzer, *Transformational Church*, 43.

launching a multiplying movement and it is possible for every church, regardless of its size.

CONCLUSION

Making disciples is the very heart of the church's mission; it is not an optional extra. The current missional breaches are a direct result of the lack of disciple making happening in our churches and through those who attend. White concludes, "The church must rethink evangelism, no longer can we be simply event-driven. The church must view evangelism as both a process and an event."[85] The American church finds itself in a peculiar place where growth, sustainability, and viability are becoming increasingly difficult. A new vision of church ministry must be embraced; a vision that not only invites people to "come and attend" church, but more importantly, "come and see" Jesus. Reaching this generation will involve relational investment with unchurched people, apologetical influence, and conversion with the goal of making disciples through the methods and model of Jesus. Ultimately, the challenge for the evangelical church in America today is to no longer follow the methods and programs of the previous ecclesial movements, but rather to follow the invitation of Jesus to "follow me" and replicate his example in engaging with a lost world. The invitation to the church is to embrace a full hermeneutic of the Great Commission as its disciple making mission and to follow the careful strategic process through which Jesus turned a group of ragged uneducated disciples into world-changing disciple makers. In writing of Jesus' command to "follow me," Bonhoeffer states, "The object of Jesus' command is always the same, to evoke wholehearted faith, to make us love God and our neighbor with all our heart and soul. This is the only unequivocal feature in his command."[86] As Bonhoeffer writes those words, he finds himself in an emerging Nazi culture adamantly opposed to the truths of Scripture, yet his response to the invitation of Jesus was to love his neighbors regardless of how difficult this would become in the years leading up to the war. The challenge is the same for the church today. Though the American church is not facing a militant regime, it does find itself surrounded by a secular culture that is moving farther and farther away from Christ. Postmoderns will only be reached if the church has a heart motivated by love, equipped to invite them to "come

---

85. White, *Meet Generation Z*, 109.
86. Bonhoeffer, *Cost of Discipleship*, 227.

and see," and prepared to show them what it means to follow Jesus, fish for men, and multiply fruit.

The work of the church must be in making disciples who make disciples, and this vision must be shared by church leaders as the one true mission. The breach of mission can only be shored up through this approach. If church leaders are not themselves disciple makers, it is hard to imagine that church members and ministries will follow the process of Jesus and be obedient to the Great Commission. Far too many pastors are not modeling disciple making to their congregation because they are too busy with programmatical planning and thinking of a new strategy to grow the church. Some pastors see this type of relational disciple making as too time-consuming and lacking immediate results. In a time when pastors are under a great amount of pressure to perform and produce results, the temptation is to look for programs that promise fast growth. The most "Jesus-like" activity that a pastor can accomplish is simply to invest in a few with the expectation of replication and multiplication. It will not involve announcements in the bulletin or signup sheets, but rather a personal invitation to journey together in becoming mature followers of Jesus. This type of relational investment will likely result in disciples who are reaching their culture through a "come and see" missional disciple making lifestyle. Craig Etheredge reminds church leaders of the exhilaration of missional disciple making:

> There is nothing more satisfying in ministry than making disciples. Record attendances come and go. Large events come and go. Building projects and mission trips come and go. But the one thing that will satisfy you in ministry is pouring your life into a few people and watching them do the same thing.[87]

The command to make disciples is an urgent call to the church. The perpetuity of the *missio Dei* is dependent upon how well one generation can reach the next. Programs, buildings, budgets, attendance, and even denominations will fade, but missional disciple makers never fade because they are investing their lives in others. Etheredge states:

> The church in America today desperately needs to return back to making disciples. The lives of those far from God are at stake. How will this world be reached? How will the nations hear the gospel?

---

87. Etheredge, *Bold Moves*, 215.

Toward a Faithful Missional Future

They will hear it from men and women who are sold out to Jesus and know how to multiply their lives in others.[88]

The movement of disciple making that Etheredge is referring to will not come as a result of church calendar events, pre-packaged programs, or a pulpit presence only, it will take something much more intentional. Postmodern America is not unreachable, but it will take an approach that focuses on equipping believers to get out of their pews and enter the lives of those who are not in current fellowship with Christ. Coleman challenges the church, "One must decide where he wants his ministry to count—in the momentary applause of popular recognition or in the reproduction of his life in a few chosen ones who will carry on his work after he has gone. Really, it is a question of which generation we are living for."[89]

The ecclesial movements of the past fifty years in American evangelicalism have resulted in limited results and this book has revealed the flaws of each, but these failures serve as a reminder that the church does not need a new movement. The greatest need is a rediscovery of the original movement that began two thousand years ago through the life, sacrifice, and consecration of Jesus to a small band of disciples. While cultural accretions will bring challenges and necessitate methodological adaptations, the missional disciple making purpose of the church has not changed. The church doesn't need a new movement, it needs to fix the missional breaches. The church is the movement that began through a promise of Jesus in Matthew 16:18 and if it fully embraces its disciple making mission, its walls will never be breached.

In response to the Church Growth Movement, the main attraction of the Church ought to be its Savior. In response to the Emergent Church Movement, the mission is grounded upon a sacred fidelity to the orthodox truths of Scripture. In response to the Missional Church Movement, the concept of being *missional* ought to be clearly expressed and defined as the *missio Dei* as lived out through people committed to being missional disciple makers to the culture in which they find themselves. The very future of the American church will depend on how well we respond to this challenge. As the tides of secularism and postmodern belief continue to grow in American culture, how well the church repairs these breaches will ultimately determine its future effectiveness.

---

88. Etheredge, *Bold Moves*, 221.
89. Coleman, *Master Plan*, 37.

Bibliography

Addison, Steve. *Movements that Change the World: 5 Keys to the Expansion of Christianity*. Downers Grove, IL: InterVarsity, 2011.

Arn, Win. *How to Grow a Church: Conversations about Church Growth*. Grand Rapids: Baker, 1973.

Barrett, Lois. "Missional Witness: The Church as Apostle to the World." In *Missional Church: A Vision for the Sending of the Church in North America*. Edited by Darrell L. Guder, 110–141. Grand Rapids: Eerdmans, 1998.

Barrs, Jerram. *Learning Evangelism from Jesus*. Wheaton, IL: Crossway Books, 2009.

Bell, Rob. *Love Wins: A Book About Heaven, Hell, and the Fate of Every Person Who Ever Lived*. New York: Harper, 2001.

———. *Velvet Elvis: Repainting the Christian Faith*. Grand Rapids: Zondervan, 2006.

Blomberg, Craig. *Matthew*. In *New American Commentary*. Nashville: B&H, 2012. https://app.wordsearchbible.lifeway.com.

Blount, Douglas K. "A New Kind of Interpretation: Brian McLaren and the Hermeneutics of Taste" in *Evangelicals Engaging Emergent: A Discussion of the Emergent Church Movement*. Edited by William D. Henard and Adam W. Greenway, 109–128. Nashville: Broadman, 2009.

Bonhoeffer, Dietrich. *The Cost of Discipleship*. New York: Simon and Schuster, 1939.

Borchert, Gerald L. *John 1-11*. In *New American Commentary*. Nashville: Broadman and Holman, 1996.

Bosch, David J. *Transforming Mission: Paradigm Shifts in Theology of Mission*. Maryknoll, NY: Orbis, 1991.

Bounds, E. M. *Power Through Prayer*. Grand Rapids: Baker, 1972.

Breen, Mike. *Building a Discipling Culture*. US: 3DM, 2017.

Brooks, James A. *Mark*. In *New American Commentary*. Nashville: Broadman, 1991.

Bruce, A. B. *The Training of the Twelve: How Jesus Christ Found and Taught the Twelve Apostles, A Book of New Testament Biography*. Grand Rapids: Christian Classics Ethereal Library, 1871.

Bruce, F. F. *The Gospel of John: Introduction, Exposition and Notes*. Grand Rapids: William B. Eerdmans, 1983.

Burge, Ryan P., and Paul A. Djupe. "Emergent Church Practices in America: Inclusion and Deliberation in American Congregations." *Religious Research Association* (March 2014) 1–23.

———. "Emergent Fault Lines: Clergy Attitudes Toward the Emergent Church Movement." In *Journal of Religious Leadership* 15 no. 1 (Spring 2016) 5–29.

Bibliography

Caputo, J. D. *What Would Jesus Deconstruct?: The Good News of Post-Modernism for the Church*. Grand Rapids: Baker, 2007.

Carson, D. A. *Becoming Conversant with the Emerging Church*. Grand Rapids: Zondervan, 2005.

———. *The Gagging of God: Christianity Confronts Pluralism*. Grand Rapids: Zondervan, 1996.

———. *The Gospel According to John*. Leicester: Apollos, 1991.

———, ed. *Telling the Truth: Evangelizing Postmoderns*. Grand Rapids: Zondervan, 2009.

Challies, Tim. "The False Teachers: Brian McLaren." May 2014. https://www.challies.com/articles/the-false-teachers-brian-mclaren.

Chan, Sam. *Evangelism in a Skeptical World: how to make the unbelievable news about Jesus more believable*. Grand Rapids: Zondervan, 2018.

"Chuck Colson's Response." https://brianmclaren.net/chuck-colsons-response/

Coleman, Robert. *The Master Plan of Evangelism*. Grand Rapids: Revel, 1993.

Cook, David Lowell. "The Americanization of the Church Growth Movement." In *Journal of the American Society for Church Growth* (Fall 2000) 15–50.

Crouch, Andy. "Creating Culture: Our Best Response to the World Is to Make Something of it." In *Christianity Today* (September 2008) 24–29.

Csinos, David M. "'Come, Follow Me': Apprenticeship in Jesus' Approach to Education." In *Religious Education* 105 no. 1 (Jan–Feb 2010) 45–62.

DeVine, Mark. "The Emerging Church: One Movement—Two Streams." In *Evangelicals Engaging Emergent*. Edited by William D. Henard and Adam W. Greenway, 4-46. Nashville: Broadman & Holman, 2009.

DeWaay, Bob. *The Emergent Church: Undefining Christianity*. US: Theological Abstracts, 2009.

DeYoung, Kevin, and Ted Kluck. *Why We're Not Emergent: By Two Guys Who Should Be*. Chicago: Moody, 2008.

Driscoll, Mark. *Confessions of a Reformission Rev.: Hard Lessons from an Emerging Missional Church*. Grand Rapids: Zondervan, 2006.

Eims, LeRoy. *The Lost Art of Disciple Making*. Grand Rapids: Zondervan, 1978.

Erickson, Millard J. *Postmodernizing the Faith: Evangelical Responses to the Challenge of Postmodernism*. Grand Rapids: Baker Books, 1998.

Etheredge, Craig. *Bold Moves: Lead the Church to Live Like Jesus*. Colleyville, TX: DiscipleFIRST, 2016.

Ferdinando, Keith. "Mission: A Problem of Definition," In *Themelios* 33 no. 1 (2008) 46–59.

Ficedom, Georg F. *The Mission of God: An Instruction to the Theology of Mission*. St. Louis: Concordia, 1965.

Finke, Roger, and Rodney Stark. *The Churching of America, 1776–1990: Winners and Losers in Our Religious Economy*. New Brunswick: Rutgers University, 1992.

Flett, John G. *The Witness of God: The Trinity, Missio Dei, Karl Barth and the Nature of Christian Community*. Grand Rapids: Eerdmans, 2010.

Franklin, Patrick S. "Missionaries in Our Own Back Yard: Missional Community as Cultural and Political Engagement in the Writings of Lesslie Newbigin." In *Didaskalia* 25 (Fall 2015) 161–190.

Garrison, David. *Church Planting Movements*. Richmond, VA: Office of Overseas Operations of the International Missions Board, 1999.

Bibliography

Gelder, Craig Van. *The Essence of the Church: A Community Created by the Spirit*. Grand Rapids: Baker, 2000.

———. "Mission in the Emerging Postmodern Condition." In *The Church Between Gospel and Culture: The Emerging Mission in North America*. Edited by George R. Hunsberger and Craig Van Gelder, 113–138. Grand Rapids: Eerdmans, 1996.

Gelder, Craig Van and Dwight J. Zscheile. *The Missional Church in Perspective: Mapping Trends and Shaping the Conversation*. Grand Rapids: Baker, 2010.

George, Timothy. "If I'm An Evangelical, What Am I?" In *Christianity Today* (August 9, 1999) 62.

Gibbs, Eddie and Ryan K. Bolder. *Emerging Churches: Dispatches from the Emergent Frontier*. San Francisco: Jossey-Bass, 2008.

Gilbert, Greg. "Brian McLaren and the Gospel of Here & Now." February 2010. https://www.9marks.org/article/brian-mclaren-and-gospel-here-now/.

Gladwell, Malcolm. *The Tipping Point: How Little Things Can Make a Big Difference*. Boston: Little and Brown, 2002.

Goheen, Michael W. and Timothy M. Sheriden. *Becoming a Missionary Church: Lesslie Newbigin and Contemporary Church Movements*. Grand Rapids: Baker, 2022.

Grenz, Stanley J. *A Primer on Postmodernism*. Grand Rapids: Wm. B. Eerdmans, 1996.

Guder, Darrell L. ed., *Missional Church: A Vision for the Sending of the Church in North America*. Grand Rapids: Eerdmans, 1998.

———. "Missionary Structures: The Particular Community." In *Missional Church: A Vision for the Sending of the Church in North America*. Edited by Darrell L. Guder, 221–247. Grand Rapids: Eerdmans, 1998.

Gundry, Robert H., and Robert L. Thomas. *The NIV Harmony of the Gospels with Explanations and Essays*. San Francisco: HarperCollins, 1988.

Gustafson, David M. "What is Missional Disciple Making?" October 22, 2018. https://www.michaeljamesbreen.com/blog/2018/10/22/what-is-missional-disciple-making

Harris, Murray J. *Exegetical Guide to the Greek New Testament: John*. Nashville: Broadman & Holman. 2016.

Hauerwas, Stanley, and William H. Willimon. *Resident Aliens: Life in the Christian Colony*. Nashville: Abingdon, 1989.

Hecht, Susan. "Faithfully Relating to Unbelievers in a Relational Age." In *Telling the Truth: Evangelizing Postmoderns*, edited by D. A. Carson, 245-254. Grand Rapids: Zondervan, 2000.

Henard, William D., and Adam W. Greenway, eds. *Evangelicals Engaging Emergent: A Discussion of the Emergent Church Movement*. Nashville: Broadman, 2009.

Hesselgrave, David. *Paradigms in Conflict: 10 Key Questions in Christian Missions Today*. Grand Rapids: Kregel, 2005.

Hirsch, Alan. *Disciplism: Reimagining Evangelism Through the Lens of Discipleship*. Exponential Resources, 2014.

———. *The Forgotten Ways: Reactivating the Missional Church*. Grand Rapids: Brazos, 2006.

Hobbs, Herschel H. *The Gospel of John*. Grand Rapids: Zondervan, 1965.

Hughes, R. Kent. *John: That You May Believe. Preaching the Word Commentary Series*. Wheaton: Illinois: Crossway, 1999.

Hull, Bill. *Conversion and Discipleship: You Can't Have One Without the Other*. Grand Rapids: Zondervan, 2016.

Bibliography

———. *The Disciple-Making Church: Leading a Body of Believers on the Journey of Faith.* Grand Rapids: Baker, 2010.

———. *The Disciple-Making Pastor.* Grand Rapids: Baker, 1988.

———. "Is The Church Growth Movement Really Working?" In *Power Religion: The Selling Out of the Evangelical Church.* Edited by Michael Scott Horton, 139–160. Chicago: Moody, 1992.

———. *Jesus Christ Disciplemaker.* Grand Rapids: Baker, 2004.

Hunsberger, George R. *Bearing the Witness of the Spirit: Lesslie Newbigin's Theology of Cultural Plurality.* Grand Rapids: Eerdmans, 1998.

———. "Missional Vocation: Called and Sent to Represent the Reign of God." In *Missional Church: A Vision for the Sending of the Church in North America.* Edited by Darrell L. Guder, 77–109. Grand Rapids: Eerdmans, 1998.

———. "The Newbigin Gauntlet: Developing a Domestic Missiology for North America." In *The Church Between Gospel and Culture.* Edited by George R. Hunsberger and Craig Van Gelder, 3–25. Grand Rapids: Eerdmans, 1996.

Hunsberger, George R., and Craig Van Gelder, eds. *The Church Between Gospel and Culture: The Emerging Mission in North America.* Grand Rapids: Eerdmans, 2016.

Hunter III, George G. "The Legacy of Donald A. McGavran." In *International Bulletin of Missionary Research* 16 no. 4 (October 1992) 158–162.

Hunter, James Davison. *To Change the World: The Irony, Tragedy, and Possibility of Christianity in the Late Modern World.* Oxford: University, 2010.

"Increasing Rejection of Church a 'Good Thing,' Brian McLaren Says." *Baptist Global News.* December 7, 2018. https://baptistnews.com/article/increasing-rejection-of-church-a-good-thing-brian-mclaren-says/#.Y2JvinbMKUk.

"In US Decline of Christianity Continues at a Rapid Pace," *Pew Research Center.* www.pewforum.org/2019/10/17/in-u-s-decline-of-christianity-continues-at-rapid-pace/.

Kane, J. Herbert. *The Christian World Mission: Today and Tomorrow.* Grand Rapids: Baker, 1981.

Kimball, Dan. *The Emerging Church: Vintage Christianity for New Generations.* Grand Rapids: Zondervan, 2003.

Kung, Hans. *The Church.* New York: Sheed and Ward, 1967.

Laing, Mark T. B. *From Crisis to Creation: Lesslie Newbigin and the Reinvention of Christian Mission.* Eugene, OR: Pickwick, 2012.

Lawless, Chuck. "Donald McGavran, C. Peter Wagner, and Church Growth Evangelism." In *A History of Evangelism in North America.* Edited by Thomas P. Johnston, 291–302. Grand Rapids: Kregel, 2021.

Leeman, Jonathan. "We Come in Peace!" *Primer,* 7 (March 2019) 3. https://primerhq.com/issue-07/we-come-in-peace/

Lewis, C. S. *Mere Christianity.* New York: Simon & Schuster, 1996.

Macchia, Stephen A. *Becoming a Healthy Church: 10 Characteristics.* Grand Rapids: Baker, 1999.

MacIlvaine III, W. Rodman. "What Is the Missional Church Movement?" In *Bibliotheca Sacra* 167 (January-March 2010) 89–106.

Mackenzie, Ed. "Mission and the Inclusive Kingdom of Jesus: Assessing the Missiological Approach of Brian McLaren." In *Missiology: An International Review* 43 (2015) 258–269.

Marty, Martin E. *Righteous Empire: The Protestant Experience in America.* New York: Dial, 1970.

BIBLIOGRAPHY

Marty, William H. *The World of Jesus: Making Sense of the People and Places of Jesus' Day.* Bloomington, MN: Bethany House, 2013.

McCord, H. Richard. "Ecclesial Movements as Agents of a New Evangelization." *United States Conference of Catholic Bishops.* 2012. https://www.usccb.org/beliefs-and-teachings/how-we-teach/catechesis/catechetical-sunday/new-evangelization/upload/ecclesial-movements-mccord.pdf

McGavran, Donald A. *The Bridges of God.* Eugene, OR: Wipf and Stock, 2005.

———. *Effective Evangelism.* Philipsburg, NJ: Presbyterian and Reformed, 1988.

———. "My Pilgrimage in Mission." In *International Bulletin of Missionary Research* (1986) 53–58.

———. *Understanding Church Growth.* 3rd edition. Grand Rapids: William B. Eerdmans, 1990.

———. "Will Uppsala Betray the Two Billion?" In *Church Growth Bulletin: Institute of Church Growth* 7 no. 6 (July 1971) 233–241.

McGavran, Donald A., and George Hunter, III. *Church Growth: Strategies that Work.* Nashville: Abingdon, 1980.

McIntosh, Gary L. "Church Movements of the Last Fifty Years in North America." In *Great Commission Research Journal* (January 2010) 40–49.

———. *Donald A. McGavran: A Biography of the Twentieth Century's Premier Missiologist.* USA: Church Leader Insights, 2015.

———. "The Life of Donald McGavran: Coming of Age." In *Great Commission Research Journal* 10 no. 2 (Spring 2019) 160–192.

McLaren, Brian. *A Generous Orthodoxy.* Grand Rapids: Zondervan/Youth Specialties, 2006.

———. "The Homosexuality Question: Finding a Pastoral Response." https://www.thebereancall.org/content/homosexuality

———. *The Last Word and the Word After That.* San Francisco: Jossey-Bass, 2008.

———. *A New Kind of Christianity: Ten Questions that are Transforming the Faith.* New York: HarperCollins, 2011.

———. "Q & R: Is the Emerging Church Movement Fizzling Out?" (April 14, 2012), https://brianmclaren.net/q-r-is-the-emerging-church-movement-fizzling-out/.

———. *The Secret Message of Jesus: Uncovering the Truth that Could Change Everything.* Nashville: Thomas Nelson, 2006.

———. "What about trying to convert people?" December 31, 2012. https://brianmclaren.net/q-r-what-about-trying-to-convert-people/.

———. *Why Did Jesus, Moses, the Buddha and Mohammed Cross the Road? Christian Identity in a Multi-Faith World.* London: Hodder & Stoughton, 2012.

McLaren, Brian, and Tony Campolo, *Adventures in Missing the Point: How the Culture-Controlled Church Neutered the Gospel.* Grand Rapids: Zondervan/Youth Specialties, 2006.

McNeal, Reggie. *The Present Future: Six Tough Questions for the Church.* San Francisco: Jossey-Bass, 2003.

McKnight, Scot. "Five Streams of the Emerging Church." *Christianity Today Online* (January 19, 2007). http://christianitytoday.com/ct/2007/february/11.35.html.

———. "McLaren Emerging." *Christianity Today Online* (September 26, 2008). https://www.christianitytoday.com/ct/2008/september/38.59.html.

———. "Review: Brian McLaren's 'A New Kind of Christianity.'" *Christianity Today Online.* (February 26, 2010). http://www.christianitytoday.com/ct/2010/.

Bibliography

McRainey, Will. *The Art of Personal Evangelism*. Nashville: B&H, 2003.

Miles, Delos. Introduction to Evangelism. Nashville: Broadman, 1983.

Minatrea, Milfred. *Shaped By God's Heart: The Passion and Practices of Missional Churches*. San Francisco: Jossey-Bass, 2004.

Moltmann, Jürgen. *The Church in the Power of the Spirit: A Contribution to Messianic Ecclesiology*. New York: Harper & Row, 1977.

Moore, Russell. "Is America Post-Christian?" https://www.russellmoore.com/2015/05/26/is-america-post-christian/.

Mouw, Richard J. "The Missionary Location of the North American Churches." In *Confident Witness, Changing World*. Edited by Craig Van Gelder, 3–15. Grand Rapids: Eerdmans, 1999.

Murphy, Michael P. "Suspicious Minds: The Spirituality of the Postmodern Nones." https://www.americamagazine.org/issue/suspicious-minds.

"The Nature of Evangelism." https://lausanne.org/content/covenant/lausanne-covenant#cov.

Neill, Stephen. *Creative Tension*. London: Edinburgh House, 1959.

Newbigin, Lesslie. "Can the West Be Converted?" In *International Bulletin of Missionary Research* 11 no. 1 (January 1987) 2–7.

———. *Foolishness to the Greeks: The Gospel and Western Culture*. Grand Rapids: Eerdmans, 1986.

———. *The Gospel in a Pluralist Society*. Grand Rapids: Eerdmans, 1989.

———. *The Household of God: Lectures on the Nature of the Church*. London: SCM, 1953.

———. *Mission in Christ's Way: Bible Studies*. Geneva: WCC, 1989.

———. *The Open Secret: An Introduction to the Theology of Missions*. Grand Rapids: Eerdmans, 1995.

———. *The Open Secret: Sketches for a Missionary Theology*. Grand Rapids: Eerdmans, 1978.

———. "The Ordained Foreign Missionary in the Indian Church." In *International Review of Missions* 34 (1945) 86–94.

———. *The Other Side of 1984: Questions for the Churches*. Geneva: WCC, 1983.

———. *Signs Amid the Rubble: The Purposes of God in Human History*. Grand Rapids: Eerdmans, 2003.

———. *Unfinished Agenda*. Edinburgh: St. Andrew, 1993.

Niebuhr, H. Richard. *Christ & Culture*. New York: HarperOne, 1996.

"Nones on the Rise," *Pew Research Center*. https://www.pewforum.org/2012/10/09/nones-on-the-rise/

Ott, Craig. *The Church on Mission: A Biblical Vision for Transformation Among All People*. Grand Rapids: Baker, 2019.

Pagitt, Doug. "Response to Mark Driscoll's The Emerging Church and Biblicist Theology." In *Listening to the Beliefs of Emerging Churches, Five Perspectives*. Edited by Robert Webber, 19–48. Grand Rapids: Zondervan, 2007.

Payne, J. D. *Kingdom Expressions: Trends Influencing the Advancement of the Gospel*. Nashville: Thomas Nelson, 2012.

Pickett, J. W., A. L. Warnshuis, G. H. Singh, and D. A. McGavran. *Church Growth and Group Conversion*. 5th Edition. South Pasadena, CA: William Carey Library, 1973.

Platt, David. *Follow Me: A Call to Die, A Call to Live*. Wheaton, IL: Tyndale House, 2013.

———. *Radical: Taking Back Your Faith from the American Dream*. Colorado Springs, CO: Multnomah, 2011.

Bibliography

Prebble, Edward. "Missional Church: More a Theological (Re) Discovery, Less a Strategy For Parish Development." In *Colloquium* 46 no. 2 (2014) 224–241.

"Rainer Receives McGavran Church Growth Award; Wright Speaks at Southwestern," *SBC Digest.* www.baptistpress.com/resource-library/news/sbc-digest-rainer-receives-mcgavran-church-growth-award-wright-speaks-at-southwestern/.

Rainer, Thom S. *Autopsy of a Deceased Church.* Nashville: Broadman & Holman, 2014.

———. *The Book of Church Growth: History, Theology and Principles.* Nashville: Broadman, 1993.

———. "Church Growth at the End of the Twentieth Century: Recovering Our Purpose." In *Journal of the American Society of Church Growth* 6 (1995): 59–72.

Rainer, Thom S., and Ed Stetzer. *Transformational Church: Creating a New Scorecard for Congregations.* Nashville: B&H, 2010.

Richardson, Rick. *You Found Me: New Research on How Unchurched Nones, Millennials, and Irreligious are Surprisingly Open to Christian Faith.* Downers Grove, IL: InterVarsity, 2019.

Rohde Ross P. "Practical Considerations for Postmodern Sensitive Churches." http://www.postmission.com.

Roxburgh, Alan J. "Equipping God's People for Mission." In *Missional Church: A Vision for the Sending of the Church in North America.* Edited by Darrell L. Guder, 183–220. Grand Rapids: Eerdmans, 1998.

Roxburgh, Alan J., and M. Scott Boren. *Introducing the Missional Church: What it is, Why it Matters, and How to Become One.* Grand Rapids: Baker, 2009.

Saler, Robert. "The Emergent Church and Liberal Theology: Ships in the Night?" In *Currents in Theology and Mission* 42 no. 2 (April 2015) 113–118.

Schwarz, Christian A. *Natural Church Development: A Guide to Eight Essential Qualities of Healthy Churches.* St. Charles, IL: ChurchSmart, 2000.

Scudieri, Robert J. *The Apostolic Church: One, Holy, Catholic, and Missionary.* Fort Wayne, IN: Lutheran Society for Missiology, 1995.

Selmanovic, Samir. "The Sweet Problem of Inclusiveness." In *An Emergent Manifesto of Hope.* Edited by Doug Pagitt and Tony Jones, 189–200. Grand Rapids: Baker, 2007.

Shaw, David M. "The Already and Not Yet Kingdom." https://au.thegospelcoalition.org/article/already-not-yet-kingdom/

Shenk, Wilbert R. "Newbigin in His Time." In *The Gospel and Pluralism Today: Reassessing Lesslie Newbigin in the 21st Century.* Edited by Scott W. Sunquist and Amos Yong, 29–48. Downers Grove, IL: IVP, 2015.

Shogren, Gary S. "The Wicked Will Not Inherit the Kingdom of God: A Pauline Warning and The Hermeneutics of Liberation Theology and of Brian McLaren." In *Trinity Journal*, (2010): 95–113.

Smith, Gordon T. *Consider Your Calling: Six Questions for Discerning Your Vocation.* Downers Grove, IL: IVP, 2016.

Smith, Gregory A. "About Three-in-Ten U.S. Adults Are Now Religiously Unaffiliated." *Pew Research Center.* December 14, 2021. www.pewresearch.org/religion/2021/12/14/about-three-in-ten-u-s-adults-are-now-religiously-unaffiliated/.

Smith, R. Scott. *Truth and the New Kind of Christian: The Emerging Effects of Postmodernism in the Church.* Wheaton, ILL: Crossway, 2005.

Spader, Dann. *4 Chair Discipling: Growing a Movement of Disciple-Makers.* Chicago: Moody, 2014.

Bibliography

———. *Walking as Jesus Walked: Making Disciples the Way Jesus Did*. Chicago: Moody, 2011.

Stetzer, Ed. "The Emergent/Emerging Church: A Missiological Perspective." In *Evangelicals Engaging Emergent: A Discussion of the Emergent Church Movement*. Edited by William Henard and Adam W. Greenway, 47–91. Nashville: Broadman & Holman, 2009.

Stetzer, Ed., and Mike Dodson. *Comeback Churches*. Nashville: B&H, 2007.

———. "Missional and Missions: Getting Our Language Right." https://edstetzer.com/blog2/missional-and-missions-getting-our-language-right.

———. *Planting New Churches in a Postmodern Age*. Nashville: Broadman & Holman, 2003.

Stetzer, Ed., and Mike Dodson. *Comeback Churches*. Nashville: B&H, 2007.

Streett, Alan R. "An Interview with Brian McLaren." In *Criswell Theological Review* 3 no. 2 (Spring 2006) 5–14.

Strobel, Lee. *Inside the Mind of Unchurched Harry and Mary*. Grand Rapids: Zondervan, 1993.

Sweet, Leonard. ed. *The Church in Emerging Culture: Five Perspectives*. Grand Rapids: Zondervan, 2003.

Suarez, Gustavo V. "Donald McGavran's Understanding of Conversion." In *Great Commission Research Journal* 4 no. 2 (Winter 2013) 182–201.

Taylor, Justin. "The Biggest Hole in the Gospel is the Gospel Itself." https://www.thegospelcoalition.org/blogs/justin-taylor/the-biggest-hole-in-our-gospel-is-the-gospel-itself/.

Taylor, Mendell. *Exploring Evangelism*. Kansas City: Beacon Hill, 1964.

Terry, John Mark. *Church Evangelism: Creating a Culture of Growth in Your Congregation*. Nashville: Broadman & Holman, 1997.

Thomas, Norman E., ed. *Classic Texts in Mission and World Christianity*. Maryknoll, NY: Orbis, 1995.

Tinter, Melvin. "Reversal or Betrayal? Evangelicals and Socio-political Involvement in the Twentieth Century." In *The Churchman* 113 no. 3 (1999) 18–22.

Towns, Elmer. *An Inside Look at Ten of Today's Most Innovative Churches*. Ventura: CA: Regal, 1990.

"Unchurched Report," *Lifeway Research*. http://lifewayresearch.com/wp-content/uploads/2017/01/BGCE-Unchurched-Study-Final-Report-1_5_17.pdf.

Van Der Avoort, Ryan. "Don't Divorce Christian Apologetics from Discipleship." The Gospel Coalition. August 4, 2021. https://africa.thegospelcoalition.org/article/dont-divorce-christian-apologetics-from-discipleship/

Van Engen, Charles. "Bridges of God: The Mission Legacy of Donald Anderson McGavran." In *Great Commission Research Journal* 1 no.1 (Summer 2009) 27–32.

———. "Centrist View: Church Growth is based on an evangelistically focused and a missiologically applied theology." In *Evaluating the Church Growth Movement: 5 Views*. Edited by Gary L. McIntosh and Paul E. Engle, 121–164. Grand Rapids: Zondervan, 2004.

Van Gelder, Craig. *The Essence of the Church: A Community Created by the Spirit*. Grand Rapids: Baker, 2000.

———. "Mission in the Emerging Postmodern Condition," In *The Church Between Gospel and Culture: The Emerging Mission in North America*. Edited by George R. Hunsberger and Craig Van Gelder, 113–138. Grand Rapids: Eerdmans, 1996.

Bibliography

Van Gelder, Craig., and Dwight J. Zscheile. *The Missional Church in Perspective*. Grand Rapids: Baker Academic, 2011.

Van Hoozer, Kevin. *Hearers and Doers: A Pastor's Guide to Making Disciples Through Scripture and Doctrine*. Bellingham, WA: Lexham, 2019.

Vaus, W. *Mere Theology: A Guide to the Thought of C. S. Lewis*. Downers Grove, IL: InterVarsity, 2004.

Wagner, C. Peter. "Lausanne Twelve Months Later." In *Christianity Today* (July 4, 1975) 7–9.

———. *Strategies for Church Growth: Tools for Effective Missions and Evangelism*. Ventura, CA: Regal, 1989.

———. *Your Church Can Grow: Seven Vital Signs of a Healthy Church*. Glendale, CA: Regal, 1976.

Walters, Jeff K. "Donald McGavran's Theological Foundations for 'Effective Evangelism.'" In *Great Commission Research Journal* 2 no. 1 (Summer 2010) 50–61.

Warren, Rick. *The Purpose Driven Church*. Grand Rapids: Zondervan, 1995.

Watson, David, and Paul Watson. *Contagious Disciple Making: Leading Others on a Journey of Discovery*. Nashville: Thomas Nelson, 2014.

Webber, Robert. *Ancient-Future Faith: Rethinking Evangelicalism for a Postmodern World*. Grand Rapids, Michigan: Baker, 1999.

Westin, Paul. *Lesslie Newbigin: Missionary Theologian*. Grand Rapids: Eerdmans, 2006.

White, James E. *Meet Generation Z: Understanding and Reaching the New Post-Christian World*. Grand Rapids: Baker, 2017.

Willard, Dallas. The Great Omission: Reclaiming Jesus's Essential Teachings on Discipleship. Grand Rapids: HarperCollins, 2006.

"Willow Creek Repents? Why the most influential church in America now says, 'We made a mistake.'" *Christianity Today Online*, www.christianitytoday.com/pastors/2007/october-online-only/willow-creek-repents.html.

Wilson, Carl W. *With Christ in the School of Disciple Building: The Ministry Methods of Jesus*. Colorado Springs, CO: NavPress, 2009.

World Council of Churches, *The Church for Others: Two Reports on the Missionary Structure of the Church*. Geneva: WCC,1967.

The World Mission of the Church: Findings and Recommendations of the Internal Missionary Council, Tambaram, Madras, India, December 12 to 29, 1938. London: International Missions Council, 1939.

Yaconelli, Mike, ed. *Stories of Emergence: Moving from Absolute to Authentic*. El Cajon, CA: EmergentYS/Grand Rapids: Zondervan, 2003.

Zacharias, Ravi. "An Ancient Message, Through Modern Means, To A Postmodern Mind." In *Telling the Truth: Evangelizing Postmoderns*. Edited by D. A. Carson, 18–29. Grand Rapids: Zondervan, 2000.

Ziman, Johnathan. *The Life of Jesus, A Chronological Account from God's Word*. Grand Rapids: Baker, 2010.

www.ingramcontent.com/pod-product-compliance
Lightning Source LLC
Chambersburg PA
CBHW051736230426
43670CB00012B/2050